Understanding Crypto Fundamentals

Value Investing in Cryptoassets and Management of Underlying Risks

Thomas Jeegers

Apress®

Understanding Crypto Fundamentals: Value Investing in Cryptoassets and Management of Underlying Risks

Thomas Jeegers
Vienna, Austria

ISBN-13 (pbk): 978-1-4842-9308-9   ISBN-13 (electronic): 978-1-4842-9309-6
https://doi.org/10.1007/978-1-4842-9309-6

Managing Director, Apress Media LLC: Welmoed Spahr
Acquisitions Editor: Smriti Srivastava
Development Editor: Laura Berendson
Coordinating Editor: Mark Powers
Copy Editor: Kimberly Burton-Weisman

Cover designed by eStudioCalamar

Cover image by Luemen Rutkowski on Unsplash (www.unsplash.com)

Distributed to the book trade worldwide by Apress Media, LLC, 1 New York Plaza, New York, NY 10004, U.S.A. Phone 1-800-SPRINGER, fax (201) 348-4505, e-mail orders-ny@springer-sbm.com, or visit www.springeronline.com. Apress Media, LLC is a California LLC and the sole member (owner) is Springer Science + Business Media Finance Inc (SSBM Finance Inc). SSBM Finance Inc is a **Delaware** corporation.

For information on translations, please e-mail booktranslations@springernature.com; for reprint, paperback, or audio rights, please e-mail bookpermissions@springernature.com.

Apress titles may be purchased in bulk for academic, corporate, or promotional use. eBook versions and licenses are also available for most titles. For more information, reference our Print and eBook Bulk Sales web page at http://www.apress.com/bulk-sales.

Printed on acid-free paper

*To you, the readers who take
their financial future into their hands*

Table of Contents

About the Author

Thomas Jeegers studied economics and computer science, with master's degrees from the Catholic University of Louvain and Maastricht University and an MBA from INSEAD.

Specialized in financial risk management and blockchain technology, Thomas has worked in finance for the past ten years. In parallel to his work, he completed the advanced financial certifications Chartered Financial Analyst (CFA) and Financial Risk Manager (FRM), as well as multiple blockchain certifications from institutions including INSEAD and Oxford University. He is now also a frequent speaker at events on blockchain and cryptoassets.

About the Technical Reviewer

Yamini Sagar is the founder/CEO of Instarails, a company that provides instant global payment rails. She has over 20 years of experience in tech, blockchain, and payments and has a track record of building innovative products. Yamini has worked at renowned companies like Intercontinental Exchange NYSE, BitPay, and Bakkt. She has been an amateur investor in cryptos since 2018, and her favorite is Bitcoin. When she's not working, Yamini enjoys reading about emerging technologies and sharing her insights on the latest trends.

Disclaimer

This book is not a recommendation to buy cryptoassets but rather a structured analysis of what they are, why they may be appropriate for some investors, and what such investors ought to consider. In this regard, several disclaimers are necessary.

First, I am not a financial advisor. The contents of this book should be regarded as educational, not as financial advice.

Second, cryptoassets are subject to high price volatility and more legal uncertainty than traditional investments. Facing this volatility and uncertainty is not appropriate for all investors.

Third, the cryptoasset space is evolving very rapidly. Every effort was made to provide up-to-date sources at the time of publication. However, it may no longer be the case when you read these lines. I can, therefore, hold no responsibility for outdated information or decisions (financial or otherwise) made based on the material covered in this book.

Any investor, in cryptoassets or otherwise, should assess whether a particular investment fits one's specific needs. They include risk-return characteristics, liquidity, time horizon, tax status, and other unique features. Any investment should be considered as part of the investor's total portfolio, not as an independent investment. Furthermore, one is responsible for doing one's own investment research, especially in regard to understanding the underlying risks. If you do not have the ability or desire to perform such an assessment, refer to a financial advisor who could tailor portfolio recommendations based on your unique needs and characteristics.

Preface

I decided not to invest in cryptoassets—many times. However, recent developments changed my mind.

On a Saturday evening in the autumn of 2012, I sat with friends for a session of our newly-formed think tank in Brussels. It was my turn to bring up a mind-provoking topic. Our group had diverse expertise ranging from engineering to IT and physics. Leveraging my economics background, that day's topic was the revolutionary potential of complementary currencies. Indeed, monetary systems working in parallel to a traditional single-currency model can benefit local communities in countless ways. At the time, I was not even aware of Bitcoin's existence. Still years ahead of cryptoassets becoming mainstream, alternative currencies were an obscure idea that needed to emerge.

This visionary concept would change everything. In the same way steam, electricity, and the Internet triggered the first, second, and third industrial revolutions, reframing society's use of currencies could initiate a fourth industrial revolution.

A couple of months later, I heard about Bitcoin for the first time during an economic conference in Zurich. Yet, despite my unwavering belief in alternative currencies' potential, I considered that this new digital currency was not worth its trading price, $70 apiece.

I then specialized in regulatory risk management and eventually became the local expert on blockchain technology in Germany's third-largest bank. However, given the underlying risks, I still argued in April 2016 that $430 per bitcoin was grossly overpriced. Despite blockchain's promising future, this nascent technology could not be relied upon to replace current ways of working in finance or our monetary system. Yet.

Even after completing an MBA in Singapore in 2018, I doubted investing in cryptoassets was worth the risk. I believed that past returns orders of magnitude above the highest-performing traditional asset class did not justify the lack of fundamentals. Ultimately, Bitcoin and other cryptoassets relied exclusively on trust that a peer-to-peer network would keep working. Too much could go wrong. While Bitcoin was a fascinating use case of technology as a monetary system, its likelihood of failure was exceptionally high.

During 2021's market bull run, Bitcoin and other cryptoassets made the headlines again. Thanks to recent developments in the cryptoasset industry, their adoption skyrocketed. Institutions formerly loudly advocating against cryptocurrencies changed their mind. Many of these institutions started offering cryptoasset services; some even invested considerable amounts in such assets.

Another increase in value ensued. By one order of magnitude. For the seventh time in a decade.

The last few years passed multiple milestones in cryptoasset history. We witnessed El Salvador become the first country to adopt Bitcoin as legal tender, and the financial industry evolved to leverage cryptoassets' potential. It established cryptoassets as an asset class. Regulatory uncertainty dropped, likely making cryptoassets the asset class with the most attractive risk-adjusted expected return.

For a decade, I have been too risk-averse to dare set foot in the crypto arena. However, still highly risk-conscious, I believe it is now time to step in for most investors—even risk-averse ones like me.

And I am not the only one who feels this way.

I don't think there is anything more important in my lifetime to work on [than Bitcoin].

—Jack Dorsey, CEO of Twitter and Block (previously Square)
June 4, 2021, Bitcoin 2021 Conference

Bitcoin is a bank in cyberspace, run by incorruptible software, offering a global, affordable, simple, & secure savings account to billions of people that don't have the option or desire to run their own hedge fund.

—Michael Saylor, CEO of MicroStrategy
December 17, 2020, Twitter

Paper money is going away. And crypto is a far better way to transfer value than a piece of paper, that's for sure.

—Elon Musk, CEO of Tesla, SpaceX, and Twitter
February 19, 2019, interview with ARK Invest

Something like bitcoin is going to be successful, and it's going to enable a whole new way of doing finance.

—Richard Branson, Founder of the Virgin Group
October 21, 2016, Twitter

PayPal had these goals of creating a new currency. We failed at that, and we just created a new payment system. I think Bitcoin has succeeded on the level of a new currency, but the payment system is somewhat lacking.

—Peter Thiel, Co-founder of PayPal,
February 2015, interview with The Buttonwood Gathering

[Bitcoin] is a remarkable cryptographic achievement. The ability to create something which is not duplicable in the digital world has enormous value.

—Eric Schmidt, former CEO of Google,
March 2014, Computer History Museum

Bitcoin is the beginning of something great: a currency without a government, something necessary and imperative.

—Nassim Taleb, *New York Times* best-selling author
March 20, 2013, Ask Me Anything (AMA) on Reddit.com

I think the Internet is going to be one of the major forces for reducing the role of government. The one thing that's missing, but that will soon be developed, is a reliable e-cash, a method whereby on the Internet you can transfer funds from A to B without A knowing B or B knowing A…

—Milton Friedman, Economics Nobel Prize laureate 1999,
interview with the NTU

This book started as my notes on the optimal crypto investment strategy. It uncovers the exceptional potential of cryptoassets and their specific risks. Debunk the myths, set up a meaningful investment portfolio, and get to terms with this volatile new world.

Feedback

I welcome any feedback and suggestions for possible future editions of the book. Please feel free to share any thoughts by emailing me at `thomas@thomasjeegers.com`.

Introduction

An investment in knowledge pays the best interest.

—Benjamin Franklin

Fundamental analysis is the concept of thoroughly researching an asset's economic value and the drivers for its price. In the case of a stock, it involves understanding the underlying company's business and financial statements. In the case of a commodity, it involves understanding the commodity's inventory and seasonal cycles, government policies, and related markets, as well as the drivers of supply and demand for it. The fundamentals of a stock and the fundamentals of a commodity are therefore wildly different.

Likewise, the fundamentals of cryptoassets are also unique. They involve understanding how digital information can have value, what drives this value, and how the cryptoasset ecosystem impacts it. However, similarly to any tradable asset, the market price of a cryptoasset ultimately boils down to supply and demand.

Fundamental analysis is used for long-term investment. It differs *fundamentally* from technical analysis, which analyses an asset's monthly, weekly, daily, or even intra-daily price patterns to predict short-term moves. In other words, fundamental analysis is the investor's tool, the same way technical analysis is the speculator's tool. Assets subject to fundamental and technical analyses span debt to equity, real estate to derivative products, currencies to traded funds, and any security. Of course, cryptoassets do not escape scrutiny.

However, they differ in the type of asset at hand. In particular, blockchain technology makes Bitcoin the first digital asset that is scarce and cannot be counterfeit. It is achieved by decentralizing the asset, meaning that there is no unique network owner. Through an ingenious combination of multiple technologies, it enables worldwide transfers of value settled in minutes and permanently, without requiring any intermediary. These characteristics make Bitcoin and other cryptoassets the logical next milestones in the development of a global society's monetary and financial system. It is not a revolution but rather an evolution—the natural next step in the history of money and finance. They not only offer monetary digitalization but also, and much more importantly, decentralization.

INTRODUCTION

As this book covers in detail, decentralization makes cryptoassets the base for a strictly superior monetary model compared to paper-based currencies emitted by governmental entities or private banks. Indeed, with sufficient adoption, cryptoassets offer greater value in all three core functions of money: unit of account, store of value, and medium of exchange.

In addition, the consequences of this disruption reach far beyond the monetary system. In an increasingly digital society, sharing digital assets needs fair and transparent rules. It is not only valid for money but also for identity, property titles, music, and art, among many other use cases. As a result, virtually all industries will be impacted, directly or indirectly, by cryptoassets and their underlying technology, blockchain. In particular, Chapter 3 presents multiple ways blockchain technology revolutionizes the world as a driver for the greater good.

This book primarily covers the potential of cryptoassets as part of the next monetary system and as a new asset class for investments. In particular, it analyzes cryptoassets from an economic and financial perspective, following principles of value investing. In other words, the aim is to identify what this new asset class is worth. The book identifies and measures fundamental pillars of cryptoassets to help assess their genuine value. It also balances the picture by highlighting the underlying risks, both financial and non-financial. Specifically, it is structured following critical questions that any investor, experienced or new, should ask before investing. *Why* is this asset class valuable? *What* is this asset class made of? *When* is the right time to invest? *Where* should one invest? *How* should one invest in terms of investment strategy and risk management? And finally, *which* valuation methods exist and are appropriate for cryptoassets? This book does not recommend any particular investment but provides the framework necessary to make more informed cryptoasset investment decisions. It enables an understanding of why they have true economic value and hints at how to measure it. It is the starting point for serious long-term cryptoasset investors rather than the answer for short-term speculators looking for get-rich-quick schemes.

Besides, outstanding cryptoasset resources already exist. This book does not seek to replace but rather complement them with a focus on value investing. Covering technical aspects of cryptoassets and blockchain technology too deeply would divert the focus from this book's purpose. All intricacies behind this technology would barely even fit in a book of their own. Therefore, this book only covers blockchain technology's high-level functioning. In particular, it does not cover the following topics.

- Advanced cryptography and dApps programming. Interested readers and programmers should refer to the in-depth book *Mastering Blockchain* by Imran Bashir [1].

- Non-fungible tokens (NFT). Interested readers should refer to *The NFT Handbook* by Fortnow and Terry [2].

- Cryptoasset taxation. Tax considerations of cryptoassets are wildly different for every country and rapidly evolving. Interested readers can refer to the extensive book *Taxation of Crypto Assets* by Schmidt, Bernstein, Richter, and Zarlenga, second edition (2023), covering tax law for cryptoassets in over 40 countries [3].

- Technical analysis (TA). The book focuses on the long term, not short-term horizons considered in technical analysis. The macro thesis presented here will likely take several years, possibly decades, to play out. Short-horizon crypto traders should refer to books on swing trading (short term) or breakout trading (medium term).

Since Bitcoin is the first cryptoasset and because its market value is roughly half of all cryptoassets' value combined, there is a corresponding focus on this particular asset. Nevertheless, many more cryptoassets followed in Bitcoin's wake, with purposes extending much beyond Bitcoin's original value proposition.

As the author, I feel compelled to highlight that what I do not know about cryptoassets is much broader than what I do know. In particular, while I have superficial experience in these fields, I am neither a programmer nor a professional investor with decades of experience. In addition, the exceptional pace of development of the cryptoasset industry makes it impossible to closely follow all things happening in the cryptoasset space. Nevertheless, I believe this book makes a compelling case for cryptoassets, their rightful place in a balanced investment portfolio, and the risks investors face as of 2023.

Some readers may believe they missed the opportunity. Many teenage cryptomillionaires made the headlines over the last decade. Some early investors and innovators even became billionaires through the early gains of the industry. As this book shows, it is not too late to profit from the innovation, far from it. Actually, it is just the beginning. If a human life represented the development of cryptoassets, it would currently be at the toddler stage. It can barely stand on its own feet, but it still has a lifetime of development ahead. Crises will surely pave its teenage years, but the best is yet to come.

INTRODUCTION

Regardless of one's opinion on cryptoassets, their proof of concept redefines how we think about trust. The technology behind them could become the most transformational innovation for society since the Internet—not big data, artificial intelligence, or self-driving cars but blockchain. What was once in the hands of a powerful few, for better or worse, can now be in everybody's hands—or nobody's hands, depending on how one looks at it.

PART I

Why Consider Crypto Investments?

CHAPTER 1

A Brief History of Money

Central banks in their present form would no longer exist; nor would money... The successors to Bill Gates could put the successors to Alan Greenspan out of business.

—Mervyn King, 1999

The history of cryptoassets, like this book, begins with money. In particular, with the established monetary system. Understanding what makes money and how it has evolved is essential to understand the value proposition of cryptoassets—Bitcoin in particular. Therefore, let us start with the basics by going back several millennia to identify the fundamentals of money. As you will see, they naturally make a case for what is coming next.

What Makes Money?

As human societies emerged millennia ago, the need to exchange value became crucial. Direct trades of value in a barter system, such as individuals exchanging eggs for fruits, had severe limitations. A barter system only works when one individual wants to buy what another wants to sell, while the seller also wants something the buyer has to offer. In addition, goods traded must have similar value. For example, a seller would not want to exchange a house that took months to build for a few eggs. Moreover, even if one could gather enough eggs, the trade would still be unattractive since eggs are perishable and inappropriate for transactions of considerable value. A medium of exchange, a form of money, had to arise to facilitate trade and economic activity.

In all societies, media of exchange would naturally emerge. However, they would not all be equally appropriate. A medium of exchange requires several characteristics to become an optimal form of money. Nothing dictates what should or should not be

T. Jeegers, *Understanding Crypto Fundamentals*, https://doi.org/10.1007/978-1-4842-9309-6_1

money, but some features make for better forms of money. For example, sound money needs to have value in the eyes of as many potential trade participants as possible to broaden its usability. Also, it should hold its value through time. For instance, it should not be perishable, like the eggs in the previous example. Optimally, it should also be countable and divisible into smaller units to facilitate transactions of little value and transportable to enable users to carry their wealth. Finally, an optimal form of money would have all units worth the same and be indistinguishable from one another, a characteristic known as *fungibility*.

In the fourth century BCE, Aristotle established the following critical characteristics as the base for sound money [4]. In particular, money should be

1. a medium of exchange
2. a unit of account
3. a store of value
4. durable
5. portable
6. divisible
7. fungible

Forms of money used by societies over time only partially fulfilled these characteristics—from seashells to beads, cattle, grain, salt, tobacco, skins, silver, and even gold.

The founder of the Austrian School of Economics,[1] Carl Menger, challenges the popular thinking that a medium of exchange becomes money by authority, for example by law dictated by the state [5]. Instead, he considers money as a special case of other assets (commodities) with a remarkably high degree of "saleability" (*Absatzfähigkeit*). A saleable item is readily marketable at any convenient time without incurring a material

---

[1] This school of thoughts is a branch of economics focusing on the results of individual actions in line with rational decisions following economics incentives. Its early proponents were Austrians, which gave it its name. Nowadays, it contrasts predominantly to the Keynesian school of thoughts, which promotes extensive government control in all economic matters.

decrease in the selling price. In other words, it represents the degree to which a seller can dispose of the asset at a fair economic price. Menger identifies the following six criteria affecting an asset's saleability.[2]

1. the number of potentially interested buyers
2. their purchasing power
3. the quantity available of the good compared to the total unsupplied quantity that the market wants of it
4. the divisibility of the asset
5. the level of market development and speculation and
6. the legal and regulatory limitations imposed on transacting the asset

The criteria summarized by Aristotle on the one hand and by Menger on the other are critical in understanding why an asset makes a good form of money. By extension, they are crucial to evaluate the potential for such money to become valuable. These lists are also helpful in assessing how a change in any criterion affects the asset's valuation. For example, improving market development or reducing regulatory limitations on transactions would increase the asset's saleability and value.

Rational individuals facing several potential media of exchange will naturally tilt toward the "better" forms of money, that is, those with greater saleability. Even if one does not need the asset, the mere knowledge that others may need it is sufficient to incentivize acquiring it. Indeed, the owner of the better medium of exchange maximizes his ability to purchase goods in the future. Individuals arriving at the marketplace with less saleable assets (e.g., rare antique writings) find themselves at a disadvantage compared to individuals with more saleable assets (e.g., gold coins). The less saleable asset must first be converted to a more saleable asset before the owner can perform any further trade.

---

[2] Menger also identifies five criteria conditioning the geographical limits to the saleability of an asset and seven criteria conditioning its limits through time. Such spatial and temporal criteria are similarly important in assessing the value of an asset as a medium of exchange, but beyond the scope of this book. The interested reader should refer to the original text [5].

It ensued in every society that better forms of money (i.e., with a higher degree of saleability) tended to be hoarded. At the same time, comparatively inferior forms of money lost attractiveness. One tends to exchange less saleable for more saleable assets because doing so is in one's best interest. Thus, the preceding criteria, not the pressure of a central authority, enabled specific forms of money in a free economy to become the most appropriate medium of exchange. These criteria enabled one particular asset to emerge as the best form of money among all potential candidates.

Precious Metals As Money

In early societies, precious metals were desirable for their utility and beauty. Gold and silver, for example, shone from the Far East to the Western world as ornaments. They were less prone to corrosion (contrary to iron or copper), so they could last generations. In other words, they had high durability. Also, since they carried much value in relatively small weight, they enabled the portability of one's wealth. At the same time, their relative scarcity made the unsupplied quantity that the market demanded proportionally larger than the available quantity. These characteristics positioned them well as assets with a high degree of saleability.

Before metals such as silver or gold became the officially state-backed medium of exchange, individuals already used them as such. Many individuals bought them because of their intrinsic characteristics of durability, portability, divisibility, and especially store of value. It enabled them to transfer value across space and time. This interest, in turn, increased their saleability. Precious metals became money because traders following their self-interest effectively used them, not because an authority imposed them as currency. As metallurgy improved, the malleability and subsequent standardization in shape, quality, and weight of these metals further enhanced their attributes of sound money (namely fungibility and divisibility), which made them even more saleable. They became the de facto money in most of the civilized world. However, it is essential to understand that money is a social construct, not a regulatory one. Regulations and state backing only followed and strengthened this pre-existing social construct.

Storing Value

The concept of saleability introduced by Menger is closely related to that of a store of value. In particular, his first and third criteria[3] are worth investigating further to understand what makes an actual store of value.

Paraphrasing Menger's first criterion, there must be a demand for the good. If the demand for a good is non-existent, it is worthless, regardless of its supply characteristics. For example, if a mediocre artist paints only five paintings over his lifetime, it does not automatically make them valuable. There must be interested buyers for the paintings to have value. In other words, a good store of value has a high demand. With population growth and increasing prosperity in early societies, the demand for shiny metals was growing, especially for gold and silver.

Menger's third criterion of the saleability of an asset relates to relative scarcity, which is measured by the *stock-to-flow ratio*.[4] The *stock* of an asset is the total existing usable quantity of the asset. For example, while unmined gold still exists in difficult-to-reach areas, its *stock* is the quantity of available gold usable by individuals. On the other hand, the asset's *flow* is the quantity that can be added to its stock per unit of time—for example, the number of tons of gold mined in a year.

An asset with a high flow relative to its stock renders the stock of the asset worth little because the stock can increase significantly with time. For example, if the stock of copper in an economy at the beginning of a year is 100, and its yearly flow is 50, then the stock at the end of the year would sum up to 150, assuming no loss, destruction, or corrosion of the stock. A copper holder cannot expect the asset to remain scarce because a substantial proportion, compared to the existing quantity, can rapidly increase the stock. An asset with a high flow compared to its stock quickly loses any scarcity it might have had. By extension, only assets with a small flow compared to their stock (or high stock-to-flow ratio) can be potential stores of value because only such assets remain scarce.

---

[3] The number of potential interested buyers and the quantity available of the good in relation to the total unsupplied quantity that the market wants of it.

[4] The book *Whither Gold?* from Antal Fekete provides a more in-depth discussion of the relationship between the stock-to-flow ratio and the saleability of an asset [58].

Regarding their stock-to-flow, assets are not equal. Far from it, actually. First, any perishable product (e.g., apples, eggs, nuts), corrodible asset (e.g., iron, copper), or other consumable commodities (e.g., zinc, nickel) have a low stock-to-flow because no stock can accumulate over extended periods. At the same time, the flow represents a substantial portion of the asset's stock. Only durable (non-perishable) assets can apply as potential stores of value. Gold, for example, ranks well as a durable asset because its chemical stability makes it virtually indestructible.

Second, an actual store of value must be an asset whose flow does not vary much with the stock's market price. Economists refer to this characteristic as the price elasticity of supply. For example, if the market value of copper suddenly increased dramatically, many individuals would become copper producers to leverage the opportunity. As a result, the quantity of copper produced would rise accordingly. In other terms, the flow would increase until the asset is no longer scarce and its price drops to its long-term economic level. So, copper production (its flow) depends heavily on its market price. In economic terms, copper is an asset with a high price elasticity of supply. However, this price-to-supply relationship is almost non-existent for gold. History has shown that even when the price of gold increased dramatically, its production remained almost unchanged. In particular, the increase in the global gold stockpile did not exceed 2% in any year since World War II. In 2006, despite a 36% increase in the market price of gold, the annual production decreased in both 2006 and 2007.[5] In other words, gold's supply is not affected much by changes in its market price. Gold has a low price elasticity of supply.

Growing demand and marginally increasing supply made gold the optimal store of value throughout the past few millennia. While silver ranks better than other commodities, it is still second to gold in these characteristics. For this reason, people typically only used silver as a medium of exchange for transactions of small value.

---

[5] See Chapter 3 of *The Bitcoin Standard* by Saifedean Ammous [56].

From Money to Currency

Money and currency are not the same thing. Money is the natural medium selected by individuals to conduct transactions. On the other hand, governments impose currency on their citizens for these transactions. They can be the same and typically start as such. However, many times in history, governments have let their currency gradually drift away from money. These episodes ended badly, often in disasters of epic proportions. A few examples follow.

Gold and silver established themselves as money for most of the past five millennia. Sound money enabled civilizations to flourish and push the boundaries of humankind's development. Thanks to the coinage of these metals, the great Greek civilization, half a millennium BCE, became the world's most prosperous society and kept expanding. It established a free-market economy with an effective tax system and became the world's first democracy. However, in 431 BCE, Athens entered the Peloponnesian War against Sparta, which lasted almost two decades, much longer than anticipated. As the war went on, funding it became challenging and soon impossible. To ease the problem, Athenian authorities creatively mixed copper with the gold and silver they gathered from taxes to melt new coins. They could increase the number of coins they had on hand and suddenly spend more than their revenue. This creative development became the first currency debasement in history. Gold and silver were no longer traded based on their weight but rather on the historical value of coins. Athens had just created the first government currency. In the few years that followed, citizens progressively realized the trick and stopped accepting these coins as genuine gold or silver. The new currency quickly became worthless, Athens lost the war, and its prosperity ended. What remained of the country became a conquest of the next great civilization, Rome.

The Roman Empire was next in line to reach the heights of the world's dominant civilization. However, after centuries of prosperity, the emperors' greed led Rome to unaffordable wars. Similar to the Greeks, Romans funded wars by debasing their currency. They shrank the size of coins and mixed cheaper metals to produce new ones. The debasement was initially slow and minimal. From the original denarius containing 95% silver under Augustus, only 50% remained under Caracalla two centuries later. However, once the process started, emperors minted more currency at increasing rates, trying to escape price increases. In the middle of the third century CE, the silver content in a denarius dropped to only 0.5% within a couple of decades. The unavoidable consequence materialized as the Roman Empire sank into hyperinflation. In these two decades, known as the Crisis of the Third Century, prices increased by nearly 1000% (i.e., multiplied by a factor of 10). Troops hired by the emperor would only accept payment in gold for their services, thereby plainly denying the value of the official currency. Toward the end of the century, the situation temporarily stabilized after the assassination of dozens of short-term emperors. However, the process quickly resumed. Under Diocletian in 301, a pound of gold traded for 50,000 denarii. By the year of his death, in 337, it increased to 20 million denarii, corresponding to 40,000% inflation.[6]

Figure 1-1. *Denarius under Augustus (Source: Classical Numismatic Group, Inc.* http://www.cngcoins.com; *Wikimedia, public domain)*

Episodes of hyperinflation are not limited to ancient history. For example, in sixteenth-century England, the Great Debasement under Henry VIII rhymes with the preceding stories of Greece and Rome. To finance wars in France, the English King ordered the reduction of precious metals in coins by replacing them with cheaper metals. As a result, the formerly prestigious English currency quickly disintegrated and disappeared from circulation. The same pattern arises in all cases: unaffordable wars require increasing the currency supply, leading to price increases, ruining the nation, and ending in a collapse of the currency.

---

[6] *Inflation and the Fall of the Roman Empire*, J. R. Peden, Mises Daily Articles [66].

In the next century, on the European continent, small German states repeated the same mistakes in the Thirty Years War. Under the Holy Roman Empire, only a few princes had the right to mint coins. The Empire was, in theory, under a bimetallic standard, with large gold coins of high value and silver coins for smaller denominations. While coin alteration was punishable by death, enforcing the sentence was difficult. As a result, this period became known as the *clipping and culling times* (*Kipper- und Wipperzeit*), following the recurrent clipping of coin edges and careful selection of the best coins. Little remained due to debasement from the original coins made of valuable metals. Coins progressively lost their valuable content until becoming exclusively copper. As in previous examples, hyperinflation settled, and an economic crisis followed. People stopped accepting coins as payment, and the currency became worthless.[7]

The Ascension of Paper Currency

In eighteenth-century France, this pattern appears again, but with elements of novelty: central banking and paper money. After the death of the French King Louis XIV, the Duke of Orléans Philip II took over the regency of the country until the eleven-year-old successor to the throne, Louis XV, came of age. The duke found the country buried under unimaginable war debt the previous monarch had accumulated. France's tax revenue did not even cover the interest payments on that debt.

The "remedy" came in May 1716, as the French government established a central bank with the power to print paper currency. In a few months of currency printing, France could not only pay interest on its debt but also reimburse that debt entirely. However, as in previous cases, inflating the currency supply inevitably led to rampant prices. By January 1720, prices were increasing at 23% monthly. Rents and real estate prices, for example, had increased 20-fold since the beginning of this money-printing frenzy. In February 1720, banks stopped redeeming paper currency for gold or silver. It became illegal to transact in precious metals, which were confiscated from anyone found in possession of them. When banks reopened in May of that year, gold, silver, and copper ran out as people were desperate to exchange the worthless paper currency for real money. Ultimately, these four years of hysteric money printing drove the country and a large part of Europe into a depression that lasted decades.

---

[7] *Money and trust: lessons from the 1620s for money in the digital age*, Schnabel and Shin, Bank for International Settlements [72].

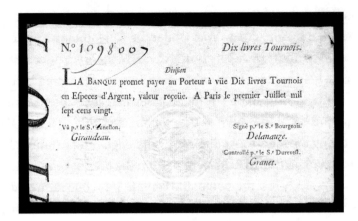

Figure 1-2. *Paper currency note issued by France's Banque Royale in 1720 (Source: National Numismatic Collection at the Smithsonian Institution; Wikimedia, public domain)*

Using paper currency only resumed in France during the Revolutionary Wars toward the end of that century. Similar to its predecessor, the new French paper currency (the assignat) became legal tender. And similar to its predecessor, the currency supplier (the National Assembly) printed increasing amounts of the new currency. Despite critics pointing out that this approach risked the same fate as money-printing earlier in the century, the supply of assignats grew from millions to billions in a few short years. As expected, the new currency lost all of its value less than a decade after its creation.

Figure 1-3. *Assignat of 1792, a short-lived legal tender paper currency in France (Source: Design: Nicolas-Marie Gatteaux - Lettering: Jean-Baptiste Gérard; Wikimedia, public domain)*

Another noteworthy episode of printing frenzy happened under the Weimar Republic in Germany at the beginning of the twentieth century. As in all previous examples, it started with a war. At the outbreak of World War I, Germany abandoned its gold-bound currency, the gold mark, for the paper mark. The republic started to use cheap metals like iron, zinc, and aluminum to mint new coins and increased the number of paper marks 4-fold over the war period.

The devastating impact of excessive currency supply did not materialize until after the war because people were holding on to savings during wartime, avoiding unnecessary spending. In a couple of years after the end of World War I, prices increased more than tenfold, wiping out over 90% of people's savings value.

When war reparation payments to France became due, the printing press accelerated its frenzy. The price of a gold mark increased from 15 marks in 1920 to 100 thousand marks in July 1923, 13 million marks in September, and 1 trillion marks in November of that year. Typical banknotes in circulation grew from 10 marks in 1920 to 100 trillion marks in 1924. October 1923 alone saw prices increase by 29,500%, while printing presses emitted another 500 quadrillion new paper marks daily.[8] As in previous examples, the paper currency lost all of its value, and the nation collapsed and ultimately returned to a gold-backed currency.

Figure 1-4. *Weimar Republic's banknote of 100 trillion marks in 1924[9] (Source: National Numismatic Collection, National Museum of American History; Wikimedia, public domain)*

---

[8] *German Hyperinflation 1922/23*, Amankwah, Goulding, Krausbeck, Mwenda, and Schweigert [67].

[9] The German word *billion* counterintuitively means *trillion* in English, not billion.

Central Banking and Fractional Reserve Banking

On the other side of the Atlantic Ocean, a major financial development happened over the same period. Until the outbreak of World War I, the United States and most of the developed world backed their currency with gold. Since the new supply (the flow) of gold compared to its stock was minimal, there was no inflation. Back-and-forth wealth transfers happened from one country to another as the relative price of goods adjusted, but they summed up to zero. Inflation was virtually non-existent, enabling people to store their wealth. It changed for the United States in 1914 when it created a private bank, the Federal Reserve, a.k.a. the Fed, with the authority to print US currency. The Fed is independent of the US government, has no budget, undergoes no audit, has no supervisor, and is accountable to no one.[10] As the Fed describes itself, it lends to the US government by creating new currency.[11] The "money" lent is new currency created out of thin air. As should be clear by now, no new value arises; printing just dilutes the value of all existing dollars. Also, the Fed does not back any new dollar with real value, such as gold.

This questionable scheme becomes even more contentious when considering the fractional reserve banking system that goes with it. When a commercial bank holds deposits from the public, only a fraction of that amount has to stay in the vault. Instead of holding on to deposits, the bank lends out most of them. In the United States, the Fed sets the reserve requirement. This way, it controls how much currency flows into the economy. Assume a 10% reserve requirement. When Alice deposits $100 at her commercial bank, say ING, the bank can lend out $90 to Bob while it keeps $10 in its vault.[12] Bob buys stuff from Charlie with that money, and Charlie deposits the $90 he just earned into his account at his commercial bank, say Wells Fargo. This bank, in turn, keeps $9 (10%) on hand and lends the remaining $81 out to Dan. Dan buys stuff from Erin, who saves the money at her commercial bank. At this point, Alice has $100 in her bank account, Charlie has $90 in his, and Erin has $81. All of this is happening with the original $100 from Alice. The process does not stop there but continues further. A 10% fractional reserve ratio enables commercial banks to "create" up to nine times that amount of money: the $100 can end up as $1,000 in circulation.

---

[10] *The Case Against the Fed*, Rothbard [57].

[11] *Putting it Simply*, Federal Reserve Bank of Boston [87].

[12] In practice, the money is not kept physically in a vault but on the bank's financial account at the central bank.

That is how banks create money—by the stroke of a pen when someone takes out a loan. Moreover, interest is due on the total amount lent by the commercial banks. If the interest rate on loans is 5%, $45 of interest must be repaid yearly, on top of the borrowed $900. And all of this arises from the original $100 deposited by Alice. The only way to pay off interest is by getting it abroad or raising more debt. At the scale of the entire economy, it is mathematically impossible to repay both the debt and the interest on the debt because money must come from somewhere. Therefore, the current monetary system relying on fractional reserve banking is a sort of legalized pyramid scheme.

The Great Depression

The 1920s represent a shift in financial culture from the pre-war era. Citizens were no longer saving but investing, which was enhanced by the low-interest rate environment. Loans that were formerly almost exclusively used by corporations gradually extended to private individuals. People borrowed to buy a house, a car, or even stocks. Due to the easy money and loan-enabled buying, everything became a bubble: consumption goods, real estate, the stock market, and more.

The most severe economic depression of the past century followed at the end of that decade. It ended up having a devastating impact on economies and the lives of people the world over. Prominent theorists from the Austrian School of Economics, Friedrich von Hayek and Murray Rothbard, attribute much of the depression to the money supply expansion of the 1920s, driving unsustainable credit bubbles.[13]

As the bubbles popped and prices dropped, many people could not repay their existing loans and stopped requesting new ones. Consequently, as in any depression under fractional reserve banking, the money supply contracted, which drove additional price decreases and massive wage drops. An unprecedented number of banks failed, wiping out people's life savings. In September 1931, the United Kingdom defaulted on its gold obligations, which created panic in all other nations. Fearing that the same would happen to the United States, a run for gold ensued at the expense of the US dollar. Once more, currency's value in the street diverged from its stated value due to an excessive supply of paper currency versus stable "real" money—gold. People increasingly

---

[13] *America's Great Depression*, Rothbard [70].

redeemed their paper money for the gold supposed to back it until banks could no longer deliver it. The US government faced no choice but to sever the peg between its currency and gold.

Figure 1-5. *US one-dollar bill under the gold standard (1928). It still holds the "will pay to the bearer on demand," which was removed upon the end of the gold standard. (Source: Wikimedia, public domain)*

In 1933, the US government under Franklin Delano Roosevelt published FDR's Executive Order 6102. With this order, the US government effectively confiscated all "gold coin, gold bullion, and gold certificates" from US citizens, threatening non-compliers with heavy fines or even jail time.[14] However, even this drastic measure was not enough to enable the government to service its debt obligations. A few months later, the United States defaulted on gold clauses in all contracts. Simply put, the government officially declared it would not reimburse loans it had contracted, both among its population and abroad. The United States repaid loans with the country's paper currency but not with real value, gold. One year later, the United States devalued its currency to gold by 59%, thereby admitting it had overvalued its dollar.

It took another decade and a second World War before nations across the world resumed a gold standard. This major decision in worldwide monetary history happened in a small area of New Hampshire called Bretton Woods.

---

[14] *Blockchain Revolution*, Tapscott and Tapscott [29].

The Bretton Woods Era

At the dawn of the post-war era, in 1944, the world's major powers established a set of rules on monetary, financial, and commercial relations known as the Bretton Woods system. The United States, Canada, Western European countries, Australia, and Japan agreed to set up a monetary policy to ensure stable exchange rates by tying their respective currencies to gold.

In addition to a set of rules, they established institutions to regulate the international monetary system. These institutions included the International Monetary Fund (IMF) and what is now known as the World Bank. The objective was to increase cooperation between countries and ward off currency devaluations that would give its perpetrator a competitive trade advantage over other countries.[15]

The subsequent international economic success of returning to the gold standard was phenomenal. The following thirty years became known as the *Glorious Thirty*,[16] also known as the *Golden Age of Capitalism*, characterized by sustained elevated levels of economic growth in industrial countries. While the need for post-war reconstruction contributed to this recovery, the gold standard was also a crucial growth driver as it imposed discipline on governments. If a government wanted to spend money, it needed to have gold first, so it needed to have or collect real value first.

The Return to Fiat Currencies

Nevertheless, the United States tried to escape this obligation by printing more dollars than it had gold to cover for. As foreign governments noticed the trick, they increasingly redeemed their dollars for gold. In the early 1970s, the United States had to act to stop real value from leaving the country.

---

[15] When a country devalues its currency, the price of local goods becomes comparatively more attractive for foreign buyers. Foreigners therefore tend to buy more goods from the country with the devalued currency, which therefore benefits from increased exports, hence a competitive trade advantage.

[16] In original French, *Trente Glorieuses*, by the French demographer Fourastié.

In the summer of 1971, US President Nixon ended the convertibility of the US dollar to gold. This decision effectively marked the end of the Bretton Woods era. Since other major powers kept central bank reserves mainly in US dollars, they followed suit in abandoning their fixed exchange rate to gold. As a result, currencies became fiat,[17] backed only by trust in the government's goodwill.

However, removing the gold standard was removing the discipline imposed on governments. With this change to fiat currency systems, governments could spend as much as they wanted by printing more of their currency. They could run unchecked deficits for years without the need to balance out their budget. As history has shown in the examples in this chapter, one cannot create new value by printing more of a currency. The value of newly printed currency comes from the existing currency in circulation. Every new dollar dilutes the value of all existing dollars. Printing new dollar bills effectively transfers purchasing power from people and corporations with savings toward the printing entity. It is a tax on savings in the form of decreasing value of these savings. As Nobel Prize laureate Milton Friedman put it, "Inflation is taxation without legislation."

As economic theory predicted, increased prices followed, as these currencies lost purchasing power when governments printed them. As shown in Figure 1-6, post–Bretton Woods, citizens' life savings held in cash lost half their value in a matter of years: in the case of the US dollar, in less than a decade. This value erosion continued over the rest of the century and beyond. In particular, $100 set aside in 1971 was only worth about $20 one generation later, in 2001. Despite the relative political stability, cash not backed by gold proved again to be an ineffective store of value.

---

[17] The Latin word *fiat* translates as "let it be done." Fiat "money" is therefore considered money only by decree, as it has no intrinsic value beyond its function as a medium of exchange.

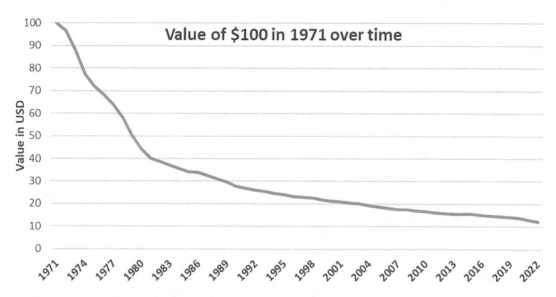

Figure 1-6. *Value of $100 in 1971 over time until 2022, reflecting US inflation measured by the Consumer Price Index in the post–Bretton Woods era (Source: Macrotrends (*www.macrotrends.net*) and own workings)*

This value erosion of currency is not unique to the US dollar; the Japanese yen, Swiss franc, and pound sterling followed a similar trend as their corresponding central banks kept printing more of their currency.

While the preceding figures are already unfortunate for savers, whose value of savings melted over time like ice cream in the sun, the reality is even harsher. It is due to these figures using the Consumer Price Index (CPI) to measure inflation. The CPI understates inflation due to its use of the "constant level of satisfaction" concept in its computation. In particular, the CPI measures the price of a basket of goods defined by the spending habits of consumers. However, it does not consider the changes in spending habits as a reaction to inflation.

To illustrate this, assume consumers typically eat sirloin steak once a week before an inflationary episode in which all prices double. Consumers whose salaries remained flat must change their spending habits. They replace the weekly sirloin steak with chicken breast. Chicken breast after the inflationary episode may cost the same as sirloin steak before this episode. While real inflation would indicate a 100% increase (prices doubled), the CPI indicates 0% inflation: the basket of goods changed such that it costs the same before and after the inflationary episode. Indeed, consumers spend the same amount before and after, but the quality of the underlying items decreased. In other words, the metric to compute the CPI is directly influenced by what it measures. Real inflation is, therefore, much higher than what the CPI suggests.[18] It implies that purchasing power decreased at an even higher rate than depicted above.

Nonetheless, this drop in purchasing power of fiat currencies represented an opportunity for gold holders. In particular, over the first decade of the post–Bretton Woods era, the market price of one ounce of gold was multiplied by 16. It grew from $40 in the summer of 1971 to above $600 before the decade's end. In other words, the real value did not vanish; instead, it merely transferred from holders of fiat currencies to holders of "real" money, gold.

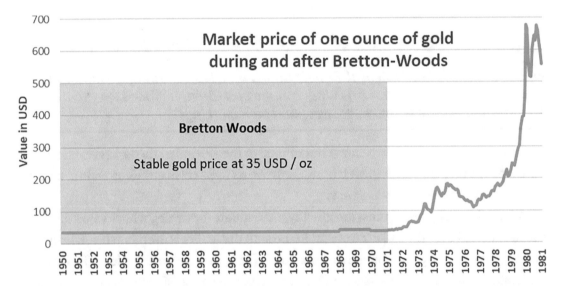

Figure 1-7. *The market price of one ounce of gold during and after the Bretton Woods system, measured in US dollars (Source: Macrotrends (*www.macrotrends.net*) and own workings)*

---

[18] This bias, referred to as the *substitution effect*, is partially taken into account in the CPI computation within the same "item category" (e.g., "steak") to reflect consumers switching to cheaper brands. However, CPI computation does not consider consumers changing item categories, such as moving from steak to chicken or from car to bus tickets.

Increasing the Pace of Printing

The last 15 years of the 1900s are marked by sustained macroeconomic stability, as monetary policies focused on taming inflation rather than increasing output and limiting unemployment. However, the new century began with a crisis as the dot-com bubble popped, driving the United States and the developed world into another recession.

To fight it, central banks reduced interest rates.[19] However, artificially reducing rates incentivizes commercial banks to lend more money to corporations and individuals. The increase in private lending materialized, especially in the real estate sector. The refinancing of existing mortgages at historically low rates soared, and the financing of the subprime market boomed. Cheap credit made real estate prices reach new records, much higher than their economic value. This bubble grew for a few years, then popped in 2007, which brought about another crisis: the Great Recession. Multiple factors intensified the crisis but are beyond the scope of this book. However, it was noteworthy how central banks reacted to another crisis while their interest rates were already historically low. After lowering interest rates even further (in negative territory, previously described as impossible in finance textbooks), the following monetary tool inputted even more liquidity into the system. Technically, central banks called it quantitative easing, but fundamentally, it was simply more currency printing.[20]

Due to this cheap financing, most governments reached record levels of debt. For example, the US debt-to-GDP ratio soared from 62% in 2007 to 90% in 2010. It increased from 62% to 80% in the EU over the same three-year period. In the private market, such unsustainable deficit situations typically end with bankruptcy. However, in the case of modern governments, central banking enables to print more to devalue debt and thereby temporarily escape default.

---

[19] The Fed reduced its fund rate from 6.50% in late 2000 to 1.00% mid-2003. Similarly, the ECB progressively decreased its main refinancing rate from 3.75% in late 2000 to 1.00% in mid-2003.

[20] Quantitative easing is when central banks buy bonds with newly created currency. It brings more liquidity (currency) to the financial system and maintains bonds' interest rates artificially low (below their "natural" or equilibrium level) so that they are more affordable by the emitter, typically governments. Governments therefore benefit from artificially cheap financing.

Over the following decade, an unprecedented wave of new regulations flooded the financial system. Financial and regulatory authorities tried to upgrade a failing system instead of rethinking it from the ground up. While they strived to improve the legacy system, a radically new one emerged. Rather than striving to increase trust in a fiat-based financial system, the new one would make trust no longer necessary. This is when Bitcoin took off.

The COVID-19 Pandemic

At the end of the 2010s, governments worldwide desperately needed to return to more sustainable financials. The central banks' reaction to a series of recent crises had added an exceptional amount of new liquidity to the financial system. Then, unfortunately, a pandemic broke out. As in previous crises, the currency printing press was the economic weapon used to fight.

The purest measure of the currency supply is the size of a central bank's balance sheet. Indeed, when the central bank prints currency, its balance sheet expands.[21] At the end of 2019, the balance sheets of four of the world's largest central banks (the Federal Reserve, the European Central Bank, the Bank of England, and the Bank of Japan) summed up to just short of 16 trillion dollars. This figure increased to over 26 trillion dollars less than two years later.[22] In other words, 38% of all US dollars, euros, British pounds, and Japanese yen ever created were printed between 2020 and 2021. In the case of the US dollar alone, this figure increases to over 52%.[23] As noted throughout this chapter, history has shown that such a printing frenzy does not fare well for currency holders.

---

[21] The central bank buys bonds (extending its asset side) with previously non-existent currency that is added to a digital account (extending its liability side).

[22] FactSet, J.P. Morgan Asset Management, most recent available data as of December 31, 2021 [59].

[23] *Value of assets on the Fed's balance sheet from August 2007 to January 2022*, Statista [68].

The price of assets is typically expressed in a fiat currency. An alternative would be to express them in "the size of the central bank's balance sheet." Fundamentally, the denominator (e.g., USD) is replaced with the central bank's balance sheet size to obtain a ratio. For example, the value of the US stock market over the size of the Fed's balance sheet, instead of expressing it traditionally as the value of the US stock market in US dollars. This new ratio indicates the value of an asset in comparison to the quantity of one particular currency in circulation. This approach reveals that assets' real value is not growing as fast as typically presented. Instead, they maintain their relative value over time, as shown in Figure 1-8.[24]

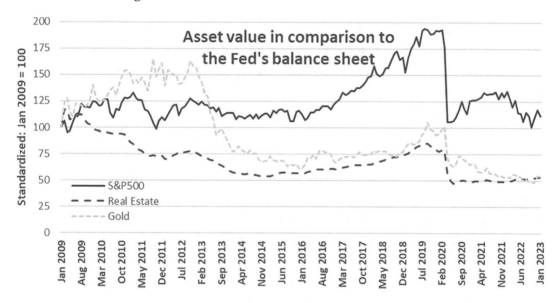

Figure 1-8. *US stock market (S&P500), real estate (US median home price), and gold expressed in proportion to the Fed's balance sheet from January 2009 to January 2023. Standardized: January 1, 2009's value = 100 (Source: Federal Reserve (federalreserve.gov/monetarypolicy), Macrotrends (*`www.macrotrends.net`*) and own workings)*

---

[24] The drop in the first half of 2020 corresponds to the increased liquidity brought by the Fed.

Figure 1-8 indicates that stocks, real estate, and gold did not diverge too far from their starting point. In particular, they all mainly remained between 50% (half as large) and 200% (twice as large) as their starting point. Also, they tend to revert toward a mean value. In other words, the change in assets' real value over time is not drastic. It is not that stocks, real estate, or gold are in a bubble; the bubble is in the central banks' balance sheets.

Where to Go from Here?

The last sections covered milestones in monetary history, where civilizations thrived under gold standards and collapsed when they moved away from them. Every attempt to separate currency from money, be it by reducing the precious material content of coins or moving to a fiat standard, ended with catastrophic consequences.[25]

Aware of this reality, authorities in recent history resorted multiple times to confiscating gold to refill their reserves of real value.[26] Citizens saw their life savings wiped out, with no recourse but to accept the new reality. The last couple of decades went through a tremendous flood of currency supply in economies worldwide. The amount of currency in circulation is multiple times larger than a decade ago. Unfortunately, history suggests a gloomy ending for this scenario.

As traditional macroeconomics concludes, increasing a country's money supply causes a proportional increase in its price level.[27] Or, as former Federal Reserve Chair (1987–2006) Alan Greenspan put it, "In the absence of the gold standard, there is no way to protect savings from confiscation through inflation."

The case presented in this chapter is not against any specific entity. Any central authority with currency printing power tends to print an excessive amount of currency because failure to do so would bring another authority into power. In particular, the entity that prevails typically promises more "free" stuff for voters, regardless of whether

---

[25] Only a few examples were covered to highlight the pattern that emerges every time, regardless of geography or time, but history provides plenty more examples along the same lines.

[26] E.g., Poland in 1919, United States in 1933, Australia in 1959, United Kingdom in 1966.

[27] See for example *International Economics Theory and Policy* (2023), 12th Edition, Krugman, Obstfeld and Melitz, Chapter 15 [93].

voters are the general population or a private council. Of course, the "free" stuff is not free but financed by devaluing existing currency units. Printing is moving value from people's savings to newly printed currency notes. This Darwinian argument indicates that the problem is not any specific government but a structural issue of wrong incentives. Indeed, for any central authority with this power, the incentive for printing currency is too strong to resist, be it for providing more welfare or more warfare. An authority with the power to print currency naturally prints an economically excessive amount of that currency. This process continues until the economic imbalance causes a monetary crash and a complete currency meltdown. Only when it returns to an "unprintable" money standard, such as gold, can the economy recover on a sound monetary basis and restore the balance.

The silver lining of the monetary crises throughout history has actually been a golden lining. Investments in gold not only maintained their value through time but even soared in value during crises. Gold remained the ultimate store of value for long-term investors because it was a high stock-to-flow asset. No asset has ever come close to gold in this regard—until recently.

The Highest Stock-to-Flow Asset of All Time

As covered in detail later in the book, hard-coded features of Bitcoin limit the ultimate number of bitcoins to 21 million. Also, the flow of new bitcoins halves every four years, making Bitcoin an ever-increasing stock-to-flow asset. No authority can choose to emit more bitcoins, even if the authority's existence depends on it. Neither governments, central banks, companies, miners, counterfeiters, nor anybody else can mine bitcoins faster than Bitcoin's supply schedule imposes. This is the ultimate guarantee of supply limitation. Bitcoin is superior to gold as a high-stock-to-flow asset since its stock-to-flow ratio keeps increasing, and its new supply is entirely independent of its market price (i.e., it has a zero price elasticity of supply; its supply is perfectly inelastic to price).

Bitcoin also scores higher than gold for core characteristics of money covered at the beginning of the chapter. Bitcoin is neither perishable nor corrodible, as its durability is infinite. It also surpasses gold in portability since it can be conveniently exchanged with a smartphone. Its level of divisibility is far superior, as one can split a bitcoin into 100 million subunits instantly and at no cost. It is also more fungible than gold, as one does not need to doubt the quality of coins or bullion. Bitcoin is also gaining traction as a unit of account (for example, many exchanges express other cryptoassets as a fraction of Bitcoin) and is already more established as such than gold. Finally, its use as a medium of exchange is growing worldwide at a tremendous pace. In particular, commerce increasingly accepts Bitcoin payments, both online and physically, in virtually all countries. In addition, it has already become the legal tender currency in El Salvador, and other countries are following suit.

In terms of the saleability of the asset, Bitcoin similarly scores remarkably high on all criteria, except two of them, for which it is still evolving: (1) the level of market development and speculation, and (2) the legal and regulatory limitations imposed on transacting the asset. As Bitcoin is still a relatively new asset, it did not reach its maturity on these levels yet but is improving quickly. In particular, Chapter 10 presents multiple metrics testifying to this maturity growth. These developments suggest that Bitcoin could soon become the most pristine form of money that humanity has ever known, taking over this title from gold.

As part of its value proposition, Bitcoin would establish a separation of money and state. Indeed, Bitcoin as a form of money is independent of the state's interests. No state can produce it to pursue its own goals at the expense of savers in that form of money. Adoption of Bitcoin would re-establish discipline in governments that the gold standard once imposed, thereby enabling people to save the value of their work in non-dilutable money.

Key Concepts

Money is whichever medium is chosen by individuals to transact. Better media of exchange gather critical characteristics, among which is the ability to store value over time. For the best part of the last five millennia, gold fulfilled this function best because its flow (new quantity of the asset available) remained small compared to its stock (existing usable quantity of the asset), even when its price soared. The limited supply combined with growing demand for gold placed it above any other asset as a store of value. Bitcoin is a new alternative to gold, gathering the crucial characteristics that made gold successful and improving on characteristics such as portability, divisibility, durability, and fungibility.

History is populated by episodes of governments drifting away from gold as currency, then frenzied printing of the new governmental currency (most often to fund wars or to service debts contracted because of wars). However, each of these episodes ended brutally, often with nation-destroying consequences. Returning to a gold standard has always been the only viable way to recover stability and resume prosperity. Money printing in the past two decades has increased to levels much larger than in previous crises, especially since the COVID-19 pandemic broke out. Unfortunately, history suggests a gloomy ending for this scenario. More pristine forms of money, such as gold or now Bitcoin, offer a once-in-a-generation opportunity to benefit from the wealth transfer that the unavoidable upcoming monetary crisis will generate.

Extension Questions

What are the incentives for governments to choose a gold standard vs a fiat standard?

Would a dual standard be desirable, where federal reserves are held partly in gold and partly in Bitcoin?

Why did citizen continue using fiat currencies in 1971 when their peg to gold was severed?

CHAPTER 2

Complementary Currencies

All money is a matter of belief.

—Adam Smith

While Bitcoin makes a compelling case against gold as pristine money, Bitcoin is unlikely to replace gold entirely because of gold's millennia-long cultural establishment. Instead, a more likely scenario is that they coexist, like television did not replace the radio entirely but only took a share of its market. Given recent developments, it will also likely coexist with national currencies, such as dollars, euros, or yen, as a payment medium. In fact, it is already increasingly doing so. Such a system will effectively have multiple currencies (accepted media of payments) running in parallel. While a multiple-currency model sounds unusual, it is a notion that already exists and whose many benefits have been praised for decades by monetary visionaries.[1] This chapter investigates why it is the case.

---

[1] See in particular Lietaer and Dunne's *Rethinking Money* (2013) [8], and Peter Moers' Community Currency Systems: A Co-operative Option for the Developing World? (1998) [86]. Bernard Lietaer, one of the designers of the European Currency System, notably dedicated his career to promoting the ground-breaking potential of multi-currency economies.

T. Jeegers, *Understanding Crypto Fundamentals*, https://doi.org/10.1007/978-1-4842-9309-6_2

Structural Imbalances

Today's financial and monetary system is unstable. Over the last half-century (1970–2017), the International Monetary Fund identified "151 banking crises, 236 currency crises, and 74 sovereign crises" [6]. It sums up to ten financial disasters annually or one every five-to-six weeks.

While financial regulators keep producing more pages of regulation for every aspect of the sector,[2] the system's stability is unaffected, still undergoing similar numbers of financial disasters year after year. Despite the unprecedented wave of new regulations following 2008's Great Recession, most of Southern Europe's sovereign debts became seriously questionable: 94% of the Venezuelan population is living in poverty due to economic crises [7]; the Argentinian Peso, the Turkish Lira and the Lebanese Pound lost over 95% of their value; and many more countries suffer from economic disasters. While some of these issues originate outside the financial and monetary systems, these systems fail to keep the economy afloat in the face of challenges. Even as recently as May 2023, major US bank failures indicate that the existing (and extensive) regulation is not an effective back-stop to the current system's flaws.

The upcoming analysis suggests that problems in our fragile system remain because the underlying issue is structural: rooted in our fundamental approach to money. Instead of treating symptoms of economic crises, an effective solution would address the root cause of these disasters. A structural issue needs a structural solution.

A Procyclical Monetary System

Of all the many ways of organizing banking, the worst is the one we have today. [...] Change is, I believe, inevitable [8].

—Sir Mervyn King, Governor of the Bank of England

---

[2] The author used to work as a regulatory risk manager in a major commercial bank in the mid-2010s, where his work included analyzing new financial regulations. At the time, 10 to 30 new financial regulations (some hundreds of pages long) were published weekly.

The economy works in cycles. When business is good and people are optimistic, the economy expands. However, when troubles arise and confidence in the future drops, the economy contracts. Long-term cycles last many decades,[3] while within them, shorter-term cycles also take place, lasting only a few years, typically less than a decade.

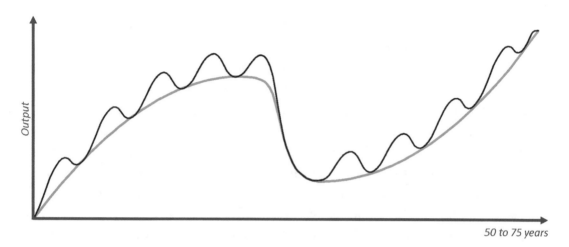

Figure 2-1. *Representation of economic cycles, with short-term cycles on top of a long-term cycle*

A crucial consequence of fractional reserve banking systems is that banks' behavior is procyclical. Banks are willing to lend money when the economy is expanding, and people want to borrow to start new businesses. As described in the previous chapter, a bank loan creates "new" money for the economy, thereby supporting its expansion. When things turn sour, however, banks are more careful in giving out loans, and people feel less confident in taking out any. As a result, the quantity of money in the economy decreases with the lower borrowing, which enhances the economy's contraction.

The procyclical nature of our current monetary system is critical in understanding today's economy. It means that when the economic horizon is bright, the system encourages credit exuberance and the creation of debt bubbles. In contrast, low credit availability deepens economic recessions when financial clouds appear.

---

[3] Ray Dalio describes these cycles as "long-term debt and capital market cycles" lasting roughly 50 to 75 years [60]. In traditional economics, it corresponds to the Kondratiev wave, typically lasting 45 to 60 years.

Monetary and Financial Sustainability

The current monetary system is a human invention several hundred years old. It emerged for medieval societies without much thought, let alone research, on how to structure it for the long term.

Modern science, however, provides a solid rationale for structuring a better system. Monetary visionaries[4] studied how natural ecosystems work, thrive, and collapse. Complex networks have predictable outcomes—from plants in biological systems to electrons in electrical circuits. In particular, natural ecosystems are sustainable; they have been there for millions of years, much longer than humans and our monetary arrangement. Research on such systems draws compelling parallels with the monetary ecosystem. Indeed, money in the economy is similar to blood in the human body, energy in organisms, or even information on social media. They are the basic flows enabling their ecosystem to operate. Left alone, excesses move to fill in deficits until the system reaches an equilibrium. For example, when electrons get too close, they repel each other so that the energy level where they orbit tends toward neutrality. When a living being overexerts itself, fatigue builds up and compels it to rest to maintain balance. Similarly, when the price for a good is temporarily lower than its equilibrium level, more people purchase it; the increased demand raises the price until it returns to its equilibrium level, where supply equals demand. Left alone, systems adjust to reach a balance.

The universality in the structure of these complex flow networks (money, blood, energy, or information) makes core characteristics driving their survival comparable. Insights from natural ecosystems can help build a more robust economy and avoid all-too-recurrent and devastating financial disasters. Arguably the main finding of this research is that an ecosystem thrives in the long run when it balances two opposite features: efficiency and resilience.

---

[4] For example, Bernard Lietaer, Jacqui Dunne, Christian Arnsperger, Sally Goerner, Stefan Brunnhuber, and Peter Moers.

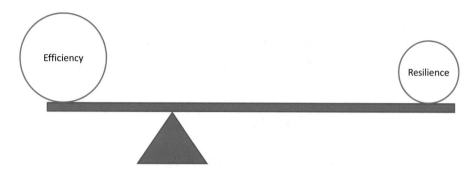

Figure 2-2. *A critical characteristic of a sustainable ecosystem: balancing efficiency and resilience*

Efficiency is the quantity of a flow that is processed in a system over time, it is the system's throughput. It is also the only feature that the traditional monetary system optimized. Having a single currency is the most efficient system: different actors have a common transaction medium, they do not need to worry about the relative valuation of currencies, and their prices are all denominated in the same unit. These benefits make the throughput of a single-currency system extremely high. They make the system *efficient.*

However, the other critical feature, *resilience*, has mostly been ignored. *Resilience* is the ability of a complex network to deal with change; its capacity to survive and adapt to a changing environment. As the frequency and impact of recent financial disasters have shown, our economic system worryingly lacks resilience.

Perhaps counterintuitively, nature does not optimize for efficiency but for a healthy combination of efficiency and resilience. Indeed, any natural ecosystem lacking resilience would no longer be here to be studied today. Similarly, a system lacking efficiency would not have survived and thrived over the ages.

Research on natural ecosystems identifies that both efficiency and resilience depend on a central characteristic: diversity.[5] However, its impact goes in opposite directions: more diversity increases the resilience of an ecosystem while, at the same time, it decreases its efficiency.

In the case of the monetary system, higher diversity means using more than a single currency. In other words, organizations and citizens would use different currencies in parallel for different purposes. For example, they could use a local currency, a regional

---

[5] Writings on the topic actually also identify a second characteristic, the "interconnectedness" of the system, but its analysis goes beyond the scope of this book.

one, and a global one. Alternatively, they would use one currency in one community and another currency in a different community. Such local and community currencies have many benefits presented in the following sections.

Multiple-Currency Systems

Multiple currencies working in parallel have been the standard for most of the past two millennia. Over this timeframe, the wide acceptance of gold coins made them optimal for international trade, while local coins, typically made of less valuable metals, supported local transactions. As a result, merchants who dealt with local and distant peers regularly switched from one currency to another.

Modernization established national currencies that became increasingly unique and increasingly *efficient*. However, over the past couple of centuries since Adam Smith, the traditional economics discipline barely ever questioned the assumption that a single currency was the optimal way for the monetary system to operate.

Yet, even today, we are making regular use of complementary currencies, however small they are in proportion to legal tender currency trades. When booking a flight, for example, you can use Air Miles as a substitute for payment with legal tender currency; hence, it is a form of complementary currency. Of course, usability is limited; only a few buyers exist (the airline companies using them), and purchasing with Air Miles is only for specific travel-related services. Nevertheless, their mere existence proves that even today, people frequently use complementary currencies, though often unknowingly.

Many complementary currency systems in use today extend beyond corporate loyalty strategies—for example, cooperative currencies. By their typically local nature, communities craft them for local purposes. For instance, they can have specific goals such as preserving the environment, incentivizing local trades, empowering less fortunate members of society, or other social purposes.

In Haiti, for example, the Small Farmers Alliance created a "tree currency." Farmers receive tree credits by planting trees or maintaining tree farms. These credits are exchangeable for goods and services such as training sessions and livestock. In its first few years of existence, this model contributed to planting 6.5 million trees while at the same time increasing local incomes, sometimes as high as doubling them.

TimeBanking[6] is another community currency that exchanges services based on the principle that one hour is one hour, regardless of the service performed. For example, if Alice teaches cooking to Bob for one hour, she gets one hour of credit from Bob. Alice can then spend this credit getting her car fixed by Charlie, who can have Bob mow his lawn or mentor his kids. No traditional currency is exchanged, only the time credits within the community. One of the objectives of TimeBanking is to connect people, create relationships and strengthen bonds within a community through acts of goodwill and reciprocity. This model follows the principle of equity, valuing everyone's time equally. TimeBanking is estimated to be used by tens of thousands worldwide, split into hundreds of TimeBanks.

The Local Exchange Trading System (LETS) is another mutual credit system working similarly to TimeBanking. However, instead of using time as a base for credit, it lets community members negotiate the rate at which to render services. For example, one could pay 12 LETS for an hour of cooking lessons, 14 LETS to fix a car, and 10 LETS to mow the lawn. The community similarly maintains the balance of each member with credits and debits upon every service rendered. This system also enables to apply skills that would otherwise be unused to solve needs that would otherwise be unaddressed.

The possibilities and structures of such currencies are limitless. However, they often have in common that they are tapping into idle resources (e.g., time that would otherwise be spent on less productive tasks) to address unmet needs (e.g., reforestation or tutoring). Consequently, people at the bottom of society typically do much better in a society with a dual currency system.

Contrary to most legal tender currencies, cooperative currencies are usually run by the community or a non-governmental organization, not traditional banks or governmental entities. Therefore, the community, not a central authority, determines the quantity of that currency in circulation.

In total, more than 4,000 such cooperative currencies were already mature before the first bitcoin ever appeared[7] [8]. The arrival of cryptocurrencies vastly increased this number, on top of increasing access through digitalization.

---

[6] See timebanks.org for more information.

[7] This number was established based on complementary currencies with an online presence. Many more such currencies certainly exist but without web visibility.

The Wörgl Experiment

Specific historical examples provide empirical evidence for complementary currencies' benefits to economies. In 1932, the consequences of the Great Depression were ravaging Europe through high unemployment and low transaction levels. In this dire situation, people held on to money as security for uncertain times. In the small Austrian city of Wörgl, with a 35% unemployment rate, the mayor addressed the problem by convincing the town hall to issue stamp scrips. Stamp scrips are a form of credit, which in this case were backed by 5,000 Austrian schillings deposited in a local bank. Fundamentally, it was a form of complementary currency used as a transaction medium in parallel to the legal tender currency.

The result of this experiment dwarfed the greatest hopes. In the first year after their issuance, the local stamp scrips had circulated among the population 463 times, which was 14 times faster than the legal tender currency. The same amount of value therefore created 14 times more jobs and transactions than traditional shillings did. While the rest of Europe continued to experience economic difficulties for years, the city of Wörgl prospered, with lower unemployment rates and higher living conditions for its citizens than in any comparable city in the region.

Further evidence of benefits from complementary currencies comes to light in the neighboring country, Switzerland.

The Swiss Miracle

In 1934, from the ashes of the Great Depression rose an important credit network in Switzerland: the *Wirtschaftsring* (German for "Economic Circle"), or WIR.[8] The Swiss Wirtschaftsring is a centralized credit clearing system with over 50,000 members and is the largest and longest-surviving community currency. Users of the WIR system can use WIR credits and debits to purchase from suppliers and sell to customers as an alternative to the Swiss franc. While most users are small and medium-sized companies, some households are also part of the network. The goods exchanged are broad and diversified,

---

[8] The three-letter word "WIR" is an abbreviation for *Wirtschaftsring* and the German word for *we*, fitting nicely with the local features of this non-governmental currency.

ranging from legal services to second-hand cars and paintings.[9] Today, WIR transactions clear in seconds via smartphones.

While using traditional currencies involves settling corporate trades after a specific number of days (for example, a 2% discount if paid within 30 days or net if paid within 90 days), the WIR system enables immediate settlement of trades. Thus, it is a system of moneyless clearing of debits and credits with the emitting WIR bank. Creditors are therefore incentivized to trade using the WIR system of bridge financing for payments because it improves their working capital (money needed to run a company's regular operations).

Also, the debits and credits are not redeemable in the local legal tender currency, the Swiss franc. Therefore, they must remain in the system to have value, promoting local trade. Accepting WIR credits thereby gives another incentive to corporations, which become prioritized over companies accepting exclusively Swiss francs.

A major macroeconomic consequence of this system is that it behaves counter-cyclically in the short run.[10] In other words, companies use the WIR system more during recessions, where cash is scarce. Companies are more willing to use the WIR system in these challenging times because they hold on to their Swiss francs tighter. The number of WIR users peaked at over 80,000 during the 2000 crisis, testifying to this thesis. Also, WIR turnover tends to increase with unemployment in Switzerland. It is challenging to accurately measure the impact of such a complementary currency network on an economy's stability. Nevertheless, indicators suggest that providing companies with a substitute currency when Swiss francs are unavailable tends to limit the downsides of economic cycles.[11]

Incentives Due to Currency Devaluation

The current economy tends to value the present more than the future because fiat currencies lose value over time. When facing a yearly 2% decrease in a currency's value (a best-case scenario for most fiat currencies), $100 today is worth the same as $102 next year. The nature of compounding amplifies this impact many times in the distant future. Under the same 2% yearly attrition, a project needs a $724 cash flow in 100 years to be worth

---

[9] *Complementary Credit Networks and Macro-Economic Stability*, Stodder [69].

[10] See *Complementary Credit Networks and Macro-Economic Stability: Switzerland's Wirtschaftsring* by Stodder for a quantitative analysis of the WIR's countercyclicality [69].

[11] As supported by the theory that inappropriate monetary and credit conditions drive macro-instability. For example, see Colander's *Post Walrasian Macroeconomics* [71].

the same as $100 today. The unfortunate consequence of this reality is that companies favor projects with short payback periods over long-term projects. As a result, incentives are such that investing in a decade-long forest management plant in the Amazona, for example, is less attractive financially than maximizing the next quarterly earnings.

However, these incentives change with the nature of the currency. For example, a complementary currency increasing in value over time incentivizes one to value the future more than the present. A project with long-term cash flows could become more financially interesting than one with equivalent cash flows today.

A Possible Future

A world where complementary currencies become the standard could help stabilize economies, incentivize local trades, and support social communities. Several payment media established vertically (for example, global, regional, and local currencies) and horizontally (different currencies for communities with different purposes) could benefit all parties involved.

For example, Bitcoin could become a global store of value, the role historically taken by gold. Another cryptoasset could become a global payment medium, while national currencies are alternatives used for tax purposes and possible redistribution of wealth. In parallel, a regional credit network like the WIR in Switzerland would facilitate corporate transactions. In addition, a provincial currency would incentivize behaviors impacting climate, such as planting trees or recycling waste, and a local cooperative currency would support social endeavors, such as tutoring children or caring for the elderly.

If such a world sounds less efficient than the current standard in which each nation has a single currency, it is because it would indeed be less *efficient*. However, the benefits of this diversity would likely largely compensate for the lower efficiency. These include reducing the impact of economic downturns and matching unused resources with unmet needs for less fortunate members of society. Therefore, such a model has reasonable grounds to become superior. In addition, all these currencies could be digital and used seamlessly through a mobile phone, making the lower "efficiency" much less relevant than the first intuition suggests.

Key Concepts

The current economic system is deeply unstable. While designed for efficiency, it drastically lacks resilience and, as a result, is subject to frequent collapses (worldwide, about ten financial disasters every year). Insights from natural ecosystems identify that our single-currency model may be the main cause of this lack of resilience. Empirical evidence supports these findings. Indeed, cities and regions using complementary currencies in parallel to legal tender currencies have shown remarkable advances (economic, environmental, or social), where all stakeholders benefited in exceptional ways.

The permanent devaluation of fiat currencies provides incentives to value the present more than the future. A store of value (e.g., Bitcoin) not devalued over time through excessive printing and working in parallel to local currencies meant as media of payment could realign incentives for the longer-term focus of financial investments. Long-term projects could become the priority over short-term ones, incentivizing sustainable management of resources.

Extension Questions

Assuming its legality, what are the pros and cons of a local currency running in parallel to its country's legal tender?

What could be the consequences of a world where Bitcoin acts as a global store of value, Ethereum as a global medium of payment, and national currencies as alternative local media of payments?

What does Bitcoin need to become not only a global store of value, but also the standard medium of payment and unit of account?

CHAPTER 3

Blockchain As a Force for Good

Men are only as good as their technical development allows them to be.

—George Orwell

While the previous chapters focused on money, revolutionary promises of cryptoassets extend well beyond the monetary sector. In particular, the underlying blockchain technology can become a force for the greater good through countless use cases. Here is just a glimpse of possible applications and their likely positive impact.

Decentralization

A few years ago, on a small Mediterranean island, the people of Cyprus learned the hard way a lesson that most of the world has yet to understand. While the health of their economy was in question, and banks struggled to show positive quarterly financial statements, most citizens considered themselves safely insulated from the bewildering macroeconomic affairs. Personal bank accounts were, in many cases, holding considerable amounts due to decades of hard work and saving for older days. Little would justify having financial concerns in such a situation.

Then, in early 2013, the creative concept of bail-in was first activated. Instead of letting failing commercial banks collapse under unpayable debts and go bankrupt, the financial regulators decided to use the creditors' money (mainly citizens' deposits at these banks) to pay off the bank's debt.[1] Imagine the size of your bank account suddenly

---

[1] A bail-in is the counterpart of a bail-out, in which the government saves a financial institution by "bailing it out" (i.e., by buying a large share of it or paying off debts on its behalf).

© Thomas Jeegers 2023
T. Jeegers, *Understanding Crypto Fundamentals*, https://doi.org/10.1007/978-1-4842-9309-6_3

undergoing a haircut, in a perfectly legal and recourseless way, for both uninsured (above 100,000 EUR) and insured (below 100,000 EUR) deposits. Unfortunately, this was the reality for thousands of people in a democratic and industrialized European nation only a few short years ago.

The infamous lesson in Cyprus is that the content of your bank account is not your money. It is instead a claim on money you willingly entrusted to a commercial bank. The bank is taking risks with this money and, if things go wrong, it can refuse (or be legally prevented) to repay your claim in full. So, your hard-earned money is at the mercy of centralized authorities that can refuse to return it.[2]

Now let us consider an alternative world where your money is not in a commercial bank but on a decentralized platform. A scenario made possible through blockchain technology. Instead of having a board of directors in a bank making decisions on depositors' funds, decisions are pre-programmed transparently on a shared online technology owned by the users or agreed upon by users directly. In this scenario, depositors own their money. Of course, savers can still individually choose to lend out some savings to earn a return if they wish to do so. However, they can also keep their money free of financial risk and centralized authorities' decisions if they desire.

It is sometimes challenging to convince people of the benefits of decentralization because they usually assume that they already have what decentralization would bring: ownership. Understanding decentralization means understanding that the current standard is not ownership but custody. Money in your bank account is not truly yours; you only have a claim on money held by the bank.

Privacy

At the beginning of 2018, hackers broke into India's national ID database, Aadhaar. They leaked the personal data of 1.1 billion registered Indian citizens, or one in every seven individuals on the planet. It included names, bank account details, and even biometric information such as fingerprints [9].

---

[2] Admittedly, the authority in question must be in a very bad situation and under specific circumstances for a bail-in scenario to take place, but the argument remains that it is a possibility under Europe's current framework for resolving failing banks (the Bank Recovery and Resolution Directive of 2014). As history has shown, this possibility is not only theoretical.

Just three years later, on the other side of the planet, in April 2021, Facebook made the headlines with another security breach. It followed a series of infamous security incidents and data leaks at the company, which exposed the personal information of hundreds of millions of users. The 2021 breach impacted over half-a-billion users and revealed full names, birthdays, locations, email addresses, and other personal information [10].

While privacy issues are not new, they have been the cause of growing concerns over the last decade. Governmental and corporate failures to secure confidential information about their citizens and users have been much too recurrent. The two earlier examples are, unfortunately, only two of many. Although individuals highly value their private information, a government or a company does not appreciate this confidential data at the same level. And since custodians undervalue our data, it typically ends up under-protected. For example, Facebook keeps millions of user records, including accounts and passwords, in plain text, accessible by thousands of Facebook employees [11].

Here again, blockchain technology is a game changer. The latest advances in cryptography enable blockchain to be the database of choice for confidential information, where owners of the information (citizens) keep ownership of their data. Indeed, one technically does not need personal details saved on a centralized governmental or corporate database. Instead, users only need to prove that they are who they say they are or that they own what they claim to own without revealing any more information than is strictly necessary. This can be achieved through cryptography.

In particular, zero-knowledge proof (ZKP) is a cryptography concept where one person can prove to another that a fact is true without revealing anything more. For example, if I want to buy alcohol in the United States, I need to prove that I am at least 21 years old. Typically, I would hand over my ID card to the merchant (or upload it online), where he can check my identity and age. However, in this process, I reveal much more than required. I am sharing my name, nationality, and all other information on my ID, which the merchant does not need. The merchant does not even need to know my exact date of birth, but only that I am at least 21. Instead, with ZKP technology, I can swipe a card (or use a platform online) that returns "true" or "false" to the question of whether I am at least 21 years old. Through cryptography, I can prove that this information is genuine and unforgeable. Confidential information is maintained, and the merchant receives the necessary information. Of course, buying alcohol is not the primary use case of this technology, but just an example that is easy to understand. ZKP can be similarly used for proving ownership of a house, creditworthiness, membership to a club, and countless other cases, without sharing anything more than required.

The objective is not to hide information but to protect oneself from possible data breaches, hacks, or leaks that could happen to whichever system stores this information. Encrypting this information and using a blockchain to convey it prevents any company or government from storing the information without sufficient protection. It enables people to regain control of their identity and become self-sovereign for their confidential data. Not only would it enforce the right to be forgotten, but it would also make compliance (for example, to GDPR) cheaper and easier.

Blockchain technology can also address the opposite problem—the inability to officially register one's personal data through traditional means.

Inclusion

In 2019, UNICEF identified that every fourth birth in the world is unregistered, and the proportion of unrecorded births is increasing. Developing countries in Southeast Asia and Africa drive this figure, as the complexity of the process and registration fees may be dissuasive for parents. Unfortunately, lacking official birth registration often excludes children from access to essential services such as healthcare or education. In addition, lacking registration puts these children at an even greater risk of exploitation [12].

Obtaining a proof of identity should be simple and affordable. Again, blockchain technology provides these benefits by removing barriers to access. Simple processes provide access to inexpensive and unfalsifiable proof of identity, secured by state-of-the-art cryptography. In addition, removing barriers to access for greater inclusion is not only valid for identity but also for services such as banking.

About 2 billion people worldwide do not have a bank account and are thus excluded from many economic opportunities. Even more so than for birth registration, access fees can be dissuasive, transaction fees prohibitively expensive, and minimum amounts required. With blockchain technology, no bank account is necessary to participate in the economy. It is not even necessary to have a formal proof of identity to do so. As a result, cryptoassets enable higher inclusion of the unbanked, more simply and cheaply than any technology has enabled thus far.

Admittedly, blockchain usage requires users to have access to the Internet. And unfortunately, many of these 2 billion unbanked people do not. However, as Internet infrastructure expands, an increasing number of people can join an economy that was previously inaccessible to them.

Private Property

The year 2022 forced millions of Eastern European citizens to flee their countries. Seeking refuge elsewhere, many lost almost everything they owned, as they could not transport their wealth across borders. In many cases, the few belongings they carried physically were confiscated or stolen from them. Besides the crisis in Ukraine, the United Nations High Commissioner for Refugees flags at least another dozen emergencies worldwide, where people often face analogous disasters.

While much of one's wealth resides in physical objects, part lies in online money accounts. Unfortunately, this money is not always easily transportable as the institutions behind it are often reticent to enable withdrawals when they are most needed. Also, international transfers can be limited to specific amounts and are subject to high fees.

In contrast, Bitcoin enables holders to carry wealth regardless of circumstances. By memorizing a 12-word seed phrase, one can resume transacting with a Bitcoin wallet from anywhere on the planet. One can own private property regardless of conflicts, financial institutions' limitations, or states' political agendas.

For this reason, countries most at risk are leading cryptoasset adoption. For instance, Chainalysis' 2022 Global Crypto Adoption Index ranks Vietnam, Philippines, Ukraine, and India as the countries with the highest crypto adoption [13].

Free Speech

In October 2022, the financial technology giant PayPal updated its acceptable use policy (AUP), warning users that they would be charged a $2,500 fine for "promoting misinformation." This update triggered an instantaneous reaction from the public, vocally opposing this limitation to free speech. For example, David Markus, PayPal's former president, tweeted his utmost opposition to this update.

> It's hard for me to openly criticize a company I used to love and gave so much to. But @PayPal's new AUP goes against everything I believe in. A private company now gets to decide to take your money if you say something they disagree with. Insanity.

—David Markus

While PayPal quickly reversed course, this imprudent update raised concerns in communities worldwide about the power of centralized authorities. In particular, it strengthened the case for decentralized systems to protect the public from financial institutions' ability to seize people's funds. Safeguarding freedom of speech implies that people should be able to freely express ideas without fearing repercussions threatening their life or finances.

For this reason, journalists and activists worldwide are already using cryptoassets, particularly Bitcoin, to transact. Not only are they facing a low risk of seeing their funds confiscated by institutions disagreeing with them or with different interests, but at the same time, they are also increasing their privacy.

Inflation

Per the World Bank database, 28 countries had an average yearly inflation rate of two digits or more over the twenty years ending in 2021.[3] These countries represent over 1.3 billion people whose national currency is unreliable enough to store value earned through work.[4] Moreover, in 2022, inflation increased significantly worldwide, worsening the situation.

As presented in Chapter 1, inflation reflects the increased quantity of a currency in an economy. It happens through incremental currency made available by the central bank and credits created by commercial banks. In other words, letting central banks print currency at will opens the door to possibly unlimited inflation.

The higher the credibility of a central bank, the higher the trust that future inflation will remain close to the target. However, even comparatively credible central banks have difficulty maintaining this target, as the incentives to print more currency become overwhelming under challenging times. For example, despite the European Central Bank's mandate to keep inflation below 2%, the Euro Area's year-on-year official inflation rate was above 10% in October and November 2022. As previously covered, actual inflation is likely even higher due to the metric used to compute the official level of inflation. Even in the case of the ECB, trust in the ability to tame inflation is eroding.

---

[3] Inflation measured through CPI over 2001–2021; last database update on September 16, 2022.
[4] With a 10% inflation rate, a currency loses half its value in about seven years.

In contrast, Bitcoin automates the role of a central bank with absolute credibility. Nobody will ever mine bitcoins faster than the code imposes. Therefore, the future inflation rate is known with absolute certainty and is unchangeable, regardless of circumstances. In 2023, Bitcoin's inflation rate is about 1.5% and will continuously decrease until it reaches 0% around the year 2140.

Environment

As of 2023, the total electricity consumption for securing the Bitcoin network is as high as the total energy consumption of Switzerland. This record energy usage is the cause of recurring attacks on cryptoassets by environmentalists. However, upon more informed analysis, this industry's emergence is a net benefit for the environment, as exposed next.

First, the high energy consumption argument does not apply to all cryptoassets. Most cryptoassets do not rely on an energy-intensive mechanism to secure their network but on alternatives consuming much less energy. For example, the more widespread proof-of-stake mechanism consumes less than 1% of the energy consumed by a proof-of-work mechanism. For instance, a transaction on the Solana blockchain only uses 2,707 Joules or less energy than three Google searches [14]. To set records straight, the high energy consumption of the industry is almost exclusively coming from Bitcoin mining, a process explored in detail in Chapter 6. For now, just remember that Bitcoin mining consists of thousands of computers worldwide partaking in a race by consuming computer power to earn ("mine") new bitcoins, thereby securing the network from external attacks.

Second, cryptoassets could replace most of the current financial industry. They have already started to replace banking services, payment transfer companies, brokers, clearing houses, and more. The outdated infrastructure they replace is highly energy-consuming. Even at its peak consumption, the cryptoasset industry consumes only a fraction of the energy the current inefficient infrastructure uses. For instance, a May 2021 study by Galaxy Digital establishes that Bitcoin's energy consumption is less than half the energy consumed by the traditional banking system alone [15]. Transitioning from the traditional financial system to a cryptoasset-based system would materially decrease total energy consumption.

However, these first two arguments are only minor in addressing the energy-consumption issue that cryptoasset critics put forward. The fundamental arguments they ignore are the following.

The proof-of-work consensus mechanism securing the Bitcoin blockchain creates a market for energy where efficient energy sources have a competitive advantage. For example, natural and renewable geothermal energy in countries like El Salvador can now be valued and traded globally. However, mining Bitcoin is only interesting financially where and when energy is exceptionally cheap. For instance, it is only meaningful when it cannot power anything else useful. If that energy could serve any purpose besides mining Bitcoin, it would be advantageous for the producer to use it for that alternative purpose. As a result, Bitcoin's energy consumption would not have otherwise gone to powering a US household or lighting a German highway. Instead, it is energy that would otherwise be lost because the demand on the electricity grid at that place and time is exceptionally low. Since excess energy cannot be effectively stored, using it to secure the Bitcoin network benefits all users worldwide while preventing energy from going to waste. In addition, countries rich in natural and renewable energy can now trade previously unusable excess energy to benefit local communities.

Critics of Bitcoin's energy consumption fail to understand that Bitcoin does not provide incentives to mine where energy can power other valuable purposes. It is in stark contrast to Christmas lights, for example, which plug where and when energy is necessary to fulfill basic needs such as warming a home or cooking food. Another example is clothes driers, typically using energy where it is valued the highest—big cities—and consuming more energy than Bitcoin mining worldwide.[5]

In addition, the energy used to mine Bitcoin comes primarily from renewable sources. The Bitcoin Mining Council, gathering 53 mining companies representing half of the global network, revealed in its Q4 2022 report that 59% of Bitcoin mining uses renewable energy, a figure higher than for any country in the world and growing rapidly. Independent institutions and academic bodies researching the same topic confirm this finding. In comparison, the share of renewable energy used to power the energy grid is only about 31% in the United States and below 22% worldwide. Securing the Bitcoin network is therefore a much greener endeavor than using most other technologies. Besides, Bitcoin mining efficiency and its sustainable electricity mix continuously evolve for the better. For instance, Bitcoin's mining efficiency improved by a factor of 58 over the past eight years [16]. This phenomenal improvement means the cost of securing the Bitcoin network dropped by more than 98% over this period. Not only is the Bitcoin network secured in a much greener way than most technologies, but it is also increasingly more efficient in doing so.

---

[5] World Economic Forum, "Why the debate about crypto's energy consumption is flawed" [73].

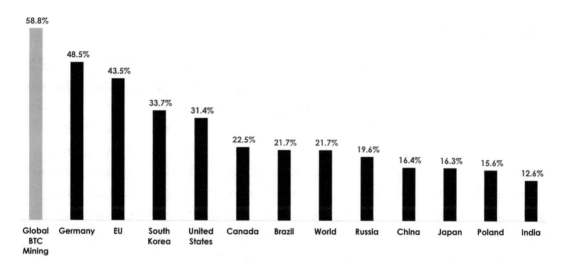

Figure 3-1. *Sustainable power mix: Bitcoin mining vs. countries (% of TWh) (Source: Bitcoin Mining Council Q4 2022 report [16])*

Furthermore, Bitcoin mining incentivizes the financing of renewable power infrastructure around the world. For example, wind turbines and hydropower plants are often in shortage when demand on the grid is high. However, they produce excess energy when demand is low—lost energy that producers cannot store or trade to recover investment costs. With the option to mine Bitcoin, they now have the means to put this excess energy to practical use and pay off their fixed costs with the proceeds. This mechanism of countercyclical energy use for Bitcoin mining compared to grid demand (reflected in energy prices) has a stabilizing impact. Investing in renewable power plants becomes more attractive with a more stable energy demand because producers can continuously benefit from their output. As a result, renewable energy revenues become more reliable, increasing incentives to finance renewable infrastructure.

Finally, new developments enable Bitcoin miners to capture flared methane and other unwanted side-products of currently polluting processes. Oil drilling, for example, is a process during which natural gas is sometimes discovered. As petroleum drilling sites often lack pipelines to redirect it, natural gas in the past has typically been released into the atmosphere or burned, referred to as *flaring*. This stranded gas can now be used to create cheap electricity and mine Bitcoin. As a result, the CO_2 output of the oil drilling processes decreases while at the same time providing extra revenue to miners [17]. Bitcoin mining thereby further contributes positively to the environment. Therefore, if it is not the case already, Bitcoin mining will soon become a carbon-negative industry.

Sustainability

In early 2022, deforestation of the Amazon rainforest rose to a 14-year high after reaching record levels in the previous two years. Deforestation is accelerating, causing permanent biodiversity loss and devastatingly impacting the climate.

Despite climate commitments and political promises, one reason for the lack of care for the world's largest rainforest is the lack of financial incentives for long-term forest management projects. As introduced in the previous two chapters, the continuous erosion in the value of fiat currencies creates a preference for short-term cash flows over long-term cash flows. Indeed, given the high pace of inflation and the uncertainty around it, investors prefer moderate returns on their investment in the upcoming quarter over large returns that may take decades to materialize.[6] A short-term return is more valuable in the eyes of investors because they do not discount it as heavily. With a currency losing value over time, the discount applied to any future cash flow increases with the time horizon. The financial value of the future is lower, misdirecting capital away from it.

Moving to a currency standard where value does not erode over time, but grows over time, would radically change financial incentives. The future would no longer be discounted, which would no longer incentivize immediate spending at its expense. Instead, projects with long-term cash flows would become more interesting financially, redirecting capital toward sustainable endeavors. Such a currency standard has never been accessible but is now technologically available for all: Bitcoin.

Transparency

The subprime mortgage crisis of 2008 was devastating throughout the world. However, countries with greater financial sector transparency suffered less from this disaster [18]. One reason is greater transparency increases incentives to "do the right thing," as market participants can better act on information.

Blockchain-based assets are typically highly transparent. For example, all Bitcoin transactions on the network are publicly shared and instantly retrievable by anybody. The underlying technology can enable greater transparency for companies and public

---

[6] A tendency known as a *high time preference* and investigated by Saifedean Ammous in *The Bitcoin Standard* [56] and *The Fiat Standard* [61].

officials at a low cost. It would most likely do so at lower costs than in the existing system. It is not to claim that full transparency on transactions and actions is necessary in all cases (though it is programmable if necessary). However, higher levels of transparency can bring more accountability. It is especially relevant in relationships with inherent conflicts of interest for people acting on behalf of others, known as the *agency problem*. For example, banks that are "too big to fail" take more risks than desired by savers, debtors, regulators, and the public. Banks benefit from the upside (higher expected profits) but do not suffer from downsides as governments would likely bail them out if things went wrong. Higher transparency on investments and spending would reduce such undesirable incentives. Public blockchains are highly transparent as they publish transactions in the public domain in an immutable ledger accessible by all.

The value of transparency to investors is even measurable in financial markets. For instance, municipal bonds are less transparent than federal bonds. Even though more municipal bonds exist than any other security, they suffer from less financial interest because they lack transparency.

Velocity

In a remote village, a stranger visits the local restaurant. He expects his date to arrive but is unsure whether she will show up. He nevertheless asks for the nicest table, where he would wait for her. The restaurant owner wants to ensure the stranger can pay and asks for a deposit before bringing the stranger guest to the table. The guest hands over a $100 bill under the condition that he can reclaim it if his date does not come. While waiting, the restaurant owner uses the bill to pay his cook. The cook swiftly runs to the neighboring barber to pay off his debt of the same amount. The barber runs to the car dealer to pay for the ongoing repairs on his car. The car dealer takes the bill and brings it to the restaurant owner to pay for his last dinner on credit. The stranger guest then leaves, taking the $100 bill back. No economic activity occurred, but all villagers are now more creditworthy, less indebted than they were just an hour before.

A high velocity of money happens when the same dollar changes hands many times rather than being stuck under a mattress as a personal saving. Moreover, as the preceding story illustrates, a high velocity of money can increase economic prosperity even when no economic activity happens. On the other hand, money locked, saved, and unused does not allow transactions to occur, which slows down the economy. Unfortunately, our current banking system locks money for extended periods with every interbank transaction. For transactions within the same jurisdiction, the settlement typically lasts about two days, during which the transacted amount cannot serve any other purpose. International transfers can even lock money for weeks.

Decentralized finance through blockchain solves this issue, shortening the settlement period from days to minutes. As it unlocks money, more prosperity can ensue, benefiting the whole system.

Foreign Exchange

When international transactions happen, currencies often must be exchanged for another (e.g., Swiss francs for euros). In 2022, the foreign exchange market accounted for $7.5 trillion daily.[7] However, a fee applies to each dollar, disincentivizing international trade and reducing economic activity. In particular, cross-border payments from the United States face an average 5% fee. In addition, foreign exchange trades take time to settle, further slowing down the economy and requiring resources to deal with its complexities.

The enormous amount lost in fees is due to the many middlemen involved and to different economies using different currencies, whose exchange rates fluctuate permanently. While the previous chapter made the case that several currencies are likely a good thing for the economy, this argument applies to currencies used in parallel to each other within the same economy (e.g., one for local trades, one for community-specific dealings, and one for global transactions). In a crypto-integrated world, international trades would not have to go through a prior foreign exchange to settle. Instead, such trades could happen on a global cryptoasset network, thereby minimizing trading fees and settlement time. A global currency is preferred for international transactions, not local currencies. It would eliminate inefficiencies implied by multiple banks and middlemen. In addition, this simplification would free up resources: hundreds of thousands of people working in foreign exchange markets could instead use their skills for more economically productive purposes.

---

[7] 2022 *Triennial Central Bank Survey of Foreign Exchange Over-the-counter (OTC) Derivatives Markets*, Bank for International Settlement [79].

Accounting

In 2018, a scandal hit BT, a British multinational telecommunication company, where a human error in the group's accounting underestimated its pension obligation by £500 million. It happened just a year after another accounting scandal at the company reduced the group's valuation by £8 billion [19].

Unfortunately, human errors and fraud in accounting are regularly slipping through companies' internal controls and auditors' verifications. Accounting scandals have come to light in the last decade at companies such as Wirecard, Wells Fargo, Toshiba, Tesco, Petrobras, and all major audit firms.

Using blockchain technology in accounting could reduce human errors and fraud, facilitating transactions and automating controls. For example, the digital signature of a contract could set up a purchase order for that contract on a blockchain. Invoices would be issued directly on the blockchain against that purchase order, and payments would be triggered immediately for these invoices. Linking separate items together in an automated and transparent way would provide all parties involved with instantaneous updates on the status of all invoices, transactions, and outstanding amounts. In addition, exhaustively auditing these records could be automatic and continuous rather than sample-based and delayed, as they are today. Automating this process would also drastically reduce auditing costs and provide transaction transparency. Many other accounting processes are automatable and can be simplified on blockchain-based systems. Such developments will likely reduce accounting scandals and human errors through more automation and higher transparency of corporate accounting processes.

Sharing Economy

When Uber's ride-hailing app entered the market, it quickly became evident that this business model was superior to traditional taxis. For instance, Uber matches occasional drivers who have a few hours to invest in increasing their income with people who need a more affordable ride than with licensed taxis. Prices follow the laws of supply and demand to clear at the level suggested by the market. In addition, rides are easily bookable through an app, making prices transparent and minimizing wait times. Despite this travel revolution, Uber is controversial due to the over-proportional share of profits that the company captures, often only leaving drivers with just enough to cover the costs of the car and the fuel.

Now imagine the service delivered by Uber, but without the company behind it. Not Uber, but also not any other company. The service delivered does not need any company to run it. Instead, the community could manage it through a decentralized platform. Matching idle drivers with riders is cheaply programmable. Also, the community can vote on issues, such as ensuring customers' safety through certifications or ratings. Rides could be even more affordable for customers and profitable to drivers since no company would capture any share of the profits.

Such a system would be part of a true sharing economy. Community-built apps, run by the people, for the people. Uber is not the only example; imagine Airbnb's service without the company Airbnb behind it. Or eBay's services without eBay. YouTube services without YouTube. Banking services without banks. Blockchain's decentralization enables a whole new world for the sharing economy, which can now operate at scale and without intermediaries.[8]

Creators' Empowerment

When an artist releases a song, the audience enjoying the music typically does not pay him directly. Instead, many intermediaries stand in between content creators and consumers: studios, record labels, agents, radios, intellectual property services, streaming platforms such as Spotify, Amazon Music, or iTunes, and more. Each intermediary takes a cut of the artist's profit, leaving him with little left to reward and refine his craft. Other creative expressions experience the same erosion of fees in the distribution chain from creation to consumption—for videos, books, paintings, or even video games.

In some cases, record labels, publishers, and other middlemen add value to the process by providing helpful feedback, targeting the right audience, or editing the creative work for the better. However, in many instances, fees are over-proportional to the delivered service. In any case, going through intermediaries or reaching out directly to fans should be the artist's choice, not an obligation implied by limited technology or industry standards.

Blockchain solutions offer this choice. An artist can now publish his work, say a song, on a decentralized server and use a blockchain for sharing it with predefined usage fees. Should one listen to the song privately, the fees can be minimal. It can be higher

---

[8] The start-up Origin already enables the creation of decentralized marketplaces, connecting users to enable the true sharing economy to flourish. See `www.originprotocol.com`.

for usage as background music for a commercial video. And for usage as a theme song of a movie, it can be even higher. The artist can be rewarded directly through crypto payments on the same blockchain and have complete transparency on the popularity of his work. Higher visibility allows other artists to identify opportunities rather than face the black box of intermediaries' fees. Drastically lower production and distribution costs enable content creators to benefit fully from their intellectual property. Moreover, users can reward them directly, and everybody benefits from higher industry transparency.

Key Concepts

While blockchain technology challenges the meaning of money, blockchain's benefits extend well beyond. In particular, it shines as a driver for ESG practices and inclusion. For example, decentralization frees people from abusive practices from institutions and governments, which do not always prioritize people's best interests. Higher security standards and data encryption enable people to recapture their online identity and limit risks related to database breaches. Blockchain also enables billions of people to access basic services such as identity certification and banking, from which they are currently excluded. Also, it enables a true sharing economy by removing unnecessary middlemen capturing over-proportional shares of profits.

Moreover, the billions of people currently facing hyperinflation risk now have a currency alternative for which future inflation is reliably known in advance. Furthermore, blockchain-based assets can drastically reduce humanity's negative impact on the environment by accelerating the transition to renewable energy. Securing cryptoasset networks such as Bitcoin leads the way through much higher usage of renewables than any country in the world. Finally, many more use cases of blockchain as a force for good are constantly being developed.

Extension Questions

How could blockchain technology and cryptoassets enable to establish a universal basic income?

How can blockchain strengthen local communities?

How else can blockchain or Bitcoin be a driver for the greater good?

CHAPTER 4

Portfolio Management Primer

Audentes fortuna iuvat. (Fortune favors the bold.)

—Virgil

Let us change perspective and look at cryptoassets from a financial portfolio management point of view. This chapter introduces the basics of portfolio management to assess the financial characteristics of cryptoassets. As the analysis shows, cryptoassets have been the most financially attractive investment of the last decade, even risk-adjusted, and could remain so for the upcoming one.

Price Fluctuations

While fundamentals define the economic value of an asset, supply and demand on exchanges drive its price. The difference between the price of an asset and its value creates opportunities for investors able to spot it: they can secure a return on investment when the price eventually trends toward the asset's economic value. The size and frequency of price fluctuations, known as volatility, are critical in portfolio management. Let us start by discussing how prices fluctuate, which ultimately drives both return and volatility.

© Thomas Jeegers 2023
T. Jeegers, *Understanding Crypto Fundamentals*, https://doi.org/10.1007/978-1-4842-9309-6_4

Price variations depend on trades on exchanges. An *order book* holds pending trades. It captures the price at which buyers are willing to buy and sellers are willing to sell, as well as the quantity for each trade. Table 4-1 illustrates how an order book looks and what happens when a large trade happens. Assume that Bitcoin is currently trading at $123,456.78 (a price it has not reached yet as of this writing) with the order book presented in Table 4-1.

Table 4-1. *Example of an Order Book for Bitcoin, Where the Current Price Is $123,456.78*

	Price (USD)	Amount (BTC)
Sell side	123,500.00	3.141
	123,489.24	0.318
	123,475.00	2.718
	123,468.43	0.476
	123,459.00	1.618
	123,457.55	0.693
	123,457.00	0.301
Buy side	123,456.54	0.707
	123,456.32	0.632
	123,456.00	0.774
	123,455.00	1.000
	123,453.50	0.547
	123,450.00	3.162
	123,449.99	1.414

Every row in Table 4-1 corresponds to a market participant's purchase or sell order. For example, one private individual is willing to sell 0.301 BTC for $123,457.00 per BTC (the seventh row), and another is willing to buy 1.000 BTC for $123,455.00. Both wait for the market price to move for their order to execute, as the current price is too high for the buyer and too low for the seller. Prices are sorted from highest to lowest, with prices on the sell side always higher than the current price and prices on the buy side lower than the current price. It will always be the case; otherwise, the orders would execute immediately and not be visible as pending trades on the order book.

Now assume that a large buyer would like to acquire 10 BTC for a price up to $123,500.00 per BTC. The entire sell side of pending trades visible in Table 4-1 would execute immediately. The buyer gets 0.301 BTC at $123,457.00, 0.693 BTC at $123,457.55, and so on until 3.141 BTC at $123,500.00. As a result, Bitcoin's current price would suddenly jump to $123,500.00.

Since the cryptoasset market is relatively illiquid compared to traditional stocks and bonds markets (the total volume traded in a day is substantially lower), large orders tend to move prices significantly. For example, Tesla's purchase of $1.5 billion of Bitcoin in February 2021 caused the price to surge. Large price moves create the high volatility that cryptoassets are known for. Nevertheless, as the industry matures, increasing levels of liquidity become available for cryptoassets, which tend to reduce volatility.

Risk and Return

In a nutshell, portfolio management aims to identify the optimal asset allocation to maximize expected return with as little volatility as possible. Indeed, for most investors, high financial returns and low volatility are attractive features. By convention, the industry gives the term "risk" to volatility and measures it as the standard deviation of returns. Simply speaking, the standard deviation of returns is their average deviation compared to their average.

A theory developed by Nobel Prize laureate Harry Markowitz in 1952 to optimize financial portfolios is still an elemental method financial advisors use today. This *modern portfolio theory* aims to identify the right balance between return and risk, given specific characteristics of an investor, such as willingness to take risks and time horizon. This method identifies the highest possible level of return one can expect for a given level of risk. The higher the acceptable level of risk, the higher the expected return can be.

With this background in mind, Table 4-2 compares past returns of major cryptoassets (Bitcoin and Ethereum) to different benchmarks: gold and major diversified indices (S&P500, NASDAQ, and Euro Stoxx 50). Arbitrarily selecting a time frame can significantly bias an analysis. Therefore, a standard one is used, long enough to be meaningful and recent enough to be relevant: a ten-year window ending when writing this book—from January 1, 2013, to December 31, 2022. To compare multi-year returns, one uses the *compound annual growth rate* (CAGR), which is the average yearly return of an investment, assuming continuously reinvested profits.

Table 4-2. *Yearly Return Comparison of Selected Investments over 10 Years from 2013 to 2022, Starting 2016 for Ethereum (its first full year). (Data source: Yahoo! Finance for BTC; ethereumprice.org for ETH; MacroTrends (`www.macrotrends.net`) for gold, S&P500 and NASDAQ, and investing.com for Euro Stoxx 50)*

Return	BTC	ETH	Gold	S&P500	NASDAQ	EU50
2013	+6,035%	n.a.	−28%	+30%	+62%	+18%
2014	−61%	n.a.	−0%	+11%	+22%	+1%
2015	+38%	n.a.	−12%	−1%	+23%	+4%
2016	+130%	+785%	+9%	+10%	+17%	+1%
2017	+1,268%	+9,190%	+13%	+19%	+17%	+6%
2018	−72%	−81%	−1%	−6%	+8%	−14%
2019	+87%	−10%	+19%	+29%	+34%	+25%
2020	+308%	+473%	+24%	+16%	+26%	−5%
2021	+62%	+400%	−4%	+27%	+60%	+21%
2022	−65%	−68%	−0%	−19%	−11%	−12%
Total	+124,317%	+130,242%	+10%	+169%	+770%	+44%
CAGR	**+103.9%**	**+178.6%**	**+0.9%**	**+10.4%**	**+24.1%**	**+3.7%**

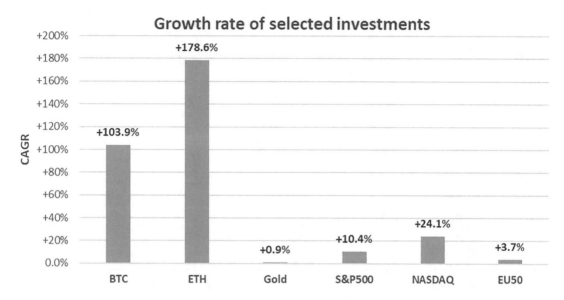

Figure 4-1. *CAGR of selected investments 2013–2022*

As Table 4-2 and Figure 4-1 indicate, the average returns of the two largest cryptoassets are orders of magnitude larger than those of more traditional investments.

However, returns are only part of the picture. Higher returns were only possible by accepting the much larger volatility of these returns. Table 4-3 presents volatility based on the standard deviation of daily, weekly, monthly, and yearly returns for the same investments.

Table 4-3. *Standard Deviation of Returns (aka Volatility or Risk) of Selected Investments over the Same Time Horizon*

Standard deviation	BTC	ETH	Gold	S&P500	NASDAQ	EU50
Daily	5.5%	6.3%	0.8%	0.9%	1.2%	1.0%
Weekly	13.1%	17.2%	2.0%	2.3%	3.2%	2.7%
Monthly	29.4%	50.4%	4.2%	4.5%	6.1%	5.1%
Yearly	1,891.1%	3,394.7%	15.1%	16.3%	22.1%	13.4%

Volatility is also orders of magnitude larger for cryptoassets than for traditional investments, regardless of the frequency of returns observed (daily, weekly, monthly, or yearly). Accessing the possibility of three- or four-digit rates of return with cryptoassets implied accepting that these investments could also lose 80% of their value in a matter of weeks.

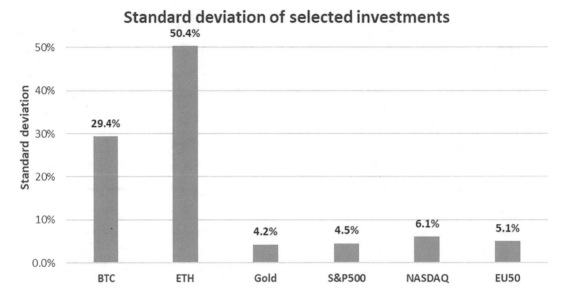

Figure 4-2. *The standard deviation of monthly returns (a.k.a. volatility or "risk") of selected investments over the time horizon*

The Sharpe Ratio

Named after the Nobel Prize laureate William Sharpe, the *Sharpe ratio* assesses the relationship between risk and return on investment. Specifically, this ratio divides the incremental return (compared to a benchmark) by its volatility. Thereby, it measures an investment's effectiveness compared to its risk in a single metric. For example, assume that a risk-free investment used as benchmark yields a 1% return. Another investment that yielded an average return of 4% with a volatility of returns of 2% has a Sharpe ratio of 1.50, computed as the incremental return of 3% (=4% − 1%), divided by its volatility of 2%.

Algebraically, it is as follows.

$$Sharpe\ ratio = \frac{incremental\ return}{volatility} = \frac{4\% - 1\%}{2\%} = 1.50$$

This metric is beneficial because it enables comparing investments with different risk profiles. For example, investing in a stock with an expected return of 10% is not better per se than investing in another stock with an expected return of 8% if the risk of the former is materially higher than the risk of the latter. The Sharpe ratio enables like-for-like comparisons.

Assuming a risk-free rate of return of 1%, Table 4-4 presents the Sharpe ratio of the previous investments using daily, weekly, monthly, and yearly data.

Table 4-4. *Sharpe Ratio of Selected Investments, Using the Same Time Frame and Assuming a Risk-Free Rate of Return of 1% As the Benchmark*

Sharpe Ratio	BTC	ETH	Gold	S&P500	NASDAQ	EU50
Daily	0.05	0.07	0.00	0.03	0.05	0.01
Weekly	0.14	0.18	0.01	0.09	0.14	0.03
Monthly	0.27	0.32	0.00	0.18	0.31	0.07
Yearly	0.41	0.45	0.07	0.65	1.13	0.26

Based on this metric, large and diversified traditional indices are in the same order of magnitude as major cryptoassets, suggesting that the increased return of cryptoassets is roughly proportional to the increased volatility of these returns.[1]

---

[1] Investors may be interested in performing a similar analysis but, instead of the Sharpe ratio, using the Treynor ratio or Jensen's alpha, by using the S&P 500 or the NASDAQ as a benchmark. However, a similar conclusion would be drawn from such approaches.

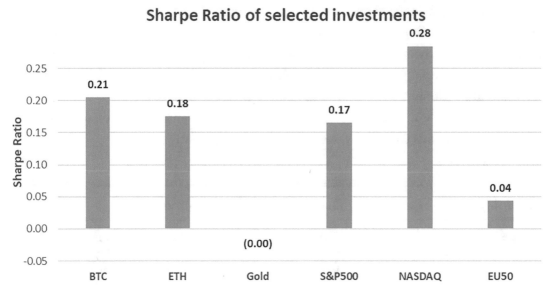

Figure 4-3. *Monthly Sharpe ratio of selected investments, using the same time frame and assuming a risk-free rate of return of 1% as the benchmark*

The Sortino Ratio

One shortcoming of the Sharpe ratio is that when returns are largely volatile on the upside, the ratio goes down the same way as when returns are volatile on the downside. However, the financial risk of these two situations is vastly different. True risk for an investor is the risk of losing money or, at least, the risk of not reaching a target level of return. The possibility of either matching the target return or largely overshooting it should not play a role in assessing an investment's riskiness.

This shortcoming is precisely what the Sortino ratio aims to address. Named after Frank Sortino, this ratio differentiates *good* volatility from *bad* volatility. Instead of simply using the standard deviation of returns, as the Sharpe ratio does, it removes the effect of upward price swings on the standard deviation to focus on the volatility of returns below a target return. This target return replaces the risk-free rate of return from the Sharpe ratio's formula.

In terms of their Sortino ratio and assuming a target rate of return of 5%, the previously covered investments fared as follows for daily, weekly, monthly, and yearly data.[2]

Table 4-5. *Sortino Ratio of Selected Investments, Using the Same Time Frame and Assuming a Target Rate of Return of 5% As the Benchmark*

Sortino Ratio	BTC	ETH	Gold	S&P500	NASDAQ	EU50
Daily	0.04	0.07	−0.02	0.02	0.05	0.00
Weekly	0.14	0.24	−0.05	0.05	0.14	−0.01
Monthly	0.49	0.63	−0.13	0.12	0.36	−0.03
Yearly	18.86	4.57	−0.37	0.56	n.a.	−0.27

The verdict reached by the Sortino ratio for these assets over the last decade is clear. When only considering "bad" volatility as a risk metric, the excess return of major cryptoassets largely overcompensates the increase in financial risk compared to traditional investments.

---

[2] The Sortino ratio only considers the standard deviation of observations below the arbitrary target, ignoring the other ones. It cannot be computed for yearly NASDAQ data over this period because the NASDAQ's yearly returns were not below 5% during any year of the horizon. The formula would therefore require to "divide by 0", which is mathematically impossible.

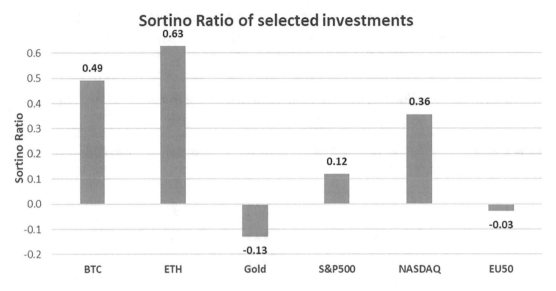

Figure 4-4. *Sortino ratio of selected investments, using the same time and assuming a target rate of return of 5% as the benchmark*

Simple Analysis of Return for Investors

While the preceding analysis favors cryptoassets, another more intuitive approach simplifies the case even further. While high volatility is, per se, undesirable, it is not a major concern for long-term investors. Indeed, if I invest for a four-year horizon and my investment is multiplied by ten or more, I do not care much about what volatility it experienced over this period. Such a return would be an order of magnitude larger than what I could expect from any traditional investment. The only values that are truly important for many investors are the entry price and the exit price.

An example makes it more tangible. If I entered a long position (bought) in Bitcoin in May 2017, I would buy one bitcoin at its all-time high (at the time) for $2,000 a piece (i.e., the first time bitcoin passed this milestone). If I had sold it four years later, in May 2021, for $50,000, I would have made a substantial return. In particular, I would have multiplied my investment 25 times (i.e., a 2400% return over four years), corresponding to a 124% CAGR. Does it matter that the price went wildly up and down over this period? I could have bought it cheaper in July 2017 and sold it for over $64,000 in April 2021, making even bigger gains in an even shorter period. Indeed, a part of the opportunity is lost, but my annual return is still many times higher than what I would have earned on the stock market[3] or with bonds[4]. Volatility is only a second-order concern in such a case.

Correlation and Diversification

The idiom "do not put all your eggs in one basket" takes life in portfolio management through the concept of correlation. Typically, one expects some financial assets to perform well at certain times while others perform poorly in the same period. Indeed, a local or firm-specific event can affect one company without impacting others. For example, political upheaval in Africa can affect the region without too much impact on the other side of the world. This simple fact implies that diversifying one's portfolio is beneficial because it enables one to lower one's level of risk without impacting one's level of expected return. For example, one is better off investing some capital in American technology stocks, some in Chinese manufacturing sites, some in European residential real estate, some in physical gold, and some in Australian municipal bonds than investing all of it in any of these categories.

Correlation is the degree to which assets tend to move together. If one asset tends to increase when another increases, these assets are positively correlated. If one asset tends to decrease when the other increases, they are negatively correlated. If they evolve independently of each other, then they are uncorrelated. Correlation can therefore be represented on a spectrum from perfect negative correlation (–100%) to perfect positive correlation (+100%). The center of this range, 0% correlation, indicates uncorrelated assets.

---

[3] Over the same period, the S&P500 went from $2,300 to $4,200, yielding an 83% increase over a four-year period, which is a 16% CAGR.

[4] US Treasury bonds for this period are around the 1% annual return. More risky corporate bonds would yield marginally more, but still far below returns mentioned here.

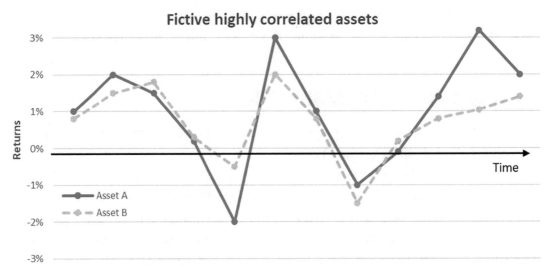

Figure 4-5. *Example of positively correlated asset returns (correlation coefficient = 85%; i.e., tending to evolve in tandem over time)*

Even if there is some degree of positive correlation between most assets, the fact that they are not perfectly positively correlated (i.e., not moving exactly in the same direction and at the same time) implies diversification benefits. The higher the positive correlation between assets, the lower the diversification benefits of having these assets in the same portfolio.

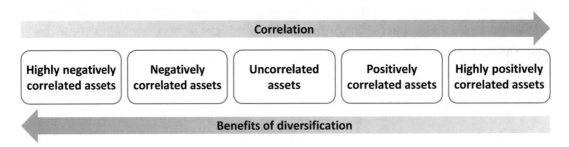

Figure 4-6. *Representation of the relationship between correlation and diversification benefits between assets*

All risk is not diversifiable, though. Systematic risk relates to macroeconomic events—to the economic system as a whole. It will always remain in any portfolio. On the other hand, unsystematic risk, or firm-specific risk, can be diversified away. For example, a new tax could benefit one industry at the expense of another. An investor with capital invested in each industry hedged this tax risk, as the gain on one investment offsets the loss on the other. Diversification can lower a portfolio's level of risk without lowering its expected return.

A portfolio manager's job is to pick investments that maximize expected returns while keeping risk as low as possible. While client-specific criteria also play a part (time horizon, willingness to take risk, marginal tax rate), generally speaking, it boils down to maximizing return for a defined level of risk. Diversification across asset classes and within asset classes helps achieve that goal.

The birth of cryptoassets enables portfolio managers to access a new asset class from which they can pick investments for their portfolios. As long as this new asset class is not perfectly positively correlated (+100%) to their existing portfolio, diversification benefits emerge from adding cryptoassets to it.

Table 4-6 presents the pair correlations between investments selected earlier over the last decade.

Table 4-6. *Correlation of Monthly Returns Between Pairs of Selected Assets, over the Same Time Frame*

	BTC	ETH	Gold	S&P500	NASDAQ	EU50
BTC		44%	1%	24%	20%	16%
ETH			25%	19%	18%	15%
Gold				5%	2%	−1%
S&P500					68%	80%
NASDAQ						44%
EU50						

A correlation is typically considered *moderate* when it is above 50% and *strong* when it is above 75%. While Table 4-6 indicates a correlation close to the "moderate" threshold within the asset class of cryptoassets (44% between Bitcoin and Ethereum), it shows that cryptoassets have little correlation with gold and with the three major indices selected (below 25%), at least over the timeframe selected.[5]

---

[5] Note, however, that since 2020, the level of correlation of cryptoassets with the NASDAQ (which is an index massively tilted toward tech companies) has increased significantly.

Adding cryptoassets to a traditional portfolio can materially improve the prospects of that portfolio, not only due to the high returns presented previously but also due to the low level of correlation with other asset classes. Diversification benefits make it meaningful to have a non-zero cryptoasset allocation in any investment portfolio, even if one ignores the high returns they provide.

Fiduciary Duty of Portfolio Managers

Entrusting a portfolio manager with one's capital comes with trust from the investor and commitment from the portfolio manager. Indeed, the portfolio manager is obligated, as per his mandate, to act in the investor's best interest. This obligation is called a fiduciary duty. Therefore, he must thoroughly research each potential investment and build an optimal portfolio for that investor. And the optimality of the portfolio considers, among others, its risk-return characteristics.

The substantial diversification benefits of adding cryptoassets to a financial portfolio therefore make it a duty for all portfolio managers worldwide to invest part of their capital in cryptoassets. At the very least, they have to offer this possibility to investors willing to gain exposure to the highest-performing asset class of the decade.

Among these portfolio managers are investment funds, mutual funds, and pension funds. As of the end of 2020, pension funds alone hold over $56 trillion of assets, most of which are in the United States.[6] However, these traditional investment firms do not yet have broad access to cryptoasset investments. Recent regulatory developments suggest it is poised to change in the coming months and years. Once this new asset class becomes investable for pension funds, investing just 2% of their assets under management in cryptoassets would more than double the size of the cryptoasset sector as of May 2023.

Other institutional investors face a similar situation to pension funds in that they currently face major barriers to investing in cryptoassets. In addition, their assets under management are many times larger than pension funds. Due to their fiduciary duty and the recent regulatory developments in the cryptoassets industry, it is reasonable to assume that most of these financial institutions will soon enter the cryptoasset space. Their entry into cryptoassets will likely be a game-changer for the asset class size, similar to the situation that arose in the late 1990s when commodities became an

---

[6] Data per Statista, https://www.statista.com/statistics/421220/global-pension-funds-assets/, May 23, 2022.

investable asset class for institutions. Consequently, when it happens, the sizable flow of institutional capital into cryptoassets will likely increase many cryptoasset prices by large multiples.

Key Concepts

Essential concepts of financial portfolio management are return and volatility (known as *risk*). Over the last decade, the average return and volatility of cryptoassets have been orders of magnitude higher than those of traditional equity and commodity investments. However, the relationship between the two—excess return per unit of financial risk— indicates that cryptoassets were by far the most financially attractive investment of the past decade.

In addition, cryptoassets show relatively low levels of correlation to traditional investments (i.e., they do not tend to fluctuate in the same direction at the same time). This lack of correlation makes cryptoassets good instruments to diversify financial portfolios. Given the fiduciary duty of portfolio managers in financial institutions to act in the best interest of their investors, investing in cryptoassets will likely soon be a requirement as per their mandate. Once this happens, the size of the cryptoasset market is due to increase by a multiple of its current size.

Extension Questions

For a typical pension fund, what would be the optimal percentage of assets under management to invest in cryptoassets?

What about other institutional investors, such as major investment funds?

Are the historical rates of return of cryptoassets indicative of their future expected returns?

PART II

What Are Cryptoassets?

CHAPTER 5

Birth of a New Asset Class

I've been working on a new electronic cash system that's fully peer-to-peer with no trusted third party.

—Satoshi Nakamoto

While the first part of the book covered why cryptoassets are worth understanding, this second part dives into what they are in more detail. This chapter introduces how the first cryptoasset came to life, why it was meaningful, and what followed.

Genesis of the First Cryptoasset: Bitcoin

Amid the largest financial crisis since the Great Depression of the 1930s, the financial system's stability was on trial. The afternoon after Halloween 2008, the mysterious "Satoshi Nakamoto"[1] posted for the first time on a cryptography forum, the Cryptography Mailing List. Satoshi's post started with the preceding quote and contained a link to a nine-page document titled "Bitcoin P2P e-cash paper". This white paper was the conception of the first cryptoasset [20] [21].

---

[1] The true identity of the author, or group of authors, under the nickname Satoshi Nakamoto is still unknown today. While he claimed to be a middle-aged Japanese man, his English was flawless and even used idioms that can only reasonably expected to be used by native speakers. Whoever stands behind this pseudonym is a genius accomplished in cryptography, computer science, mathematics, economics, monetary history, game theory, and more.

© Thomas Jeegers 2023
T. Jeegers, *Understanding Crypto Fundamentals*, https://doi.org/10.1007/978-1-4842-9309-6_5

Bitcoin effectively came to life a few months later, just after New Year 2009, when Satoshi posted Bitcoin's genesis block on a blockchain, the underlying technology enabling Bitcoin to work.

Despite its birth in early 2009, Bitcoin's proof of concept needed a few years to come out of the shadows. The first effective valuation of Bitcoin came in the autumn of that year when the New Liberty Standard online exchange bought 5,050 bitcoins for $5.02 (1,006 bitcoins per US dollar) to publish the first formal Bitcoin exchange rate. This exchange rate was based on a simple model estimating the electricity cost needed to mine a bitcoin. Later, at the end of spring 2010, Laszlo Hanyecz completed the first commercial purchase in bitcoins. A 10,000-bitcoin transaction for a couple of Papa John's pizzas. While the $41 these bitcoins represented at the time was already too much for purchasing two pizzas, they would now be worth hundreds of millions of dollars.

From that moment onward, technology enthusiasts increasingly used Bitcoin as a digital currency. However, these transactions were not driven by ease. Instead, they aimed to show that value can be exchanged in a decentralized way without an intermediary. Indeed, this new digital currency is a true technological masterpiece as it solves issues that had never been effectively tackled.

A Solution to the Double-Spend Problem

The real innovation that Satoshi Nakamoto brought to the table is cracking the *double-spend problem* in a digital and decentralized environment.

When you send an email or a picture online, you are actually sending a copy while you still own the original locally. This approach of sending copies cannot work for money. Money needs to be scarce to have value. If anybody can send copies of a digital coin around (i.e., spend it more than once, hence the term "double spend"), there is no scarcity. Just imagine what most people would do if they could spend the same $100 several times, in several shops, without being debited this amount from their bank account. The absence of scarcity would make it worthless as it could never become reliable money. Societies have traditionally relied on third parties, like banks, to avoid the double-spend problem. If you transfer money online from your bank account, your bank ensures you no longer own the money you transferred. The bank acts as an intermediary to prevent double-spending.

Leveraging technological innovations and modern cryptography, Satoshi Nakamoto designed a technology to address the double-spend problem without necessitating any intermediary. This technology was later coined *blockchain* and is part of what is now known as *distributed ledger technologies.*

Bitcoin was the first application of value with blockchain technology, the same way emails were the first with Internet technology. Of course, emails are only a fraction of the possibilities enabled by the Internet. The same goes for Bitcoin and blockchain.

Byzantine Generals Problem

One way to understand why blockchain matters is by first acknowledging a famous issue in distributed computing systems: The Byzantine Generals problem.[2]

Two Byzantine generals want to attack a city, each from one side. If they both attack simultaneously, they know they will be victorious. However, if one of them attacks alone, his troops will be annihilated by the city's defenses. The generals do not have any preference for the timing of the attack but only care about its coordination.

The issue lies in the communication system, which is unreliable. One general must send a messenger through the city to suggest a time for the attack to the other general. However, the enemy could intercept the messenger in the city. Therefore, after sending the messenger, the general does not know whether the other general received the message. Finally, even if he receives the message, the receiving general does not know whether the enemy tampered with the message (sent another messenger instead).

These issues imply that the messenger who makes it to the receiving side must also return to the sending side to confirm delivery. However, even if he manages to go back and confirm, the sending general needs the receiving general to know that the messenger made it back to confirm. Otherwise, the receiving general would be unsure that the sending general would send his troops, as he might not have received confirmation. In other words, knowing that the other party knows is not enough. One must also know that the other party knows that one knows.

---

[2] Originally presented in 1982 by Lamport, Shostak, and Pease [62].

It does not stop there: One must also know that the other party knows that one knows that the other party knows. This problem extends to infinity, with parties never sure that they agree on timing. In its generalized form, the problem states that a part of a system may fail, and there is imperfect information on whether any part has failed. Also, the number of generals needing coordination can be much bigger than two.

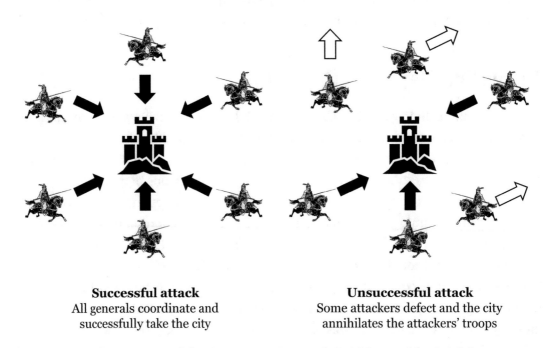

Successful attack
All generals coordinate and
successfully take the city

Unsuccessful attack
Some attackers defect and the city
annihilates the attackers' troops

Figure 5-1. *Illustration of the Byzantine Generals Problem with more than two generals*

The Byzantine Generals Problem is directly relevant in the context of decentralized money. Any actor on a monetary network may try to trick the system. For example, a dishonest person may try to send the same money twice or send money and keep it at the same time. Without any central authority to prevent such behavior, all actors on the network need to reach a consensus on who owns which amount of money at any point in time.

Like Byzantine generals, all actors on a monetary network need to coordinate under imperfect information. In particular, without knowing whether the enemy (a dishonest person) tampered with the message (the money transferred). Moreover, all members need to know that everybody on the network is aware of how much money each person has at any point in time, even in the presence of dishonest actors on the network.

Byzantine Fault Tolerance

Solving this problem is not straightforward. Solutions should avoid what is called a "Byzantine failure," where nodes[3] (generals) in the system cannot reach an agreement because one or several nodes may be failing (dishonest). A solution consists in achieving a "Byzantine consensus," where all working nodes (honest generals) accept the message sent by the broadcaster (the sending general). All working nodes agree, regardless of the possible presence of failing components. Also, they all know that all other working nodes agree. In the Byzantine context, consensus corresponds to all honest generals sending their troops simultaneously. In the monetary context, all members agree on who owns how much.

A solution to reach a "Byzantine consensus" requires two things. First, unforgeable message signatures to prove from whom the message comes. Second, relying on the assumption that the majority of nodes are honest.

Unforgeable message signatures can be achieved through cryptography. It is the process of encrypting a message through algorithms to keep it confidential.[4] In particular, a public and private key combination enables this encryption and tamper-resistant evidence of the message's originator. A node (sending general) encrypts its message with its private key. As the name implies, this key is private and cannot be forged by any dishonest node (the enemy). However, anyone can identify that the encrypted message can only come from the original node (sending general) using the corresponding public key. If the public key decrypts the message, it can only have been encrypted by the corresponding private key, testifying it is genuine.

The next chapter covers details on asymmetric cryptography. For now, it is easier to imagine these keys in the context of a physical mailbox. The public key is the address of the mailbox,[5] known by everybody; anybody can send mail to that mailbox. In contrast, only the owner holds the private key that opens the mailbox and can send from it.

The assumption that most nodes remain honest is achieved through carefully designed incentives and progressive network growth to ensure it remains decentralized. Dishonest nodes becoming the majority represent a risk in cryptoassets, analyzed in Chapter 13.

---

[3] *Nodes* is a more general term for the different actors in a system.

[4] This is where the term *crypto* in cryptocurrencies and cryptoassets comes from.

[5] Technically speaking, it is the *public address*, which is derived from the public key.

Blockchain was engineered as a Byzantine fault-tolerant system to prevent double-spending for its first use case, Bitcoin. All users agree on the chronological order of transactions through a peer-to-peer exchange of information certified by computational proof. Even if some nodes in the network become dishonest, the rest will still reach a consensus without accepting fraudulent transactions. The Bitcoin blockchain was built to be consistent with game theory in that it gives the right incentives to all actors on the network. Every actor is encouraged to act in accordance with the rules, while cheating is not beneficial in any way. This way, it is in everybody's interest to play by the book. Such technology is "technically" possible. In other words, there is a mathematically feasible way to achieve fault-proof, decentralized money transfers.

Another critical aspect remains for this technology to work—the human one. Would a community accept to deal with assets in a decentralized way, without any intermediary? As history shows, yes, it would, and it has. This story brings us to a tiny island in the Pacific Ocean.

Decentralized Money Proof of Concept: Rai Stones

Bitcoin was not the first intangible money to work without an intermediary. For centuries, the Micronesian island of Yap used a ubiquitous form of money to transfer value between individuals and villages without requiring a middleman.

This form of money is known as *Rai stones* or *Yapese stone money*: large circular stones with a hole carved in the center and scattered throughout villages on the island. These stones could weigh up to a few tons, similar to a fully grown male Asian elephant.

Figure 5-2. *Rai stone, used as money on the Micronesian island of Yap. (Source: Wikimedia, public domain)*

Contrary to Western societies' standards, the bearer does not hold value. It would be difficult, if not impossible, for any individual to transport any such stone around to transact. Instead, the community agrees on value through word-of-mouth. For example, if a farmer sells part of his land, he gets half of the rai stone at the village entrance. The buyer and seller share this information with the community to validate the transaction. Since all community members know that the buyer owned that rai stone before the transaction, they agree that it can occur. In the community's collective mind, the farmer is now the new owner of half of that rai stone, which he can use to make any purchase of that value.

Similar to an "account" of the buyer and the farmer, the value held by each community member is recorded in the memory of every other member. In such a system, money is decentralized.

Interestingly, it is not even the physical presence of the stone that gives value to it. In a famous example, a stone was being carried across the sea to a different island when the ship carrying it sank. The Yapese community agreed that the stone must still exist even at the bottom of the ocean. The stone kept its value and continued to be traded among the community.

As this example proves, money is the agreement of value in the psyche of community members. It does not need to be physical. It only needs mutual agreement. It is not so different from dealing with considerable amounts in the Western world. The Nobel laureate economist Milton Friedman compared rai stones to gold in the vault of a nation. Germany can agree to transfer the value of gold in a vault to the United Kingdom without ever moving the gold from the vault [22]. By extension, transferring money digitally with a bank transfer is also not so different—at least in the sense that no physical exchange of goods is necessary. However, a critical difference between rai stones and a bank account is that rai stones do not need any intermediary—no bank, no central authority.

Rai stones were only used among small communities as this monetary model is not scalable. Any individual, family, or community could only memorize the value split of a few dozen stones among community members. Hundreds at most. It certainly does not enable millions of daily transactions whose value must be validated and recorded in minutes. Nevertheless, the mere existence of rai stones shows that a decentralized monetary system can work and has worked for half a millennium.

Coming back to the parallel with Bitcoin, not only is it *technically* possible to decentrally exchange money through technology, but it is also *societally* possible for a community to effectively work this way. Besides, Bitcoin and cryptoassets have evolved to become a lot more than just money. Money is just where it all started. The story continues with ups and downs and many more revolutionary innovations.

Bitcoin Beyond Its Genesis

In the years following its launch, Bitcoin was only of interest to the small cryptography community where it was born. Satoshi Nakamoto regularly posted on the Cryptography Mailing List and the bitcointalk.org forum. He mostly answered early adopters' questions and published Bitcoin's source code updates on SourceForge.net. The Bitcoin community was just forming, and having a knowledgeable, though anonymous, founder behind the emerging technology provided just enough thrust to get the ball rolling.

At first, the adoption of Bitcoin picked up slowly and in waves. It took two years for the coin's price to break the $1 threshold. The nature of this innovation made potential users skeptical about whether it was a revolution, a fad, or even a scam. Wikipedia even removed the Bitcoin page from its website in July 2010 for not being noteworthy enough. Ironically, only four years later, Wikipedia started accepting donations in bitcoins.

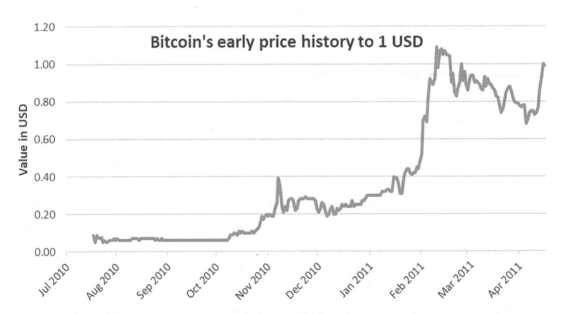

Figure 5-3. *Bitcoin's early price history (in USD). It took more than two years (from January 3, 2009 to February 10, 2011) for the price of a bitcoin to break the $1 threshold*

Bitcoin started making the headlines toward the end of 2010 when PC World magazine published an article suggesting that Bitcoin be used as payment and donation to WikiLeaks. While some saw it as an excellent opportunity to bring the innovation out of the shadows, Satoshi Nakamoto strongly opposed it.

"No, don't "bring it on"... Bitcoin is a small beta community in its infancy. You would not stand to get more than pocket change, and the heat you would bring would likely destroy us at this stage."

Then, Nakamoto started to disappear. The project was growing, interest was spreading, and Nakamoto was no longer needed. The mystery behind his true identity arguably even strengthened public interest in Bitcoin. His posts became increasingly scarcer, then stopped altogether as developers at the Bitcoin Foundation took over the role of advocate for the asset and the underlying blockchain technology. In July 2011, his penultimate post commented on WikiLeaks' new acceptance of Bitcoin as payment: "WikiLeaks has kicked the hornet's nest, and the swarm is headed towards us."

Nevertheless, Bitcoin did not collapse. Quite the opposite, its value increased by three orders of magnitude in less than three years as the unwanted attention attracted believers in the new technology.

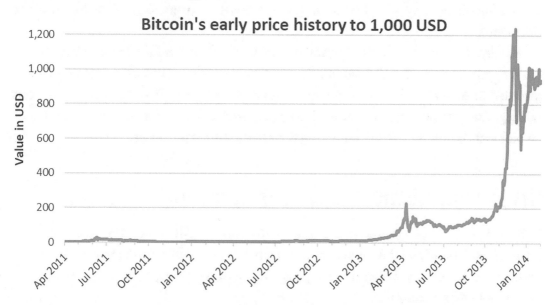

Figure 5-4. *Bitcoin's price history from April 2011 to January 2014 (in USD). Bitcoin's price increased from $1 to over $1,000 in less than three years*

In parallel, Bitcoin started to be used for illegal activities, which triggered further negative headlines. In October 2013, the FBI shut down one of the most significant online criminal marketplaces, Silk Road, which accepted payments exclusively in Bitcoin. Silk Road was like the Amazon of illicit products: you could buy any drugs, from ecstasy to LSD and cannabis seeds, as well as fake passports, and have them delivered to your doorstep in a few days.

Nevertheless, Bitcoin has never been involved in more than a tiny fraction of the illegal industry. As is often the case with any new technology, there are upsides and downsides; the real question is the net effect. The Internet in its early days was also used by fraudsters and for illegal purposes, but it was not a reason to discard the technology altogether. Blaming Bitcoin for occasional illegal use would be like sanctioning the email protocol with the justification that email can be used to facilitate phishing attacks. In addition, according to the *Chainalysis Crypto Crime Report 2023*, the total cryptocurrency value sent and received by criminal entities was "only" $18 billion in 2022, or 0.2% of all cryptoasset activity. Besides, the illicit industry's share of cryptoasset transactions continues to drop [23]. In comparison, the United Nations estimate that between 2% and 5% of global GDP (about $2 trillion to $4 trillion) is connected to criminal endeavors or money laundering. In other words, all cryptoassets are involved in less than 1% of the illicit activity industry. The currency of the illegal industry is neither Bitcoin nor any other cryptoasset. It remains fiat currencies, and in particular the US dollar.

Finally, as fraudsters eventually find out, using cryptoassets for illicit transactions is a very poor strategy. All transactions in cryptoassets such as Bitcoin or Ethereum are recorded in an open source database that can never be erased. Tracing such transactions is straightforward and can quickly lead to its perpetrator. The nature of open source cryptoassets is therefore disincentivising their use for illicit purposes.

Crypto Platforms and Smart Contracts

In 2014, a new type of cryptoasset emerged with Ethereum, the second largest cryptoasset. It builds on the same base as Bitcoin but differs in several respects. In particular, it adds a crucial feature: the possibility to program anything on it. It enables, for example, smart contracts.

Smart contracts are neither smart nor even contracts, at least not in the traditional legal sense. Instead, they are simply an if-then statement programmed into self-executing code on a blockchain. However, this seemingly trivial concept opens the door to a new world. Smart contracts enable, for example, the programming of immutable agreements specifying value flows (e.g., transactions) with automatic and instantaneous settlement without third parties. There is no need to go to court and wait for weeks or months to settle a contract. In many cases, both the court and the waiting time are obsolete.

However, the crucial element of smart contracts is not the automatic execution of a financial transaction, as this concept already exists in any bank. Instead, what is revolutionary is the decentralized nature of this action. The absence of a third party ensures that the agreement, or "contract," will be executed fairly, according to predefined rules specified in the contract's code. Besides, smart contracts are not limited to defining value flows. They enable any program to be uploaded to a sort of global computer and self-execute. Not only a value flow but also the state of any program is permanently recorded on thousands of computers, making its history unalterable.

Ethereum is the first broadly successful platform enabling smart contracts. In abstract terms, Ethereum is like an app store. Apps can be built on it. In parallel, other app stores are available: Cardano, Solana, Polkadot, and a legion of new emerging platforms. However, as of this writing, Ethereum remains the biggest by far.

In the same way that Bitcoin (capital B) is a network with bitcoin (lowercase b) (BTC) as its native currency, Ethereum is a network with ether (ETH) as its native currency. However, unlike Bitcoin, Ethereum is a programmable blockchain, and ether facilitates the flow of smart contracts. These contracts are executed on the decentralized Ethereum virtual machine, the aforementioned "global computer." While Bitcoin only allows a restricted set of instructions to verify the spending ability of users and little more, Ethereum provides a complete set of programmable instructions that enable its use as a general-purpose computer. In IT jargon, its programming language is *Turing-complete*.

A useful parallel with the Internet illustrates this difference well. The Internet relies on TCP as one possible base protocol. On top of TCP, other protocols were built to enable specific functionalities (e.g., HTTP for webpages, SMTP for emails, FTP for file transfer, and XMPP for open source messaging). Bitcoin enables only a small set of instructions; in that sense, it is like SMTP: optimized for sending emails or, in the case of Bitcoin, for sending money. Ethereum, on the other hand, is a more fundamental layer, like TCP. As it contains a complete set of programmable instructions, it enables developers to create anything of value: to build any protocol on top of it. The only limit is their imagination.

One important consequence is the possibility of disintermediating many existing functions—removing the middleman. In the financial industry, identifying unnecessary intermediaries taking a share of the value pie is straightforward; for example, a bank matching borrowers and lenders. More broadly, any financial service where a margin is captured between the need (e.g., the borrower) and the solution (e.g., the lender) can be coded and run through smart contracts. Thereby, decentralized code can replace most traditional finance: from asset management to payments, brokerage, custody, investment, derivative products, and more. These new financial solutions are called *Decentralized Finance*, or *DeFi* for short.

Of course, the power of smart contracts is not limited to finance but extends to any industry having a digital component, which is to say, most industries. Outside of finance, the need may be even bigger. Chapter 3 presented several examples, such as the music and publishing industries. Many other industries would similarly benefit from the disintermediation that smart contracts enable.

Altcoins

Any cryptoasset other than Bitcoin is called an *alternative coin* or *altcoin*. As of May 2023, they encompass more than 23,000 cryptoassets.[6]

The first altcoin, Namecoin, was launched in the middle of 2011. It was closely followed in the same year by a few other cryptoassets remarkably similar to Bitcoin. Among them, Litecoin is still in the top 20 of the most valuable cryptoassets ten years later. The number of altcoins then grew at an increasing rate. In 2014, Dogecoin was created as a joke to make fun of cryptocurrency hype. Ironically, as of 2023, Dogecoin is in the top 10 of the most valuable cryptoassets.

Not all altcoins have a real purpose in the new crypto ecosystem. Many of these cryptoassets are justifiably called "sh*tcoins" as they are unlikely to bring any value to the economy. Even if some of these cryptoassets benefited from an unprecedented rise in value during crypto bull runs (more on that in Part III), they are likely to become worthless. Some are even scams aimed at stealing money from careless investors and speculators. As a result, the crypto market will likely consolidate, with most existing coins dying while only a few useful ones get the attention and accompanying rewards.

---

[6] The exact number is available live on the homepage of CoinMarketCap (`https://coinmarketcap.com/`).

Nevertheless, some altcoins bring real utility by unlocking value that could not be tapped before. For example, a Basic Attention Token (BAT) monetizes media consumers' time watching or interacting with ads online. It enables advertisers to value precisely the attention users pay to ads. At the same time, it rewards users for that attention. As a result, advertisers benefit more from running ads, and consumers are fairly remunerated for their time and attention. BAT is making an inefficient market more efficient. Value that was lost is now unlocked.

Another example of unlocking value is Chiliz (CHZ), which enables entertainment or sports communities to monetize and engage their audience. Hypothetically, let's say you are a fan supporting the Football Club Barcelona (FCB). You can buy FCB tokens built on Chiliz and thereby get access to rebates for tickets and merchandise from the team. In addition, your tokens could also correspond to voting rights in decisions related to the club, such as the location of the next merchandise building or the shape of stripes on the next socks worn by the players.[7] Finally, if the team gains in popularity, then the value of your token may go up. You are thereby not betting on a single game but on a team. Again, this market did not exist before, or at least not to its full extent; value is unlocked.

Those are only a few examples of possibilities enabled by altcoins, among thousands of other use cases currently under development.

---

[7] Those are not real examples of benefits from this particular token, but just hypothetical possibilities enabled by the technology.

Key Concepts

Bitcoin, the first cryptoasset, was born in 2009 amid the most serious financial crisis since the Great Depression. It is built on a new technology, blockchain, which enables transacting assets digitally without requiring any trusted intermediary.

Not only is Bitcoin technically sound—the underlying technology is working—but also socially acceptable, as was proved by the existence of decentralized money for centuries in communities in the Pacific Ocean.

In its first decade, Bitcoin was used by a few early technology adopters, making some of them millionaires. The illicit industry took advantage of Bitcoin's rapid growth, bringing negative headlines, even though its use remains a negligibly small fraction of the illegal activity.

Crypto platforms, like Ethereum, were created in mid-2010 and extended the use of blockchain by enabling the decentralized exchange of self-executing code rather than just value. Other cryptoassets emerged, unlocking further value by creating previously non-existent markets.

Extension Questions

If decentralized money systems are possible, why were they only used anecdotally by small remote communities?

If a decentralized digital money model is now possible, why are not more governments worldwide embracing it yet?

CHAPTER 6

Blockchain Basics

Sed quis custodiet ipsos custodes? (But who will guard the guards themselves?)

—Juvenal, ca. 100 BCE

Understanding cryptoassets involves understanding blockchain. The first cryptoasset, Bitcoin, is only possible through blockchain, and blockchain was developed to make Bitcoin possible. While alternative technologies were subsequently developed to make cryptoassets technically possible, blockchain remains the core behind most cryptoassets.

This chapter only scratches the surface of some essential technical aspects enabling blockchain to work. A complete analysis would barely fit in an entire book. Also, the core concepts are sufficient to understand the revolutionary potential of blockchain. To draw a useful parallel, one can use the Internet and build websites without understanding how the TCP/IP protocol works. The same goes for blockchain; one can be a successful cryptoasset investor without knowing all details behind cryptographic algorithms and all types of consensus mechanisms. Nevertheless, the more one understands blockchain, the better one can identify and manage underlying risks.

Readers interested in the technical details should refer to the onboarding guide *Bitcoin, the Blockchain and Beyond* by Jean-Luc Verhelst [24] or, for more advanced reading, *Mastering Blockchain* by Imran Bashir [1].

© Thomas Jeegers 2023
T. Jeegers, *Understanding Crypto Fundamentals*, https://doi.org/10.1007/978-1-4842-9309-6_6

89

Blockchain's Main Characteristics

At its core, a blockchain is a database. In finance, one would call it a *ledger*, as it contains all the credits and debits of a digital asset since its inception. Digital assets stored on a blockchain can represent tangible assets, like real estate property titles, or be fully digital assets, like Bitcoin.

A blockchain is characterized by *decentralization*. Instead of storing data on a single computer—a centralized model—data is stored on many computers on the network. An established blockchain like the Bitcoin one is stored on hundreds of thousands of computers spread all over the planet. It is not a fully *distributed* system where all users act as information-sharing entities. Nevertheless, it is a peer-to-peer (P2P) network that does not rely on any central authority and enables anybody to become a node in possession of the entire ledger, acting as an information-sharing entity. Therefore, blockchains are between decentralized and distributed networks: all nodes can share information (distributed), but not all choose to do so (decentralized).[1]

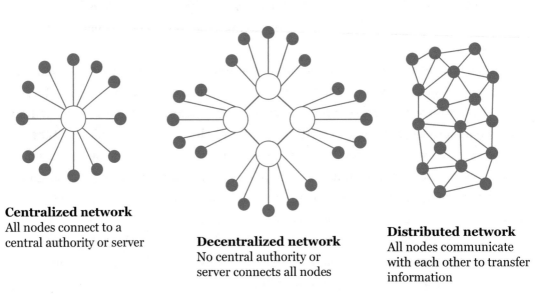

Centralized network
All nodes connect to a
central authority or server

Decentralized network
No central authority or
server connects all nodes

Distributed network
All nodes communicate
with each other to transfer
information

Figure 6-1. *Centralized, decentralized, and distributed networks*

---

[1] Vitalik Buterin brilliantly analyses what decentralization means through different axes in "The Meaning of Decentralization" [45].

The decentralized nature of blockchain networks implies that decisions regarding data are not taken by a single entity but through agreements among all network members. Also, *no central authority can shut down such networks* as transactions are *permissionless*. Indeed, no barriers to entry can be set by any central authority so that everybody can join the system and transact with anybody else on the network without requiring tedious approval processes.

Successful blockchains entail an economic guarantee that they will continue functioning as intended. This guarantee is secured by carefully designed incentives in line with game theory principles. In other words, it is in all actors' interest to behave according to the system's rules, while deviating is costly and pointless.

Another key characteristic of blockchain is that the data it stores is *immutable*. It cannot be changed. Once a transaction is successfully recorded, all nodes (computers) choosing to act as holders of the complete blockchain keep a record of that transaction and all transactions that precede it. Given the large number of independent copies, transactions approved by the network are unerasable.

Most blockchains, such as the Bitcoin one, integrate a high degree of *transparency* but are *pseudonymous*. For example, the Bitcoin blockchain does not reveal the identity of Bitcoin holders but publicly shares their pseudonyms (the wallet's digital address) and all related transactions. It differs from anonymity, where no pseudonym could be linked to a transaction.[2] In the case of Bitcoin, anybody can check online the amount held in the digital wallet of a pseudonym and all transactions it ever sent or received on the corresponding blockchain.

To achieve these characteristics, blockchain technology uses cryptography and consensus mechanisms. The following sections analyze these concepts.

A Chain of Blocks

As the name implies, a blockchain is a chain of *blocks*. Each block contains data such as user transactions, a timestamp, and a link to the previous block.

---

[2] Anonymous coins exist and are called privacy coins. However, they remain small compared to pseudonymous coins.

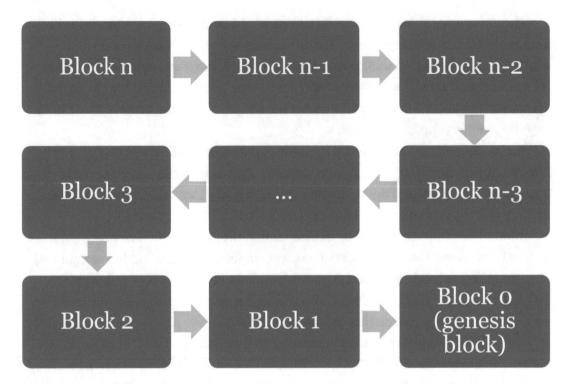

Figure 6-2. *A blockchain is a chain of blocks, where each block contains a cryptographic hash of the previous block in the chain*

The entire block content is cryptographically hashed, meaning that its content is summarized, for example, in a 64-character string. A *hash* can be considered the fingerprint of a set of digital information: much smaller than the original information but uniquely identifying it. Hashing a block gives it a unique label. Changing the slightest bit of information in the block gives the block a radically different label. Moreover, since the block contains the label of the previous block in its content, changing any information in a previous block of the chain radically changes the label of all future blocks.

Figure 6-3 illustrates how changing a tiny bit of information in the input of a hash function yields a drastically different output. This example uses SHA-256 (SHA stands for Secure Hash Algorithm), the algorithm used to hash blocks in the Bitcoin blockchain.

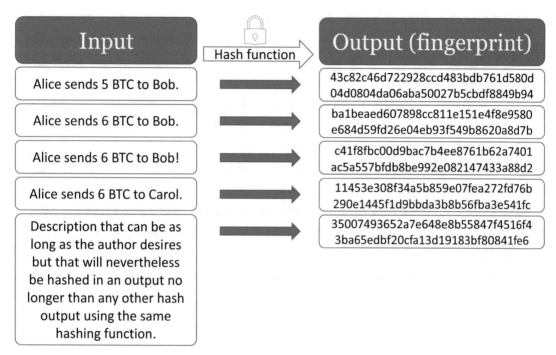

Figure 6-3. *SHA-256 hashing algorithm example. Changing the slightest information in the input yields a drastically different output*

A characteristic of this algorithm is that regardless of the length or content of the input, the output is always 64 characters long and seems random. Also, using the same input always yields the same output. However, with any given output, it is virtually impossible to reverse engineer what the input was.

One can think of a simple hashing algorithm as a mathematical algorithm, like the "square" function. For example, squaring 2 or –2 would yield the same output, 4, but given the output 4, one cannot identify the input (in this case, whether it was 2 or –2). However, the SHA-256 algorithm is much more complex, so guessing the input from a given output is virtually impossible, contrary to this simplistic example with 2 and –2.

Asymmetric Encryption

Asymmetric encryption, also known as *public-key cryptography,* enables two things. First, it enables the sender of a message to cipher it so that only specific people owning a deciphering code can decipher it. Second, it enables the receiver to ensure that the message comes from the sender (i.e., it has not been tampered with or faked by a third party). To achieve this, asymmetric encryption uses two keys, each of which is a series of seemingly random characters. The first is private, only known by its holder. The second is public and can be inferred from the private one. The keys are mathematically related, so the public key derives from the private key. However, guessing the private key from the public one is impossible.

The first function of asymmetric encryption (ciphering the message) is achieved by encoding an original message with the recipient's public key—a code that makes the original message unreadable. Only the recipient can decrypt the message because only he has the corresponding private key. You can think of this combination as a lock that only the public key can lock and only the private key can unlock.

The second function (unforgeable signature) uses the public key to establish the origin of a message. Since the public key deciphers the message, it implies that the corresponding private key ciphered this message. Only the genuine sender knows the private key, so nobody else could be the message's sender.

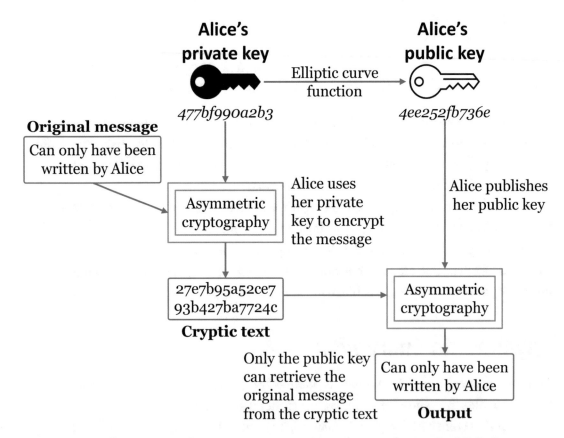

Figure 6-4. *Illustration of steps in asymmetric cryptography to establish the unforgeable origin of a message*

Asymmetric encryption proves that the holder of the private key corresponding to the public key has written the ciphered message. Since the private key is a string of characters coded on 256 bits (for the Bitcoin blockchain), it offers an exceptionally high degree of uniqueness. In particular, with 256 bits (1s and 0s), there are 2^{256} possibilities— or about as many possibilities as there are atoms in the observable universe. Unique, unforgeable signatures are thereby made possible, enabling blockchain-based mechanisms to certify the provenance of a message.

Updating a Decentralized Ledger

Adding a new entry in a ledger that is not maintained by a central authority works very differently than in a centralized model. A group of computers on a network maintaining a shared ledger must all agree on who will structure the new entry and how to add this entry to the shared ledger. To reach this agreement, there are different methods, called *consensus mechanisms*, investigated later in this chapter. This section presents a high-level series of steps that must occur regardless of the consensus mechanism. However, note that they do not strictly have to happen in this order.

First, a user requests a transaction. For example, Alice buys a car from Bob with a cryptocurrency. To pay, Alice sends a transaction request to the peer-to-peer network of that cryptocurrency using asymmetric encryption.

Second, one or several validator nodes on the network gather pending transactions in the transaction pool. One of these transactions is the one requested by Alice.

Third, a validator node creates a block with these transactions and additional information, such as the block version, the block size, a timestamp, and a hash of the previous block on the blockchain. For example, the node verifies that Alice holds the amount necessary of the cryptocurrency to perform the transaction and similarly for all other transactions gathered.

Fourth, depending on the consensus mechanism, the validator may have to perform some "work" or win a lottery against other validators and indicate this information in the block. The successful validator distributes the resulting block on the network.

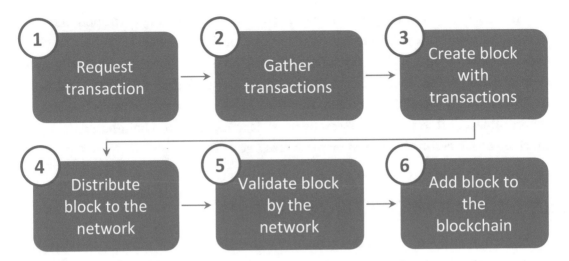

Figure 6-5. *Key steps in updating a blockchain*

Fifth, all network members verify the block's validity (i.e., whether it fulfills some pre-defined criteria). For example, they verify that the block properly refers to the last valid block on the blockchain, that the size of the block is within agreed proportions, and that the validator indeed performed its work or won the lottery.

Sixth, all network members add the valid block to their local copy of the blockchain. Alice's transaction becomes valid, and the successful validator receives a reward for its work.

The information is now on the blockchain, transparently and permanently. In other words, it is there for everybody to see, and it will never be removed.

Figure 6-6. *Visual representation of a chain of blocks, where the last block is appended to the existing chain*

Consensus Mechanisms

A consensus mechanism or consensus protocol is how agreements are reached in a decentralized system. Consensus mechanisms are how generals (as in Chapter 5's Byzantine Generals example) agree on the timing of the attack. It ensures they all know that the other parties agree, regardless of whether there are untrustworthy nodes on the network. In a blockchain context, they agree on the latest version, including who owns what. Such an agreement is a *distributed consensus* and crucial to ensuring network consistency.

Bitcoin's blockchain uses a *proof of work* (PoW) consensus mechanism. For the first decade of cryptoassets, it remained the most common method to validate blocks. During this period, however, alternative consensus mechanisms emerged to solve the drawbacks of PoW. The *proof of stake* (PoS) consensus protocol is also well-established. In particular, its adoption increased progressively over the second half of the 2010s. Ethereum even moved from PoW to PoS in September 2022. In addition, hundreds of other mechanisms exist for cryptoassets. Not all consensus mechanisms are suitable for all types of blockchains, though. For example, a mechanism such as proof of authority is more appropriate for private blockchains (more on that later in this chapter). In contrast, traditional PoW or PoS mechanisms are arguably better suited for assets meant to be used as a currency.

Let us now dive into the inner workings of blockchain specific to consensus mechanisms, starting with the first blockchain consensus mechanism, proof of work.

Updating a Decentralized Ledger with Proof of Work

Let us revisit the steps to update a decentralized ledger (see Figure 6-5) and investigate what happens under a PoW consensus mechanism.

In the first step (requesting a transaction), Alice signs with her private key the transaction she is sending to the network. She attaches her public key to the message. This process uses asymmetric encryption to cryptographically certify that Alice is the actual author of the message. In the transaction information, anybody can see that Alice's pseudonym requests to send, say, one bitcoin to Bob's public address.

In the second step (gathering transactions), the validators gather transactions from the pool of pending transactions. They only select valid transactions (i.e., those whose public key deciphers the message ciphered with the sender's private key). It is in the validators' interest to gather as many pending transactions as possible, of as big a value as possible, because they take a small fee on each transaction. That is if they are the successful validator of this block.

In the third step (creating the block), they compete to be the first to solve a mathematical problem to validate the block. It is a trivial problem with no utility, consisting of randomly running billions of hash algorithms until an output with a specific characteristic is reached by chance. For example, the hash output should start with a specific number of zeroes. Reaching such an output takes time and CPU power (electricity). This time and energy spent are the "work" referred to in *proof of work*. As this process resembles how miners quarry gold, the validators are typically called miners.

In the fourth step (distributing the valid block), the successful miner broadcasts the block on the network, indicating the selected transactions and the input that yields an output respecting the required characteristics.

In the fifth step (validating the block by the network), any node can test the submitted block (i.e., verify that the output fulfills the set characteristics). Contrary to the third step, this test is instantaneous. Indeed, with the right input, verifying that the output respects the required characteristics is straightforward.

In the ultimate step (adding the block to the blockchain), all nodes accept this new block as the latest block of the chain. As part of the block, the successful miner is rewarded with a pre-defined number of bitcoins for solving the problem. He also captures transaction fees. These rewards ensure enough miners remain on the network at any time in a competition to solve the following block.

Structure of a Block Under Proof of Work

Figure 6-7 illustrates how a block on a blockchain working with PoW is structured. It consists of two parts, a header and a set of transactions.

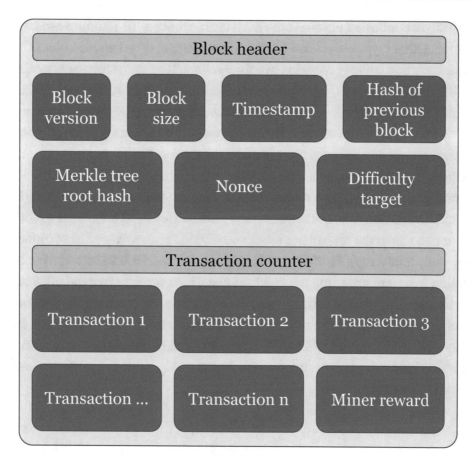

Figure 6-7. *Structure of a block on a blockchain*

As part of the header, the *block version, block size,* and *timestamp* are self-explanatory elements that provide information on the block at hand. The *previous block's hash* enables the chain to link its blocks in the correct order, like the pages of a book. The *Merkle tree* is the digital fingerprint of all the transactions in a block, allowing quick verification of whether a block includes a transaction. Each block's header includes a hash of this status to summarize all its information in only 32 bytes. A *nonce* is a number that miners change for the block's hash to yield a specific output. As Figure 6-3 shows, changing a single bit of information in a block yields a radically different hash output. Therefore, the miner changes the nonce and hashes the resulting block until he gets a block hash that begins with a specific number of zeroes. The target number of zeroes to obtain is defined in the *difficulty target*. The more miners try to solve the block (the higher the hash rate), the higher the difficulty target. For Bitcoin, this target is set so that it takes the network about 10 minutes to solve one block. Every two weeks, Bitcoin's difficulty target is adjusted based on the hash rate so that the 10-minute average is maintained. Other cryptoassets can have a different target time between blocks.[3]

The transaction counter contains two things. First, it contains transactions that were in the transaction pool (i.e., those that users submitted for recording). Since there is a maximum size to a block, not all transactions are gathered by the miner of the next block. The miner gathers as many of them as possible and selects the transactions of the biggest amount first because there is a transaction fee. The more and bigger the transactions, the higher the fee for the miner.

Second, in the transaction counter, there is a miner reward. It consists of the block reward and transaction fees. Bitcoin's block reward started at 50 bitcoins per block when it was launched, then the reward per block was divided by two every 210,000 blocks (roughly every four years). As of 2023, Bitcoin's block reward is 6.25 bitcoins per block. Transaction fees were small and negligible at first. However, now that the price of Bitcoin is in the tens of thousands of dollars, these small transaction fees have significant value. Ultimately, they will replace the block reward to incentivize miners to keep mining. In early May 2023 (block number 788,695), a surge in demand for block space on the Bitcoin blockchain caused these transaction fees to be bigger than the block reward for the first time since 2017.

---

[3] Blocks on the Solana blockchain, for example, are separated by 400 milliseconds, which therefore yields almost three blocks per second.

Bitcoin Block 788,695

Mined on May 08, 2023 12:06:27 • All Blocks

Unknown

Coinbase Message • ▤a Xd/Foundry USA Pool #dropgold/▤% ▤▤▤▤▤▤▤▤▤

A total of 1,532.75 BTC ($44,164,348) were sent in the block with the average transaction being 0.3309 BTC ($9,534.49). Unknown earned a total reward of 6.25 BTC $180,086. The reward consisted of a base reward of 6.25 BTC $180,086 with an additional 6.7007 BTC ($193,072) reward paid as fees of the 4,632 transactions which were included in the block.

Details

Hash	00000-145c6 ⎙	Depth	375
Capacity	167.57%	Size	1,757,083
Distance	2d 14h 26m 42s	Version	0×263de000
BTC	1,532.7488	Merkle Root	b6-72 ⎙
Value	$44,164,348	Difficulty	48,005,534,313,578.78
Value Today	$42,597,495	Nonce	3,488,487,704
Average Value	0.3309043176 BTC	Bits	386,260,225
Median Value	0.00000546 BTC	Weight	3,993,046 WU
Input Value	1,539.45 BTC	Minted	6.25 BTC
Output Value	1,545.70 BTC	Reward	12.95074657 BTC
Transactions	4,632	Mined on	08 May 2023, 00:06:27
Witness Tx's	4,576	Height	788,695
Inputs	5,273	Confirmations	375
Outputs	11,523	Fee Range	0-5,515 sat/vByte
Fees	6.70074657 BTC	Average Fee	0.00144662
Fees Kb	0.0038136 BTC	Median Fee	0.00099450
Fees kWU	0.0016781 BTC	Miner	Unknown

Figure 6-8. *Details of Bitcoin Block 788,695, mined on May 8, 2023 (Source: blockchain.com)*

The "Longest" Chain Is Always Right

Under PoW, when a miner completes the validation of a block, this block is appended to the chain and becomes a *candidate block*. Because of the decentralized nature of blockchain technology and the PoW consensus mechanism, two blocks may be mined at about the same time by two independent miners. It could lead to a possible "tie," as it is unclear to the network which block should be part of the blockchain.

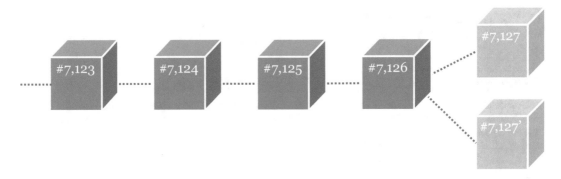

Figure 6-9. *Mining tie, where two blocks are mined at approximately the same time and are both candidate blocks*

PoW offers an elegant solution to this occasional problem: The network accepts the chain of blocks with the highest effort to build. In practice, the selected chain has the highest "chainwork" (i.e., the highest number of hashes expected to be necessary to build the chain). Miners on the network select that chain and continue mining on top of the last block of that chain.

Once the following block (or the following few blocks) is (are) mined, the tie is broken, and the longest chain becomes the uniquely valid chain. The candidate blocks that were not part of that chain are abandoned.

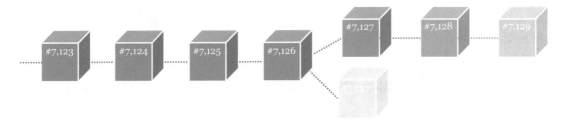

Figure 6-10. *The mining tie is broken once more blocks are mined on top of one of the candidate blocks. The abandoned block (from the non-selected chain) is an orphan block*

Through this mechanism, all users agree on which chain to use without debating or consulting each other.

It implies that a mined block does not necessarily mean that all transactions are final because it could become an orphan block. Instead, a transaction is permanently settled once a few more blocks are mined on top of the block holding this transaction. In the case of Bitcoin, with 10 minutes between blocks, it would take about 30 or 40 minutes (three or four blocks) to ensure that a transaction is permanently recorded in the ledger. This is one reason Bitcoin has been criticized as not being fit to be a medium of exchange (you would not want to wait for 30 minutes to pay for your coffee to go) and is instead seen as a store of value. Nevertheless, even such a "long" time to validate a transaction is much shorter than existing payment options, typically taking days to settle between banks (the payment is cleared in seconds but settled in days). Also, since 2017, there have been "layer 2" payment protocols, such as the Lightning Network, that circumvent this issue and enable close-to-instantaneous settlements for small-amount transactions in Bitcoin.

A dishonest node could try to tamper with a former block on the chain to double-spend, for example. However, changing any information in a former block changes the hash of all following blocks. Therefore, the dishonest node would need to solve all proof-of-work problems of all following blocks. The node would need to do so until its chain becomes the longest while the "real" chain continues to extend in parallel. As long as it is not the longest chain on the network, no other node would consider this alternative chain valid, and nobody would build on it or accept coins from it. Successfully attacking the chain would therefore require more computing power than all other nodes on the network combined. For the Bitcoin blockchain, this feat is just next to impossible.

Software Updates and Forks

As a blockchain evolves, it may need to apply changes to its core characteristics to remain relevant to the needs of the network. Such changes may include a different consensus mechanism, time between blocks, block size, and more. However, making changes to a blockchain is not straightforward because a large share of the validators on the network would need to approve and adopt the proposed new rules. To do so, the validators can freely download the latest version of the validation software and start validating blocks based on the new rules. Alternatively, they can choose not to adopt the newest version and continue validating under the older rules.

This freedom of choice can lead to two versions of a blockchain: one following the newer rules and one following the older ones. In such a case, the blockchain would encounter a fork. Such forks can be either *soft* or *hard.*

A soft fork of a blockchain happens when the newer rules still respect the older ones but become stricter. The validators using the newer rules would mine blocks that are also accepted by the validators using the older rules. However, the opposite is not true.

A validator that updated its software would not accept all blocks newly mined under the older rules. For example, assume that a change reduces the maximum size of a block from 2 MB to only 1 MB. Such a change still respects the less strict rules (i.e., a block of a maximum of 1 MB in size is also below 2 MB). However, if a miner under the old software mines a block of 1.6 MB, all validators with the updated software would consider this block invalid. Validators under the updated software would mine based on the blockchain version that includes only blocks compliant with the newer rules. Soft forks are, therefore, backward compatible. After a soft fork, only one version of the blockchain remains. The new rules would become the standard only if they created the longest chain. In other words, more than half of the miners (in terms of their hash power) must accept the new rules for them to become law.

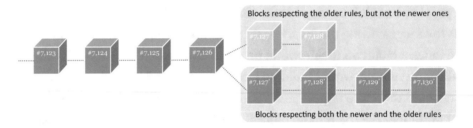

Figure 6-11. *Soft fork: new blocks are backward compatible but can only be mined under the stricter rules to be accepted by the validators under the newer software. If most validators update their software, the "new rules" blockchain becomes the longest. The other one is abandoned so that only one remains*

On the other hand, a hard fork is not backward compatible. It would, for example, include increasing the block size or changing the consensus mechanism. Such forks are controversial because they end in two incompatible blockchains running in parallel, each with its own rules.

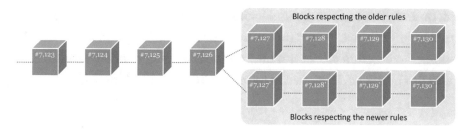

Figure 6-12. *Hard fork: new blocks are not backward compatible. Two chains exist in parallel, each with its unique rules and validators*

Forks are major events and are rare for the most established cryptoassets. However, they are also risky, as the change in rules opens the door to hackers taking advantage of an unseen bug in the new code. Therefore, they are often tested on a testnet—a dummy version of the main blockchain running in parallel.

Major forks have happened in the past, though. For example, in mid-2017, some miners theorized that block size is one factor limiting Bitcoin's scalability. They suggested increasing the block size from 1 MB to 8 MB, thereby hard-forking from Bitcoin's blockchain and creating Bitcoin Cash. On August 1, 2017, Bitcoin (BTC) holders at block 478,558 were eligible to claim an amount of Bitcoin Cash (BCH) equivalent to their Bitcoin holdings. As a result, Bitcoin and Bitcoin Cash blockchains run in parallel, are priced differently and are sometimes even considered different instruments. For example, Bitcoin could be seen as a store of value, while Bitcoin Cash as a medium of payment.

An infamous example of a hard fork relates to the 2016 disaster of The DAO, also coined the "DAOsaster." [25] The DAO[4], standing for The Decentralized Autonomous Organization, was an open source digital venture capital fund directed by its investors. They sent ethers to get tokens from The DAO, thereby voting rights. They could then vote on which start-up The DAO would invest in. In June 2016, a vulnerability in the code of The DAO enabled users to redirect $50 million, one-third of all funds of The DAO, to a private account. At the time, it represented 14% of all existing ethers. This event led to the highly controversial hard fork of Ethereum: Ethereum (ETH) reinstated the funds as before the hack, while Ethereum Classic (ETC) continued working as before. ETC proponents advocate one motto behind decentralized ledger technologies, "code is law." In their view, correcting past events would prove the lack of decentralization of the network.

---

[4] "The DAO" was a famous decentralized autonomous organization, but it is not to be confused with other DAOs that are unrelated to it and still exist.

Vitalik Buterin, the co-founder and leading developer of Ethereum, argues that as Ethereum was still in its early days (in its first year of existence) and under development, this exceptional correction would not undermine the integrity of Ethereum's values. As for BTC and BCH, ETH and ETC run in parallel, with wildly different valuations.

Public vs. Private Blockchains and Hybrids

Blockchains differ depending on whether they are public or private. A public blockchain is open to anyone at any time in a decentralized way. In contrast, a (fully) private blockchain is only partially decentralized and limited to a single organization.

Most cryptoassets mentioned in this book are based on public blockchains. However, in some cases, private blockchains can be more appropriate. Private blockchains offer higher transaction speed, lower transaction costs, and higher efficiency than public ones. As a result, they can become the favored option of private companies to manage internal data flows as an alternative to traditional databases.

What is the difference between a private blockchain and a traditional database? Technically, traditional databases use a centralized client-server model. In comparison, private blockchains are partially decentralized and use a peer-to-peer model based on cryptography. As a result, the private blockchain provides more data integrity than a traditional database but is slower and more expensive than the traditional model.

In the mid-2010s, these concepts further evolved to give birth to hybrid blockchains, also known as consortiums, which mix public and private blockchains. In a consortium blockchain, a pre-defined set of nodes would control the blockchain. For example, a dozen financial institutions could form a consortium, agreeing that two-thirds must agree for the next block to be mined. Therefore, such a model is neither a public blockchain nor a fully private one. Another hybrid alternative is to use a private blockchain that is interoperable with a public one.

Public blockchain	Private blockchain	Traditional database
Peer-to-peer model	Peer-to-peer model	Client-server model
Highly decentralized	Partially decentralized	Typically centralized
Permissionless	Permissioned	Permissioned
Immutable	Partially immutable	Mutable
Data integrity	Partial data integrity	No data integrity
Low speed	Higher speed	Highest speed
High cost	Lower costs	Lowest costs
Low efficiency	Higher efficiency	Highest efficiency

Figure 6-13. *Comparison of key characteristics of public blockchains, private blockchains, and traditional databases*

Is Blockchain Going to Replace All Databases?

The short answer is no. When given a hammer, one tends to see nails everywhere. Blockchain is a relatively new tool (a hammer) useful in some specific cases but not one to replace all other tools. Not all databases are nails. The large majority of them do not need to be decentralized. And if one needs immutability, some centralized database systems can provide it at a lower cost than blockchain solutions. Figure 6-14 summarizes in a simplified way when a blockchain is the preferred option for managing data flows.

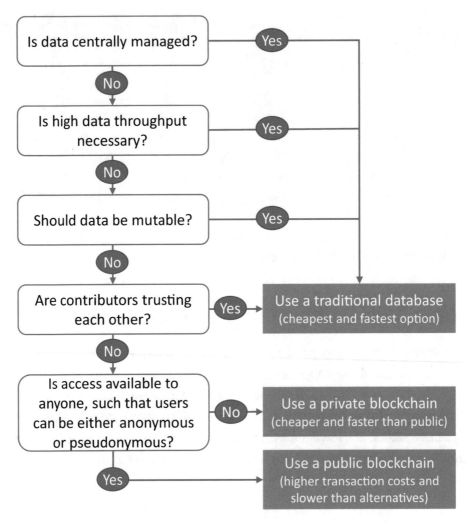

Figure 6-14. *Choice of a database based on data characteristics*

Nevertheless, in some cases, blockchains are transformational. Money is a straightforward example, but this revolution extends to insurance, identity management, music, art, supply chain, and countless other industries.

Updating a Ledger Under Proof of Stake

In the mid-2010s, an alternative to PoW, proof of stake (PoS), was developed to improve the original mechanism. In particular, it tackled the high energy consumption implied by thousands of miners competing to solve the same problem. Indeed, a crucial difference with PoW is that instead of having a winner-takes-all race to mine the next block, the PoS validator is selected before the effort is provided. This selection is based on the "stake" that the node has in the system (i.e., on the amount of the system's native cryptoasset that the node holds). In simple terms, if a node holds 2% of the existing supply of a PoS cryptoasset, then this node has a 2% chance of being selected as the next block proposer. Contrary to PoW, it does not require billions of hashes. The effort is therefore comparatively tiny.

Once the block is proposed, a committee based on members' stakes in the network assesses whether the block is valid. The members can approve or reject the block. If the block is approved by the majority (typically two-thirds), it is appended to the blockchain. The main drawback of PoS is that wealthy nodes are more likely to become validators, which tends to centralize the decision power on the network. Besides, any such tendency toward centralization is a big deal for blockchains because their main purpose is to offer decentralized alternatives to traditional, centralized models.

PoS and PoW are fundamentally different. The former is secured internally (by economic incentives in its code), while the latter is secured externally (by the number and decentralization of miners). Neither is better, the same way no car is the "best" for all purposes; some fit better in specific contexts or for specific goals.

As of 2023, PoS-like mechanisms are becoming the dominant consensus protocol for public blockchains, with the most important exception of Bitcoin.

Alternative Consensus Mechanisms

PoW and PoS are the most established consensus mechanisms but not the only ones. Hundreds of alternatives exist, combining trade-offs that make them appropriate in some cases and not in others [26].

For example, one essential trade-off is the scalability trilemma. In particular, consensus mechanisms can only have two of the following three characteristics, while the third one is only imperfect.

1. Security
2. Decentralization
3. Scalability

For instance, a consensus mechanism can create a secure and scalable blockchain but partially centralized. Similarly, it can be scalable and decentralized but with lower network security. Finally, it can be secure and decentralized but with scalability challenges.

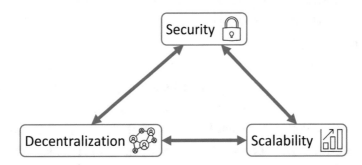

Figure 6-15. *Scalability trilemma. A consensus mechanism can only satisfy two of these three attributes perfectly*

A lack of security makes a network more vulnerable to malicious attacks. A lack of decentralization makes a network less tolerant of individual node failures. Finally, a lack of scalability limits a network's ability to process high throughput. For example, the Bitcoin blockchain famously combines high decentralization and exceptional security but has limited ability to scale intrinsically. This issue generated heated debates in the second half of the 2010s when the future of Bitcoin was under consideration. However, solutions now exist to address this issue for Bitcoin. For example, the Lightning Network enables small transactions to settle off-chain and only be occasionally posted on the Bitcoin blockchain.

To effectively assess the risks associated with a cryptoasset, one should crucially understand its consensus mechanism. This section introduces some common consensus mechanisms to give a flavor of the types of rules and protocols that can be developed to maintain the integrity of a blockchain. Note that Figure 6-16 is far from an exhaustive list.

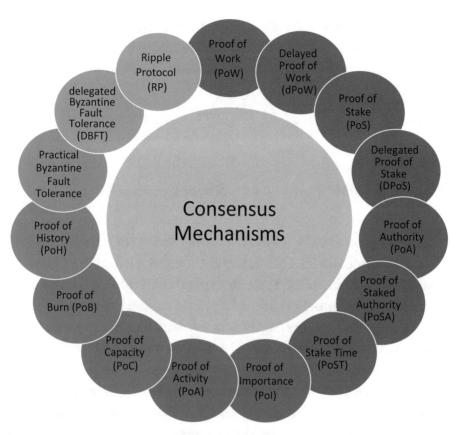

Figure 6-16. *Overview of some common consensus mechanisms (dozens more exist)*

Overall, consensus mechanisms divide into two broad groups: proof-based protocols and voting-based protocols [27]. Proof-based consensus mechanisms include proof of work (PoW), *delayed proof of work* (dPoW), *proof of importance* (PoI), *proof of capacity* (PoC), and *proof of burn* (PoB). In contrast, voting-based consensus mechanisms comprise proof of stake (PoS), *delegated proof of stake* (DPoS*), proof of authority* (PoA), *proof of stake time* (PoST), *practical Byzantine fault tolerance* (PBFT), *delegated Byzantine fault tolerance* (DBFT), and the *Ripple protocol* (RP).

Also, consensus protocols use different methods for selecting block validators. Overall, one could identify four general approaches.

1. Based on effort ("work")
2. Based on wealth or resources
3. Based on reputation or past behavior
4. Based on representation

One is arguably not better than another. However, some may be more appropriate for specific use cases. Assessing whether a consensus mechanism is appropriate can be based on how they fare in the following four fundamental properties.

1. Throughput
2. Security
3. Scalability
4. Finality

The following describes the high-level functioning of some existing consensus mechanisms.

- **Delayed proof of work (dPoW)** uses two parallel chains, where the security provided by the secondary chain enables it to append blocks on the main chain safely. Typically, it uses the Bitcoin blockchain (the most secure one) as a secondary chain to secure the main blockchain. The security comes from the main blockchain posting a hash of its status on the parallel blockchain at regular intervals. This way, it leverages the high hash power of the parallel blockchain. A crucial difference with PoW is that nodes appending new blocks on the main blockchain are elected. One benefit of dPoW is to reduce energy usage from traditional PoW mining.

- **Delegated proof of stake (DPoS)** is voting-based, similar to PoS. It consists of all network members (owners of the cryptoasset) electing representatives to act on their behalf. These representatives, called witnesses or block producers (BPs), validate transactions and blocks and are rewarded for their service. As an incentive to avoid fraud or collusion, BPs may be voted down, in which case their stake would be frozen. DPoS advocates claim it is a more democratic mechanism, as block validators are voted based on their reputation as fair stakers rather than purely on wealth. This consensus mechanism also benefits from a higher throughput than PoS but tends to be more centralized. Blockchains, including Cardano, TRON, and EOS, use DPoS.

- **Proof of authority (PoA)** is also a PoS variant, where specific trusted nodes act as block validators. The trusted nodes (the authority) earn a reputation over time, independently of their stake. They do not even have to stake anything at all. This consensus mechanism is strongly centralized as few actors have complete control over the network, but it benefits from high throughput and low fees. It is appropriate for blockchains that do not need decentralization, such as private blockchains.

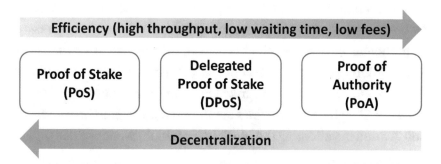

Figure 6-17. *Trade-offs between PoS and some of its variants. PoA has the highest efficiency of the three, while PoS has the highest level of decentralization*

- **Proof of staked authority (PoSA)**, a hybrid between PoS and PoA, is famous for being the consensus mechanism used by the Binance Smart Chain (BSC), one of the most established blockchains. A key difference with consensus mechanisms such as PoW or PoS is the small number of validators. In the case of BSC, the number of validators is limited to 21. Another crucial difference is that the incentive for validators in PoSA is exclusively in transaction fees, not a reward from newly minted coins. These characteristics enable PoSA to benefit from lower costs and a shorter block time than PoW or PoS.

- **Proof of stake time (PoST)** also builds on PoS by adding a time factor. The longer one holds the stake, the more valuable it becomes. Tweaks are possible, such as making the Stake Time dependent on how active the user is (a feature implemented in Vericoin, for example): the stakes of inactive users decrease over time.

- **Proof of importance (PoI)** is another voting-based consensus mechanism derived from PoS. The main difference is that to get permission to act as a validator node; one must own at least a minimum amount of the cryptoasset. Any node below the threshold is given zero importance. Above the threshold, as with PoS, the higher the amount staked, the higher the likelihood of being selected as a validator node.

- **Proof of activity (PoA)**[5] combines the most established consensus mechanisms, PoW and PoS. It supposedly combines the best of each by beginning as a PoW but resembling more PoS later in the process. In particular, once a new block is mined, the mechanism switches to PoS, randomly selecting validators based on the number of coins they own. Drawbacks of the mechanism are that the quantity of power used is still high (the main drawback of PoW), and coin hoarders are still favored in validating the block (the main drawback of PoS).

- **Proof of capacity (PoC)** moves away from using the miner's stake (as in PoS) or computational power (as in PoW) to validate transactions. Instead, it uses the available space on the miner's hard drive to store a list of possible solutions to a computational challenge. The more hard drive space is dedicated to the activity, the longer the list of possible solutions and the higher the likelihood for the miner to be selected to validate the next block. The main benefit compared to PoW or PoS is the higher resulting efficiency.

- **Proof of burn (PoB)** consists of burning coins to get the right to write blocks on the chain in proportion to the burnt coins. A miner would send coins (either the native coin of the blockchain or other coins, such as bitcoin or ether) to an unspendable address to get a reward in the native coin of the chain.

- **Proof of history (PoH)** is a series of cryptographic computations proving the time between two events, also known as a cryptographic clock. It uses a high-frequency Verifiable Delay Function to produce a series of transaction hashes (each including the previous hash as

---

[5] Both proof of authority and proof of activity use the PoA acronym.

114

one of its inputs) so that the sequence of the transactions is easily verifiable. Proving a sequence of events is the PoH key to ensuring the blockchain's integrity. This way, nodes do not need to wait for feedback from other nodes to validate the chain. PoH provides high speed for the blockchain while keeping its network secured and decentralized. It is notably used for the Solana blockchain, which posts a new block every 400 milliseconds.

- **Practical Byzantine fault tolerance (PBFT)** is a consensus mechanism replicating blocks between nodes. A primary node, elected by others, suggests a set of transactions to the rest of the network. Other nodes execute these transactions and broadcast the hash code of the resulting block. If at least two-thirds of the hash codes received correspond to the original one, the block is considered valid and appended to all local blockchain copies. This consensus mechanism benefits from remarkably high throughput and negligible waiting time. However, the number of computations necessary is high, and PBFT can only tolerate a failure of up to one-third of the network (in comparison, PoW can tolerate a failure of up to half of the network).

- **Delegated Byzantine fault tolerance (DBFT)** is a protocol in which all members get one vote, regardless of their wealth. In other words, it resembles how a country may elect a president. With this vote, members elect representatives ("bookkeeping nodes"). Among the representatives, one is randomly selected to propose the new block, which needs to be validated by the other representatives. If at least one-third disagree with the suggestion, another one is selected to propose the block. Similar to PBFT, one-third of the nodes could stall the process. However, the number of computations necessary is much smaller in DBFT.

- The **Ripple protocol (RP)** or the XRP ledger consensus mechanism (also known as *proof of correctness*) consists of a set of elected validators (the "unique node list") acting on behalf of the network. They follow an iterative process where they can add or remove new transactions until they align with enough of the other validators.

At least 80% of them must agree for the process to continue. Otherwise, the status of the blockchain remains unchanged. One major drawback is that only 20% +1 validators must be faulty for the entire process to stall.

Many other consensus mechanisms exist and are under development. The interested reader may want to look into, among others, proof of storage, proof of deposit (PoD), proof of weight, proof of reputation, proof of space, proof of stake velocity, proof of identity, proof of existence, proof of retrievability, proof of believability, and federated Byzantine agreement.

Decentralized Data vs. Decentralized Transactions

A blockchain is a decentralized database of transactions. However, it does not hold the underlying data the transactions refer to. This distinction is irrelevant when the underlying data is nothing more than transactions, like for Bitcoin. In that case, everything is on the blockchain. However, when a sizeable specific dataset is at hand (for example, for a digital song), the blockchain typically does not hold the dataset (the song) itself; instead, it only holds transactions related to the dataset.

In such a case, the blockchain must link to a database. The database can be centralized (in which case there is little interest in using a blockchain) or decentralized. One decentralized option to maintain the underlying data is IPFS: the InterPlanetary File System. IPFS marries well with blockchain as both the data transactions and the underlying database are decentralized. Introduced in 2016, IPFS is like a hard drive for blockchains. It stores not only data but also websites, applications, and more, as well as versions of this data over time.

Since copies of a blockchain exist on many computers, storing large sets of information in the blockchain itself would be inefficient. It would needlessly waste storage space on the blockchain network. Instead, cryptographic hashes of data stored on IPFS servers lighten the blockchain and increase its efficiency.

Why Is Blockchain Different?

First, blockchains are different from traditional ledgers by enabling a *trustless* exchange of information. It does not mean that there is no trust in the system or its counterparties, but rather that the element of trust is rendered irrelevant. More specifically, no trust in any other party is necessary; only trust in the continuity of a network.

The payment network is one of many possible examples, but it is straightforward to understand because it is blockchain's first application. In the traditional payment system, multiple intermediaries need to be trusted. When Alice sends money to Bob, both parties must trust their respective commercial banks, the networks enabling the transfer (e.g., the SWIFT[6] network), and the country's central bank. When payments are international, the number of intermediaries increases further. In comparison, blockchain does not rely on any central authority, thereby removing these superfluous steps and the need to trust any third party.

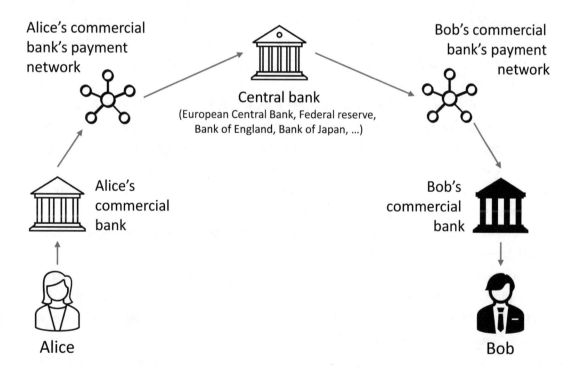

Figure 6-18. *Traditional payment flow. A money transfer from Alice to Bob requires multiple intermediaries*

---

[6] Society for Worldwide Interbank Financial Telecommunication.

In the case of blockchain, trust is only put in the cryptographic algorithm, which is open source, there for everybody to see.

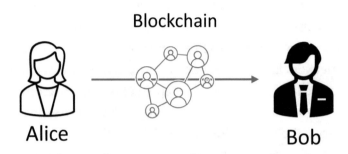

Figure 6-19. *Blockchain-enabled payment flow. A money transfer from Alice to Bob does not require any intermediary*

Also, a blockchain transaction can settle instantly at any time of the day or night, regardless of public holidays. In contrast, traditional money transfers are much slower. When you tap your credit card at a supermarket counter to buy groceries, it takes several days to settle, even if the transaction is cleared in seconds. For international money transfers, it can take weeks.

Another difference to traditional ledger systems is that a blockchain facilitates the *auditability* of any transaction or account since all transactions that ever happened are transparent and easily retrievable. Therefore, the audit is no longer a sample-based, time-consuming, and expensive process in the year after financial books closure. Instead, it becomes an exhaustive and continuous process, as the network instantly validates every transaction.

Therefore, the real value of blockchain is not just a fancy new way to organize data in a ledger. Blockchain is different because it removes the cost of trust from transactions. It removes frictions implied by sharing data with unknown third parties, such as banks. In addition, it shortens the waiting time to settle transactions from days to minutes. It also shrinks direct (e.g., transaction fees) and indirect costs (accounting, auditing, and issue settlement). By removing these frictions, blockchain can stimulate commerce and enable greater economic development, especially for those in need, such as the 2 billion people currently unbanked [28].

Key Concepts

Blockchain, part of distributed ledger technologies, was developed to enable Bitcoin to work. It is a database with the special characteristics of being decentralized, immutable, and pseudonymous. In particular, it enables the transfer of ownership of digital information without requiring trusting a third party. By removing the cost of trust, blockchains enable higher economic activity at lower costs.

It uses cryptography and consensus mechanisms to ensure data consistency despite its decentralized nature. Different consensus protocols exist, with different strengths and weaknesses, making them more appropriate in some cases and less in others, for example, for private blockchains or public blockchains.

Blockchain is a powerful new tool, but it will not replace all databases. Actually, most databases do neither need to be decentralized nor immutable.

Extension Questions

Assume you own ten bitcoins—each priced at $50,000—when a hard fork happens. Half the miners continue mining one branch of the fork and the other half the other. One block after the fork, how much is your portfolio worth?

Why was money the first use-case of blockchain?

How can you escape the scalability trilemma?

If you were to create a cryptoasset meant to be used as money, which (existent or non-existent) consensus mechanism would be most appropriate?

CHAPTER 7

Cryptoasset Taxonomies

All classifications in this world lack sharp boundaries, and all transitions are gradual.

—Aleksandr Solzhenitsyn

Note this book's recurrent use of the word *cryptoasset* rather than the more common term *cryptocurrency*. This distinction is purposeful, as cryptoassets encompass many more assets than only those meant to be currencies.

Formally, cryptoassets are digital assets secured by cryptography on a public ledger and created, managed, and exchanged on decentralized peer-to-peer networks.[1] In comparison, cryptocurrencies are one subcategory of cryptoassets. In traditional finance, currencies, stocks, bonds, commodities, real estate, and collectibles, among others, are all assets. Similarly, in the crypto universe, cryptoassets are divided into multiple categories.

Classifying cryptoassets is essential to value them accurately. Indeed, possible classifications inform how legislators might regulate and tax cryptoassets in the future. In turn, regulations and tax rules influence these assets' growth potential and risk profile. This chapter aims to provide some clarity on possible crypto taxonomies.

---

[1] Despite this formal definition suggesting decentralization as a core characteristic, some assets usually called *cryptoassets* do not include the decentralization feature (e.g., central-bank digital currencies and corporate cryptocurrencies). Also, many cryptoassets claim to be decentralized but are highly centralized in practice; more on that in Chapter 13.

© Thomas Jeegers 2023

T. Jeegers, *Understanding Crypto Fundamentals*, https://doi.org/10.1007/978-1-4842-9309-6_7

Challenges with Setting up a Cryptoasset Taxonomy

In a perfect world, a cryptoasset taxonomy would have categories that are mutually exclusive (an asset falls in only one category), commonly exhaustive (all assets have a category where they fit), and immutable (the taxonomy does not change over time). However, such a taxonomy is impossible as boundaries between subcategories of cryptoassets are blurry and rapidly changing, and new use cases are constantly emerging. Therefore, a more realistic taxonomy for cryptoassets should be constantly updated to reflect market developments.

As an example of the evolution of taxonomies, take privacy coins. Privacy coins used to be a helpful category, but now many tokens use an element of privacy in their architecture. As a result, privacy evolved from the core function of some cryptoassets to merely an attribute they can take. There are now many possible variations to achieve privacy and various levels of privacy.

Another challenge in categorizing cryptoassets is the criteria for the splits. For example, if one tried to make a taxonomy of sport types, one could wonder whether to split them according to team sports vs. individual sports or ball-based sports vs. others. For sports, as for cryptoassets, there are multiple ways to start a taxonomy. The following sections present some possible such ways.

Cryptoasset Taxonomy by Form and Function

In their 2017 bestseller *Cryptoassets,* Chris Burniske and Jack Tatar divided cryptoassets into three categories [29].

- **Cryptocurrencies** are cryptographically secured digital currencies that can be exchanged over a network.

- **Cryptocommodities** are raw digital resources that can be used as input for a finished good.

- **Cryptotokens** are finished digital goods and services.

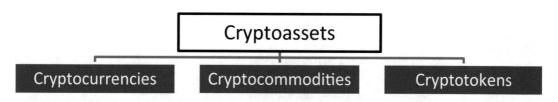

Figure 7-1. *Categorization of cryptoassets, according to Burniske and Tatar [29]*

This early classification enabled the differentiation of cryptoassets according to one fundamental characteristic: their form. However, it is also possible to build on this taxonomy by splitting categories further, based on their function, as illustrated in Figure 7-2 for cryptocurrencies and Figure 7-3 for cryptocommodities.[2]

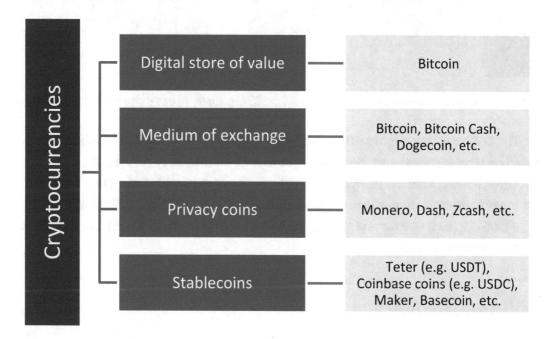

Figure 7-2. *Subcategories of cryptocurrencies, with some (possibly controversial) examples*

---

[2] These subcategorizations are not covered by Burniske and Tatar.

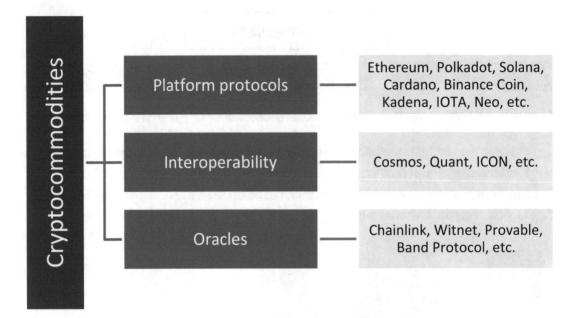

Figure 7-3. *Subcategories of cryptocommodities, with some examples*

The cryptotoken category similarly divides further, but the number of subcategories would be large (dozens) and the market size of each subcategory very small.

The following sections analyze some subcategories of cryptoassets. The objective is neither to describe how any of them works in detail nor to be exhaustive but to give a high-level overview of what the general crypto ecosystem looks like and what functions cryptoassets may provide.

Cryptocurrencies

The following subsections follow the structure in Figure 7-2.

Digital Store of Value

A store of value asset keeps or increases its purchasing power over time. It is quite different from keeping its nominal value. For example, one US dollar from 100 years ago is still one US dollar today, but it did not keep its value. While it could buy a certain amount of goods and services at the time (such as a complete meal in a major city), it can only buy a fraction of these goods and services today. The US dollar kept its nominal value but not its real value. It is not an effective store of value.

Medium of Exchange

Some cryptoassets are (meant to be) used as a medium of exchange for daily transactions. Such assets would optimally have a quick settlement time and broad commercial adoption. Optimal currency coins would also be fully fungible: one would not value one coin differently from another (for example, based on the transaction history of that coin).

Privacy Coins

Privacy coins are both a subcategory of currency coins and a function implementable in any fungible cryptoasset. As a reminder, Bitcoin is not anonymous but pseudonymous. A user's pseudonym is used to transact bitcoins, but the quantity of bitcoins held by the pseudonym and every transaction that ever happened is open for anybody to see. In comparison, privacy coins provide anonymity to users. The algorithms behind privacy coins use technologies such as ring signatures to prove that the money transfer is valid, but without revealing from where it comes.

Stablecoins

A stablecoin is a cryptocurrency tracking the value of a fiat currency or another asset. For example, they can track the US dollar's or gold's value. Stablecoins can peg to the other asset's value in several ways. In particular, tangible assets can back the stablecoin (US dollars or gold in a vault), or an algorithm can synthetically reproduce the peg.

Stablecoins benefit from low volatility in comparison to other cryptoassets. However, the ones pegged to fiat currencies indirectly lose desirable characteristics of cryptoassets, such as decentralization and trustlessness. Furthermore, due to the underlying currency's inflation rate, they are also subject to the same loss of value over time as fiat currencies, making them poor stores of value.

Alternative Cryptocurrency Taxonomy

Another helpful distinction among cryptocurrencies is their emitter. In their 2018 bestseller book *Blockchain Revolution* (updated edition), Don Tapscott and Alex Tapscott divide cryptocurrencies into three categories [30].

1. self-organizing cryptocurrencies
2. corporate cryptocurrencies
3. state-based cryptocurrencies

Bitcoin is an example of a *self-organizing cryptocurrency*. No centralized party manages it, and it is open for anyone to join. Of the three categories, it is the only one that is decentralized.

Diem (formerly Libra) is an example of *corporate cryptocurrency*, as it was initiated by a corporation, Meta (known as Facebook at the time), even though it is managed by an independent not-for-profit organization, in which Meta is merely a member.

China's Digital Currency Electronic Payment (DCEP) ("digital yuan") is an example of *state-based cryptocurrency* issued by the country's central bank, the People's Bank of China. State-based cryptocurrencies, sometimes called Central Bank Digital Currencies (CBDC), provide the issuing authority with unprecedented oversight and control over the money flows among the currency users. Moreover, compared to fiat currencies, the CBDC issuing authority's censorship ability is not only maintained but even greatly strengthened. For example, China is exploring expiration dates with its digital yuan. If unused by a specific time, the yuan you earned may expire and be made worthless. Alternatively, the issuing authority could target certain tranches of the population or even specific people to implement ad-hoc taxes or money confiscation. While decentralized cryptoassets empower people and free them from abusive authorities, CBDCs are just the opposite, the base for a real-world monetary dystopia where a central authority is all-powerful.

Cryptocommodities

The following subsections follow the structure in Figure 7-3.

Platform Protocols or Smart Contract Platforms

Smart contract platforms (or platform protocols) enable users to pay for smart contracts. For example, Ethereum requires to pay "gas fees" to run smart contracts on its blockchain. The term *gas fees* is a good analogy. The platform (Ethereum) is like a network of roads enabling cars (applications) to travel (run). Gasoline demand, and therefore its price, depends on the number of cars on the road, their size, and how much they ride. Ethereum works similarly: the more people want to run smart contracts, the higher the gas fees. Moreover, similar to bigger cars requiring more gasoline, bigger contracts also require more gas. Gas fees are therefore working as a supply-and-demand-based incentive for optimizing the network.

Interoperability

Interoperability services enable cryptoassets to interact from one blockchain to another. As an analogy, Microsoft Teams works on Windows, Linux, and Apple computers without users knowing their counterparty's operating system. Unfortunately, cryptoassets are not interoperable yet, but several cryptoasset services are working on solving this issue.

Oracles

In the cryptoasset universe, an oracle is a data feed providing real-world (off-chain) data that can be used to trigger events in a blockchain's smart contracts. Such data can include weather data, sports results, asset prices, election outcomes, and any other information that can be represented digitally. Oracles are critical to the development of the ecosystem, as many smart contracts depend on them to be functional.

Cryptotokens

As mentioned above, cryptotokens can take many different functions. Therefore, this section only illustrates some possible classifications and insights to understand cryptotokens at a high level.

Platform Tokens

A platform token is a digital asset built on a protocol (such as ERC-20 on the Ethereum blockchain or BEP20 on Binance Smart Chain) [30]. Such digital assets can be cryptocurrencies or the digital representation of assets in the real world, like cars, produce, land, or real estate.

Financial Services Cryptotokens

Financial services cryptotokens form together what is called *decentralized finance*, or DeFi. They leverage blockchain technology to remove intermediaries in traditional finance, such as banks, insurance, asset brokers, or money transfer services. They also facilitate payment settlements and enable (centralized or decentralized) exchanges to work efficiently. For example, a centralized exchange's coin enables the exchange of cryptoassets for a lower fee than would otherwise be charged.

Non-Financial Services Cryptotokens

Cryptotokens also emerged beyond the financial world. Among others, they became famous in gaming, gambling, social media, data storage, computing, digital art, and collectibles industries.

Web 3.0 Cryptotokens

Before covering Web 3.0 cryptotokens, let us briefly review what Web 3.0 is. The World Wide Web constantly evolves, but three significant waves can be identified. Web 1.0 was the first stage of the Web, defined by static read-only webpages. Pages could display text and images but not interact with users. In contrast, Web 2.0 added interactions with users and between users. As a result, content became dynamic and often generated by users. Social media are a splendid example where users generate information attracting others to the platform. While Web 2.0 focuses on the front end (where users interact), Web 3.0 upgrades the back end of the Web, the architecture. Web 3.0 organizes data for more advanced purposes, such as artificial intelligence, 3D graphics, virtual reality, or internet-of-things devices. Also, while Web 2.0 generates centralized data owned by a handful of companies, Web 3.0 enables data to be decentralized.

Web 3.0 cryptotokens facilitate data usage, storage, processing, and connectivity in a decentralized environment.

Non-Fungible Tokens (NFTs)

Among the aforementioned tokens, some are unique—like a sculpture in the physical world. In this case, they are non-fungible tokens, or NFTs for short. The NFT sector boomed in 2021, revolutionizing art by making digital art pieces unique.

The General Taxonomy for Cryptographic Assets (GTCA)

In February 2018, the blockchain and cryptoasset research company Brave New Coin launched the General Taxonomy for Cryptographic Assets (GTCA) [31]. It was a dynamic (regularly updated) taxonomy based on more than 70 metrics intended for "asset managers and traders, regulators, researchers and academics, developers and product owners, industry executives, and crypto enthusiasts." It strived to assess the strengths and weaknesses of cryptoassets consistently and objectively through a standardized and rigorous approach.

In particular, it introduced cryptographic assets as a new superclass of asset, further subdivided into two families and four subclasses of cryptographic assets. The first level of the taxonomy divided cryptoassets between "general cryptographic assets" and "protocol tokens." The first family classified assets based on more than 60 qualitative and quantitative metrics to subdivide them between subclasses. In contrast, the "protocol tokens" family assigned assets to industries so that each asset falls into a single industry. The next level of the hierarchy was significantly more granular, with more than 70 (partially overlapping) categories, such as decentralized exchange, core liquidity provider, Blockchain as a Service, dApp platform, VR-platform cryptocurrency, or social media.

Building upon the first iteration of the taxonomy, Brave New Coin updated the approach in the following years to provide a completely new framework. It categorized cryptoassets using hierarchical and morphological structures of categories to provide a 360-degree view of the asset class. These categories are organized into dimensions that represent economic, legal, international regulation, technical, and thematic factors. For example, the economic dimension is designed to classify cryptoassets based on their economic usage or purpose. This dimension also helps identify the economic properties of an asset, such as supply issuance, fungibility, industry activity, convertibility, and underlying value. Another hierarchical structure in the economic dimension is Brave New Coin's industry classification system, which comprises 10 economic sectors, 14 business sectors, 23 industry groups, 34 industries, and 108 niche markets as of March 2023. Although there is unique crypto labeling in each tier, the niche market tier was specifically developed to cater to the unique cryptoasset economy and business models.

Brave New Coin's approach already shows that there are multiple ways to build a cryptoasset taxonomy. In parallel and afterward, other companies established further taxonomies for cryptoassets.

The Digital Asset Classification Standard (DACS)

In mid-December 2021, CoinDesk Indices introduced a complete taxonomy for cryptoassets: the Digital Asset Classification Standard (DACS) [32]. This taxonomy is the crypto equivalent to the Global Industry Classification Standard (GICS) developed in 1999 by MSCI and Standard & Poor's. The GICS has been invaluable since its inception, enabling equity investors to explain financial performance co-movement within the same sector and assess comparable investment opportunities. While the GICS classifies more than 26,000 publicly traded companies worldwide, the DACS classifies at least the top 500 digital assets.[3] The DACS method to determine sector and industry exposure is standardized and transparent. The DACS could become the benchmark for cryptoasset categorization, like the GICS for equity.

The DACS is a dynamic taxonomy (revised at least monthly) that divides cryptoassets by function and in mutually exclusive categories. They split assets into three layers: sector, industry group, and industry. As of May 2023, the structure defines 7 sectors, 26 industry groups, and 40 industries, as shown in Figure 7-4 [33].

---

[3] CoinDesk Indices uses the term "digital asset" rather than *cryptoasset*.

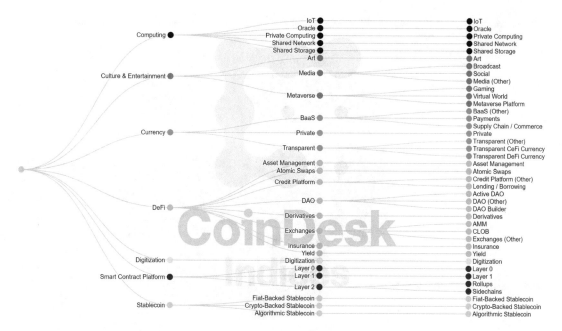

Figure 7-4. *DACS by CoinDesk Indices, as of May 2023 [33]*

So far, most cryptoassets (in market capitalization) in the DACS taxonomy fall in the currency, smart contract platform, or stablecoin sectors.

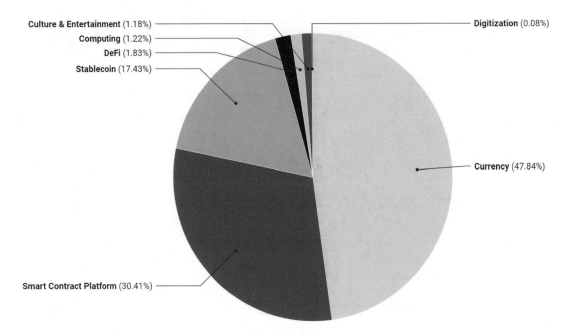

Figure 7-5. *The relative size of each sector of the DACS by CoinDesk Indices, data as of December 31, 2022 [32]*

The Global Crypto Classification Standard (GCCS)

In February 2023, the companies 21Shares and CoinGecko jointly launched another cryptoasset taxonomy—the Global Crypto Classification Standard (GCCS) [34]. The taxonomy first distinguishes between the *protocol* and the *token* levels, then subdivides between four sublevels: crypto stack, sector, industry, and token taxonomy.

While some categories within these levels are similar to categories in previous taxonomies (cryptocurrencies, oracles, interoperability, smart contract platforms), the division between *asset superclasses* is original. In particular, the taxonomy classifies assets into three *superclasses* that correspond to functions taken by traditional assets: capital assets, consumable/transformable assets, and store of value assets. Like the GTCA, the GCCS acknowledges that cryptoassets can be viewed from different perspectives and end in different groups.

Cryptoassets Technology in Layers

Another valuable classification of cryptoassets to use in parallel to previous classifications is per layer. Cryptoassets appear at various places in the value chain going from the core technology to user-friendly applications. In particular, five different layers in the crypto ecosystem can be identified, as shown in Figure 7-6.

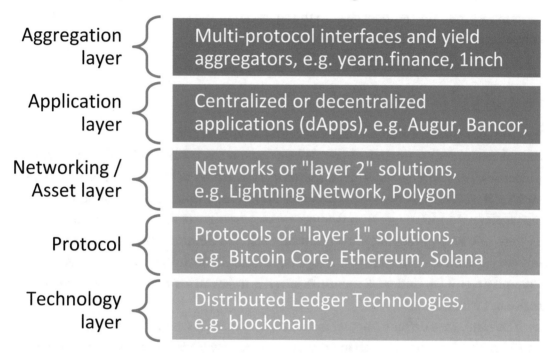

Figure 7-6. *Visualization of the crypto ecosystem in layers*

The most basic building block is the underlying technology (i.e. blockchain, or "distributed ledger technologies" to be more inclusive). This layer sets the crypto ecosystem's foundation, sometimes called *layer 0*.

Directly built on the technology is the protocol layer. It corresponds, for example, to Ethereum or the Bitcoin Core protocol. Protocols at this level define the rules on how to use a particular implementation of blockchain technology. Cryptoasset literature often refers to them as *layer 1 solutions*.

The next layer is the "networking" or "asset" layer, also known to as *layer 2 solutions*. It facilitates access for users to the protocol. For example, the Lightning Network is built on top of Bitcoin, enabling transactions to settle much faster than by interacting directly with the Bitcoin blockchain. Another example is Polygon, a framework scaling Ethereum by enabling to build and connect Ethereum-compatible blockchain networks.

Then comes the application layer, corresponding to centralized or decentralized applications (dApps). Such applications respond directly to users' needs and are typically more user-friendly; examples include Augur, Bancor, and CryptoKitties.

Finally, services leveraging the power of multiple applications (or directly from lower layers) form the aggregation layer. They, for example, aggregate yields from multiple applications to provide the best possible financial service to users.

Services from the protocol layer to the aggregation layer can be anywhere on the continuum, from centralized to fully decentralized.

Are Cryptoassets Securities?

For regulatory and taxation purposes, defining whether a cryptoasset is a security is critical. Securities are treated differently from currencies, commodities, collectibles, or properties. For example, reporting requirements can differ wildly depending on whether an asset is a security. Investment managers, for instance, must report their "assets under management," which depend on whether cryptoassets are classified as securities or as "cash or cash equivalents". More importantly, in the United States, only accredited investors can invest in securities not registered with the Securities and Exchange Commission (SEC). Under US securities law, it is unlawful to openly sell a security not registered with the SEC.

The *Howey test* defines whether an instrument qualifies as an "investment contract" or a "security."[4] In particular, an instrument is a security if it is "an investment of money in a common enterprise with an expectation of profits to be derived solely from the efforts of others."

Notice the four clear requirements for an asset to be a security as per this definition.

1. an investment of money
2. in a common enterprise
3. an expectation of profits
4. derived solely by the efforts of others

---

[4] Coming from the famous case of the US Supreme Court "Securities and Exchange Commission v. Howey Co., 328 U.S. 293 (1946)" [64].

This definition puts substance above form. In particular, a cryptoasset is a security if it behaves like a security, not based on how it came into existence (on a blockchain or not) nor based on its designation (e.g., cryptoasset, cryptocurrency, digital currency, virtual currency, coin, token).

According to this definition, arguably, all DeFi tokens are securities. Also, despite heated debates, as soon as a cryptoasset is on proof of stake (PoS), it should be considered a security. This is especially the case for PoS tokens because validating a block under PoS implies virtually no work by the staker and can therefore be considered "solely derived by the efforts of others."[5] It means that almost all cryptoassets should be considered securities, with only a few exceptions. The most notable of these exceptions is Bitcoin.[6] Mining Bitcoin clearly requires work by the miner, thereby moving it outside the Howey-test definition.

Some instead classify Bitcoin as cash or cash equivalent when it fulfills the function of a medium of exchange (like in El Salvador, where Bitcoin is legal tender). However, the growing consensus is to consider Bitcoin an intangible asset: digital property or a commodity.

Still, as of 2023, many countries have no formal regulations specifying which cryptoassets are securities. Moreover, in some countries, like the United States, there is not even a national agreement, as different regulatory institutions (such as the SEC, the Commodity Futures Trading Commission (CFTC), the Office of the Comptroller of the Currency, and the Internal Revenue Service (IRS)) consider cryptoassets differently. Nevertheless, jointly defining how to classify and regulate such assets is ongoing.

For example, the CFTC officially ruled in 2019 that Bitcoin is a commodity [35] and unofficially asserted that Ethereum is also a commodity. Aligning with that opinion, the SEC chairman Gary Gensler also repeatedly affirmed that Bitcoin is a commodity. However, until May 2023, he has always carefully avoided expressing his opinion on Ethereum's status as a security. In contrast, the SEC ruled several other PoS cryptoassets as securities. In light of this unclarity, the US president issued an executive order in 2022 to define the line between securities and non-securities in the crypto context. The Financial Stability Oversight Council replied in October of that year with a 124-page document on the corresponding risks and regulations [36]. Nevertheless, the line remains blurry.

---

[5] Defendants of the PoS consensus mechanism claim that their network (e.g., Ethereum), is not a "common enterprise" but a global platform used independently by users. This argumentation could keep open the question of whether PoS assets are securities after all.

[6] Other exceptions would mostly be some (not all) hard forks of Bitcoins.

International regulatory bodies have also not reached a greater consensus so far. They strive to establish a stance on cryptoassets as the notion of the inevitable growth of this industry settles, but the output is mainly uncoordinated. For example, the International Monetary Fund (IMF) is mandated to "safeguard the stability of the international monetary and financial system." However, while it established that the world needs global, consistent, comprehensive, and coordinated cryptoasset regulation, it does not provide insights into what such regulation should be.

The Basel Committee on Banking Supervision, part of the Bank of International Settlements (BIS), defines how to account for risks of different groups of cryptoassets. It also invites holders to assess risks underlying cryptoassets thoroughly and disclose them publicly. However, no formal BIS classification of cryptoassets as financial instruments exists yet.

Finally, the International Financial Reporting Standards (IFRS) also do not provide a definitive answer on cryptoasset classification. As of this writing, they leave it to cryptoasset holders to define which accounting category each cryptoasset falls into. See Ernst & Young's analysis "Accounting by holders of crypto-assets" for a dive into what makes a cryptoasset fall in each possible accounting category [37].

Despite regulatory uncertainty and disagreements on classifying cryptoassets, existing financial regulation can be interpreted as follows. In order not to be a security under current regulation, a cryptoasset cannot have an owning entity, so it should be truly decentralized. Satoshi Nakamoto showed us how to do that: the asset's network should neither have a board of directors nor creators able to materially influence future network developments. Once the cryptoasset functions as intended, its creators should effectively disappear and renounce all their holdings in the asset (e.g., by sending them to an unspendable address). Therefore, some existing cryptoassets may lose their security status, but it would require their effective owners to formally relinquish their managerial role for the asset's network.

Key Concepts

Classifying cryptoassets is critical to defining how they may be regulated and taxed and thereby how to value them and assess their risk profile.

However, creating a definitive cryptoasset taxonomy is impossible, as boundaries between cryptoassets are blurry and change rapidly. Classifications should therefore be constantly updated. One should use multiple taxonomies in parallel to divide assets according to different characteristics, such as their form, function, or where they lie in the crypto ecosystem.

A recent taxonomy that could become the industry standard in the future is the DACS from CoinDesk Indices. It is a regularly updated taxonomy of the main cryptoassets based on objective and transparent criteria.

As of 2023, there is no global agreement on whether or which cryptoassets are securities, and regulation is still being developed for this new asset class.

Extension Questions

What are the benefits and limitations of each taxonomy presented in this chapter?

Which subcategories of cryptoasset are here to stay, and which will disappear?

Is Ethereum a security?

CHAPTER 8

Cryptoasset Investment Types

> *If you don't find a way to make money while you sleep, you will work until you die.*
>
> —Warren Buffett

For any investment, buying at a low price and selling at a higher price is one form of return, capital gain. However, it is often not the only way to benefit from the investment. Equity investments (stocks) typically also deliver returns in dividends. Fixed-income investments (bonds) mainly deliver returns through interest. Real estate investments can deliver returns through rent.

Similarly, cryptoassets offer alternative sources of return on investment. This chapter investigates these sources. However, before that, it explores the different ways to invest in cryptoassets, from pure investment on the blockchain to indirect investments via companies with cryptoasset exposure and investment vehicles in cryptoassets.

Direct and Indirect Investments In Cryptoassets

The most straightforward way to benefit financially from cryptoassets is to buy and sell them directly. Such purchases and sales are called *spot trading* because the asset is delivered almost immediately (on the spot). For example, if you bought a bitcoin at a market price of $5,800 in March 2020 and sold it at the market price of $58,000 in March 2021, you would have made a +900% return, or 10x, in a year. Inversely, large drops are

T. Jeegers, *Understanding Crypto Fundamentals*, https://doi.org/10.1007/978-1-4842-9309-6_8

also possible. For example, if you kept the asset for 18 more months, you would have lost 66% from the March 2021 price, as it only traded at $20,000 in October 2022. Such investments can be made on centralized exchanges (e.g., Binance, KuCoin, Coinbase) or decentralized exchanges (e.g., dYdX, Uniswap, ApolloX).

However, regulation or investor mandates may limit direct investments in cryptoassets. Fortunately for investors facing such limitations, alternatives exist to get exposure to cryptoassets through indirect investments.

Exchange-Traded Funds (ETFs)

An *exchange-traded fund*, or ETF, is an investment vehicle tracking the performance of an asset or a group of assets. ETFs offer several benefits to investors compared to direct investments in the underlying asset. First, they offer portfolio diversification. By buying an ETF of an index, the investor obtains exposure to all underlying assets without needing to buy each asset separately. Second, ETFs are typically highly liquid. They can be bought and sold at a fair market price and in sizable amounts. Third, they do not require users to familiarize themselves with cryptoasset wallets. However, purchasing ETFs may be more expensive than directly buying the underlying instrument because ETFs charge an annual fee (e.g., 0.8% of the invested amount).

ETFs for the main cryptoassets are increasingly available in many countries, both *spot ETFs* and *futures ETFs*. A spot ETF simply tracks the value of the underlying cryptoasset. If Bitcoin's price goes up, then Bitcoin spot ETFs go up in the same proportion.

A futures ETF tracks the value of a "futures" of the underlying cryptoasset. A "futures" is a financial product where two parties agree that one party will buy an agreed-upon amount of an asset at a specific date for an agreed price, regardless of what the actual price of the asset is on that date. For example, Alice and Bob enter a Bitcoin futures, where Alice will buy two bitcoins from Bob for $50,000 each on December 31. Even if Bitcoin's price is below $50,000 on December 31, Alice must still buy two bitcoins from Bob at $50,000 each. And even if Bitcoin's price is above $50,000, Bob must still sell the two bitcoins for $50,000 each. Futures provide certainty about a future purchase or sale price. A Bitcoin futures ETF tracks the value at which Bitcoin futures trade on the open market.

As of May 2023, countries offering spot Bitcoin ETFs include Australia, Brazil, Canada, the Netherlands, and Singapore. In addition, spot ether ETFs are also available in multiple countries. The notable exception for spot ETFs of any cryptoasset is the United States. In particular, the Securities Exchange Commission (SEC) in the United States has rejected all spot Bitcoin ETFs applications for questionable reasons, which are being appealed in front of courts of justice.

Futures ETFs, however, are more broadly available. In particular, the first Bitcoin futures ETF has been available in the United States since October 19, 2021. As of this writing, six Bitcoin futures ETFs are approved for trading in the United States, and 25 more are awaiting approval. Similarly, many other countries offer Bitcoin and ether futures ETFs.

Companies Using Blockchain

Besides ETFs, another indirect exposure to cryptoassets is possible by investing in companies currently using blockchain technology or developing new use cases for blockchain technologies. Contrary to investing in cryptoassets directly, such indirect investments are standard (similar to investing in any company) and do not require unusual reporting or regulatory measures that would be specific to cryptoassets.

Companies with Cryptoassets on Their Balance Sheet

Similarly, one can invest in companies with large amounts of cryptoassets on their balance sheet. For example, the publicly traded business intelligence company MicroStrategy held 130,000 bitcoins at the beginning of 2023, worth over $3 billion or roughly the company's entire market capitalization. As a result, the company's stock price reflects the evolution of Bitcoin's price very closely (coefficient of correlation over 2020–2022: 93%), as shown in Figure 8-1.

Figure 8-1. *Bitcoin price (left axis) vs. MicroStrategy Incorporated (NASDAQ: MSTR) stock price (right axis) in USD from January 2020 to January 2023*

Other publicly tradable companies also hold bitcoins, though in much smaller proportions than MicroStrategy. They include Tesla (TSLA), Galaxy Digital Holding (BRPHF), and Block (previously known as Square, SQ). While buying shares of these companies may provide some indirect exposure to Bitcoin, this exposure is far from perfect. In particular, if Bitcoin's price is multiplied by ten in the coming couple of years, the value of these companies may increase, but they are unlikely to see similar 10x valuations.

Companies Providing Crypto Services

Companies mining cryptoassets or providing other crypto services are another indirect (and imperfect) investment in cryptoassets. For example, Marathon Digital Holdings (MARA) is a major Bitcoin mining company holding close to 12,000 Bitcoin at the end of 2022 and aiming "to build the largest mining operation in North America," with some 69,000 ASIC miners [38]. Mining and ASICs are explained in the next section.

Cryptoasset exchanges are another possibility. For example, Coinbase is among the most prominent public cryptoexchange in the United States and the first publicly traded one. It also holds a substantial number of bitcoins on its balance sheet (9,000 in 2022), so the exposure is dual: through its operations and Bitcoin's price fluctuations [39].

Early-Stage Cryptoasset Investing

An alternative way to gain exposure to cryptoassets consists of investing at the earliest development stage. Several offerings exist, with typically high possible rewards but also high risks.

Traditionally, when a private company decides to go public (i.e., to emit shares publicly buyable by many outside investors), it does so through an Initial Public Offering (IPO). In an IPO, investors buy a share of the underlying company. The crypto industry leveraged this established notion by developing Initial Coin Offerings (ICO). An ICO is fundamentally a form of crowdfunding that matches potential investors with founders, matching capital with an idea. It is the original way for blockchain start-ups to raise equity capital. In an ICO, investors buy a newly emitted cryptoasset in the hope of future rising value. Thereby, anybody can become a venture capital investor. The founders typically keep a large share of the cryptoasset (e.g., 20%) as a source of funds for developing the project. Despite its name using the term "coin," ICOs are not exclusively for assets meant to be currencies. Instead, all types of cryptoassets use ICOs.

ICOs started as early as 2013, the first major being Ethereum's ICO in 2014. Subsequently, most ICOs happened on Ethereum's blockchain, and their number grew exponentially in the following few years. Unfortunately, many took advantage of the ICO hype by emitting tokens not meant to become anything worthwhile. As soon as investors jumped in, scammers would pocket the funds and leave the project to die. Sometimes, founders even took advantage of the data-privacy spirit behind blockchain to hide their true identity and run the perfect scam. As founders usually lack accountability in ICOs, an alternative, *security token offerings* (STO), was created.

Unlike an ICO, an STO is backed by a company's stock or future profits. An STO is like buying a stake in a real-world company. In comparison, an ICO is like buying a token without value unless a project's promises become a reality. This difference reduces incentives for the issuing team to run away with the funds. While ICOs enable raising capital more efficiently (faster and at lower costs) and from a broader pool than has ever been possible, STOs are safer for investors. STOs take place following strict regulations to eventually become registered securities. For example, investors may be required to follow strict Know Your Customer (KYC) and Anti-Money Laundering (AML) processes to invest. This regulatory framework reduces the risk of turning out as a scam. Another crucial difference is in terms of ideology. While ICOs rely on the essential idea of removing intermediaries, STOs often rely on some middlemen to increase the reliability of the project for both issuers and investors.

Overall, ICOs and STOs improved the liquidity of historically illiquid assets and removed barriers to entry for small potential venture capital investors. As a result, what once were privileged opportunities for a few wealthy investors became accessible to the masses. They represent a major step toward the democratization of finance.

However, ICOs and STOs are not the only possibilities regarding early offerings of new cryptoassets. Alternatives emerged in the late 2010s and continued to bloom in the early 2020s. Among them are initial exchange offerings (IEO), initial DEX offerings (IDO), Maker's strong holder offering (SHO), and Initial Twitter Offering (ITO). Readers interested in these less-common offerings may consult D-Core's *Institutional Blockchain Investment Guide* [40].

Mining

Besides direct investments in cryptoassets, ETFs, or companies related to cryptoassets, another possible investment type is through infrastructure. In particular, by investing in the mining operations of cryptoassets based on a proof-of-work consensus mechanism, Bitcoin in particular.

Traditional Cryptoasset Mining

Instead of investing in a company mining cryptoassets, one can mine them directly. Chapter 6 covered mining, the process of emitting new coins (called *coinbase transactions*) for cryptoassets on a proof-of-work consensus mechanism. Such cryptoassets include Bitcoin, Bitcoin Cash, Litecoin, Monero, Dash, and Dogecoin. However, Bitcoin is by far the asset with the highest hash rate (a measure of the network's security), which is 100 times larger than the combined hash rate of all other PoW assets combined. As a reminder, miners compete in a winner-takes-all competition to validate the next block of the blockchain. To win this "race," miners run many cryptographic hashes with specialized equipment until one hits a number with specific characteristics by chance. It is similar to a lottery where the price to purchase a ticket is computing power (indirectly, electricity). The successful miner receives a reward in the form of newly minted coins.

Mining can be a profitable business, but it involves significant upfront investment, requires access to a cheap source of electricity, and has volatile profitability prospects. High investment is required to purchase specialized devices to mine on one's behalf.

In some cases, you may need a recent *application-specific integrated circuit*, or ASIC, to become relevant. Indeed, the pace of innovation makes mining rigs obsolete in a few months to a few years. It is not to say that it is impossible to mine with older rigs. However, the quantity of hashes performed by newer rigs evolves quickly, making older devices quickly uncompetitive.

Figure 8-2. *ASIC Bitcoin miner (Source: Wikimedia, public domain)*

As of May 2023, a new ASIC miner can yield over 200 terahashes (200 trillion hashes) per second. In comparison, a single block on the Bitcoin blockchain requires about 210 zettahashes (210 sextillion hashes) to find a successful nonce. This number corresponds to 350 exahashes (350 quintillion hashes) per second for ten minutes (i.e., the hash rate of the Bitcoin network as of this writing, an all-time high).

The likelihood of winning the mining lottery depends on one's relative hashing power compared to the network. As indicated in Figure 8-3, the hash rate has been growing over the past few years, reflecting better technology and more people entering the mining game to benefit from Bitcoin's increasing price. The drop of more than 50% of the hash rate in mid-2021 corresponds to China's ban on Bitcoin mining, while China produced most of Bitcoin's hash rate at the time.

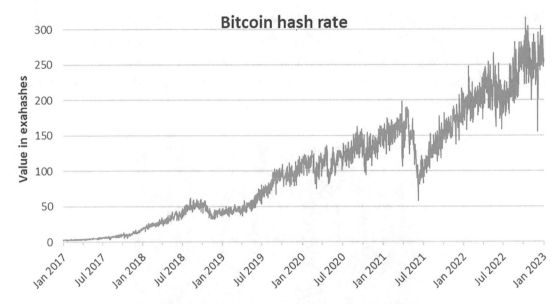

Figure 8-3. Total hash rate per second on the Bitcoin network from January 2017 to January 2023, in exahashes (Source: NASDAQ.com and own workings)

Running these mining rigs requires a high amount of electricity, making geographies with access to cheap electricity more profitable for mining purposes. For example, geothermal energy in Iceland is much cheaper than energy from the grid in New York City, making Iceland a much better location for Bitcoin mining. Since electricity production in Iceland comes almost 100% from renewable energy,[1] its sustainability is also much higher. Such mining typically happens in *mining farms*, which are warehouses with hundreds of ASIC mining rigs working in parallel. The mining farms are often placed directly next to a hydropower plant or a source of geothermal energy so that they can use the excess energy produced by the plant to mine Bitcoin. This way, the electricity production generated during supply peaks (e.g., rain season) or demand troughs (e.g., at night) can be monetized and, at the same time, secure the Bitcoin network.

As of May 2023, the price of electricity ranges from more than $0.50 per kilowatt hour in countries like Germany, Denmark, or the United Kingdom to less than $0.05 per kilowatt hour in countries like Kazakhstan, Iran, or Malaysia on average. Therefore, unsurprisingly, these latter countries are in the top 10 of the countries mining the most bitcoins. Nevertheless, even countries with a higher average cost of electricity can make

---

[1] With 73% coming from hydropower and 27% from geothermal power", as per the Government of Iceland [88].

use of occasional cheap energy (e.g., excess energy at renewable power plants) to mine Bitcoin, also bringing the United States (35% of total worldwide), Canada (10%) and Germany (5%) in the same top-10 list.[2]

In comparison, as of this writing, mining Bitcoin requires a source of electricity below $0.11 to be profitable.[3] Using more expensive energy does not make it financially interesting for miners, as the likelihood and size of mining rewards do not offset the required energy costs. Therefore, mining in high-energy-price locations is unprofitable and will lead anybody who attempts it to financial losses. In particular, the energy used to mine cryptoassets like Bitcoin is typically energy that would be lost otherwise. Indeed, if the producer could use this energy for any other purpose, it would most likely be more financially interesting to do so. Bitcoin mining, therefore, enables us to profit from lost energy. At the same time, it is not putting any strain on high energy-cost grids (e.g., in large cities of developed countries) because it provides no incentives to mine where energy costs are high.

ASIC-Resistant Mining

To curb the never-ending race to more hashing power and the ever-increasing electricity use, developers designed some cryptoassets' consensus mechanisms to be ASIC-resistant. In other words, for mining these cryptoassets, using an ASIC is not beneficial compared to using a simple Graphics Processing Unit (GPU) in a traditional computer. Furthermore, for some cryptoassets, using an ASIC is not technically possible. In these cases, mining with one's laptop at home is as likely to succeed as mining with the latest specialized equipment.

Technically, there are different methods to achieve ASIC resistance. For example, mining algorithms can be designed to require large computer memory. This requirement means more physical area on the computer chip running the algorithm. In particular, ASICs typically outperform traditional GPUs by parallelizing physical threads on a computer chip, which requires physical area. However, parallel processing becomes less useful when an algorithm step requires a wide physical area. ASICs lose their

---

[2] *Bitcoin Mining by Country 2023*, World Population Review [83].

[3] This figure is based on the following rounded numbers: hashes necessary to mine a bitcoin (210 zettahashes for a block delivering 6.25 BTC), hashes per second with the newest ASIC miners (200 trillion), their consumption (5500 watts or 5500 joules per second) and Bitcoin's current price ($28,000). It ignores the miner's purchase and set-up costs. Details of this computation are presented in Appendix B, in the appendices.

competitive advantage over GPUs, and the corresponding cryptoasset becomes ASIC-resistant. For interested readers, modern proof-of-work-based cryptoassets achieve ASIC resistance through multi-hash PoW, memory hard PoW, or programmatic PoW, and new methods continue to emerge [41].

Mining ASIC-resistant cryptoassets is more affordable for private individuals than mining non-ASIC-resistant cryptoassets. Nevertheless, access to a cheap source of electricity is still necessary to make mining activities profitable. Also, a side benefit of ASIC-resistant cryptoassets is a higher level of decentralization. Indeed, ASIC resistance creates fewer incentives for companies to establish large mining farms that could centralize the asset's mining.

As of 2023, the largest proof-of-work cryptoassets that are ASIC-resistant are Monero (XMR), Ethereum Classic (ETC), and Ravencoin (RVN).

Mining Pools

An issue with mining Bitcoin is the tiny probability of successfully mining a block for any particular individual, even though the reward is quite sizable in a successful event.[4] A solution is to join a mining pool. In such a pool, miners agree to split rewards from successfully mined blocks in proportion to the hashing power each miner contributed to the pool. For example, say a pool mines 100 bitcoins (16 blocks) in 2023, and a specific individual contributed 3% of the pool's total mining power (hash rate) over that period. In that case, this individual will earn three bitcoins (minus a pool management fee (e.g., 2%). In 2022, the top 9 Bitcoin mining pools shared 95% of the total Bitcoin mining hash rate, as shown in Figure 8-4.

---

[4] The reward is 6.25 bitcoins per block since May 2020 and until the next halving event in 2024.

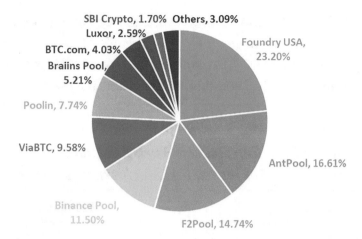

Figure 8-4. *Top 10 Bitcoin mining pools 2022, with their relative share of the hash rate (Source: BTC.com and own workings)*

Newcomers willing to mine proof-of-work cryptoassets are encouraged to join a pool but to choose it carefully. In particular, one should look for pools fully transparent on their mining equipment requirements, fee schedule, downtime history, and track record of repelling DDoS attacks.[5] Stable (without downtime and unlikely to become a victim of attacks) and transparent pools are critical to reducing risks involved in the mining process.

Staking

Many cryptoassets offer staking as possible passive income (for example, see Table 8-1). Chapter 6 introduced the proof-of-stake consensus mechanism, where stakers validate new blocks. Their likelihood of being chosen for validation typically depends (among other criteria) on the number of coins they commit (stake) to the network. These validators then earn a staking reward for their work. Becoming a validator can require a substantial minimum investment (e.g., 32 ETH for Ethereum) and a burdensome technical setup to avoid downtime (which is punishable by having one's stake slashed). However, staking pools are readily available for investors without requiring specialized equipment or a one-off investment. In particular, exchanges like Binance, KuCoin, or Coinbase offer attractive rewards for stakable cryptoassets with negligible minimum

---

[5] Distributed denial of service (DDoS) attacks are cyberattacks that can disrupt the operations of a network by flooding it with traffic.

investment thresholds. In this case, staking rewards are similar to a bond yield: The higher the staked principal, the higher the staking rewards. However, similarly to a bond, this yield is subject to financial risks. In particular, in the case of staked cryptoassets, it is subject to risks related to the asset and the platform where it is staked.

Table 8-1. *Staking Rewards in Annual Percentage Yield (APY) for Top Stakable Assets As of January 2023 (Source:* www.stakingrewards.com/cryptoassets/*)*

Cryptoasset	Ticker	Staking Reward
Ethereum	ETH	3.9%
Cardano	ADA	3.4%
Binance Coin	BNB	2.3%
Avalanche	AVAX	8.1%
Polkadot	DOT	14.5%
Polygon	MATIC	5.0%
Algorand	ALGO	6.6%
Solana	SOL	4.2%
Internet Computer	ICP	7.5%

Staking rewards typically range from the mid-single-digit to three-digit rates of return, depending on several criteria. First, stakable cryptoassets yield different staking rewards depending on their programmed features.

Secondly, the chosen platform also matters, as some platforms take a larger share of the reward and offer different conditions. Table 8-2 presents differences in staking rewards depending on the provider.

Table 8-2. *MATIC Staking Rewards in APY for the Top 5 Providers (Ranked by Total Value Staked) As of January 2023 (Source: www.stakingrewards.com/earn/ polygon/)*

Provider	Cryptoasset	Ticker	Staking Reward	Balance (in millions)
Luganodes	Polygon	MATIC	4.86%	$398
Allnodes	Polygon	MATIC	5.39%	$226
Stakin	Polygon	MATIC	5.35%	$87
stakefish	Polygon	MATIC	5.19%	$28
Everstake	Polygon	MATIC	4.85%	$15

Finally, staking rewards depend on whether and for how long the stake is locked. Nevertheless, stakes do not strictly need to be locked; most assets on most platforms can also be redeemable anytime. Table 8-3 presents differences in staking rewards depending on the lock period.

Table 8-3. *ADA Staking Rewards in APY for the Five Periods Offered by Binance As of January 2023 (Source: Binance App)*

Provider	Cryptoasset	Ticker	Staking Reward	Lock Period
Binance Staking	Cardano	ADA	1.5%	Flexible
Binance Staking	Cardano	ADA	2.7%	30 days
Binance Staking	Cardano	ADA	3.2%	60 days
Binance Staking	Cardano	ADA	4.2%	90 days
Binance Staking	Cardano	ADA	5.7%	120 days

Crypto Lending

A passive income alternative to staking is crypto lending. In crypto lending, the lender typically loans fiat money (e.g., US dollars or euros) or a stable coin (e.g., Dai or USDC) to a borrower currently holding cryptoassets. This way, the cryptoassets become collateral for the loan.

Typically, crypto loans are overcollateralized. For example, Alice lends 5,000 USDC to Bob, who currently holds five ethers priced at $2,000 each, by using the five ethers as collateral. If Bob does not repay the borrowed USDC by the loan term, Alice is entitled to sell the ethers until her loan, with interest, is repaid. In this case, the loan is overcollateralized because the market value of the collateral is twice higher than the loan's value.[6]

The collateralization lowers Alice's credit risk: she will only lose money if Bob does not repay the loan and if, in addition, the value of the collateral drops below the amount due. In this example, it would require ethers to lose at least 50% of their current value for the loan not to be repaid in full. Since Alice's risk on the loan is lower than without the collateral, she does not require a particularly high interest rate from Bob. It implies that Bob can benefit from a lower interest rate by posting collateral. He can use the borrowed amount to buy more of the cryptoasset he already holds or to buy another cryptoasset. Bob benefits from this financial setup as long as the cryptoasset appreciates at a higher pace than the loan's interest rate.

Because crypto lending exists, holders of cryptoassets can benefit by loaning out their cryptoassets and receiving positive interest rates. For example, rather than having bitcoins sitting idle on a cryptoplatform, passive income can be generated by loaning them out.

Multiple centralized and decentralized crypto platforms offer crypto lending at attractive rates (compared to traditional finance). In addition, they offer close-to-instantaneous delivery and settlement of the loan. These platforms play a crucial role in matching savers with borrowers, thereby creating a market for these loans. They differ in their interest rates, the amount of collateral, and the minimum deposit required. Interest rates typically range from less than a percentage point to two-digit rates of return, as shown in Table 8-4.

---

[6] A typical loan-to-value (LTV) ratio for lending is around 65% (i.e., a collateralization of roughly 150% (or 1.5 times) of the loaned amount). More risky collateral typically requires higher collateralization (lower LTV).

Table 8-4. *Lending Rewards in APY Offered by Binance As of January 2023 (Source: Binance App)*

Provider	Cryptoasset	Ticker	APY	Lock Period
Binance Savings	Axie Infinity	AXS	12.0%	Flexible
Binance Savings	Bitcoin	BTC	1.5%	Flexible
Binance Savings	USD Tether	USDT	5.5%	Flexible
Binance Savings	Chainlink	LINK	0.2%	Flexible

Liquidity Mining

Liquidity mining is another passive income possibility for cryptoasset holders but is more complex than staking or lending. Fundamentally, it rewards liquidity providers for their service (i.e., providing liquidity to a market).

The logic for rewarding liquidity is the following. A platform (centralized or decentralized) aims to provide high liquidity between many cryptoasset trading pairs. For a trading pair (e.g., Solana and Axie Infinity), there may be few buyers and sellers, creating an "illiquid market." In an illiquid market, buying one asset with the other can materially move the market price because there are few buyers and sellers. It typically happens when the market faces large orders and insufficient volume to absorb them. Liquid markets are valuable for platforms because such markets provide stable prices and competitive commission fees. This value translates into rewards for liquidity providers, typically a flexible interest.

Concretely, liquidity providers enter a liquidity pool containing two assets by depositing an asset (cryptoassets, fiat currencies, or stablecoins). In such a pool, the two targeted assets have a relative proportion of the pool, depending on how much of each asset is available. The provider contributes one asset (or both assets) as liquidity to the pool and gets a share of the pool in return for a claim on the two assets. The substance of the claim depends on how the relative proportion of the two assets evolves after the provider joins the pool.

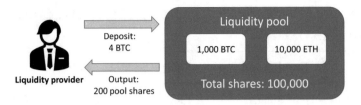

Figure 8-5. *Example of BTC-ETH liquidity pool with a relative price of 10 ETH/ BTC where a liquidity provider gets 0.2% of the pool's shares by contributing the corresponding quantity of BTC in proportion to the total pool's value*

Traders use the pool's automated market maker (AMM) to swap one asset for the other, paying a fee for the service. Rewards to liquidity providers depend on how much volume traders swap in the corresponding pool. The higher the volume swapped, the higher the total fees and the higher the return for the liquidity providers. As of May 2023, the decentralized exchange Uniswap charges a fee of 0.3% of the swapped value, and the centralized exchange Binance charges a standard fee of 0.15% (with a 50% fee rebate, paid in Binance's native coin, BNB).

Figure 8-6. *Example of BTC-ETH liquidity pool with a relative price of 10 ETH/ BTC where a liquidity provider gets 0.5% of the pool's shares, and a trader swaps 1 BTC for 10 ETH by paying a 0.3% fee for the trade*

The resulting yield for the liquidity providers can be vastly different depending on the trading pair, as shown in Table 8-5.

Table 8-5. *Examples of Liquidity Mining Trading Pairs Offered by Binance, with Vastly Different Levels of Liquidity and Yield As of January 2023 (Source: Binance App)*

Provider	Trading Pair	Liquidity	Total Yield
Binance	USDT/DAI	1,548,984 USDT + 2,802,152 DAI	1.16%
Binance	BTC/ETH	1,203 BTC + 17,398 ETH	1.38%
Binance	AAVE/BTC	5,925 AAVE + 22 BTC	3.03%
Binance	ADA/BUSD	1,610,694 ADA + 623,816 BUSD	5.10%
Binance	AXS/BNB	19,761 AXS + 756 BNB	6.31%
Binance	GALA/BNB	8,019,080 GALA + 1,509 BNB	16.11%

A concept to understand before using liquidity mining is *impermanent loss*. The relative quantity of each asset in the pool determines the value of the liquidity provider's share. When a large volume of one asset in a pair enters or leaves a liquidity pool, the share of assets in the pool changes. As a result, the investment value of the liquidity provider can be lower than it would have been by just holding on to the assets. Due to this change, the investment is subject to unrealized loss (compared to simply holding to the asset). This unrealized loss is termed impermanent loss. However, impermanent loss only becomes material when the relative value of the assets in the pool changes wildly.[7] In addition, returns from providing liquidity typically more than compensate impermanent losses.

Yield Farming

Yield farming involves locking up cryptoassets to get the highest possible passive income. Passive income typically comes from underlying staking, lending, or liquidity mining.

---

[7] Specifically, the impermanent loss in percentage is $2 \times \dfrac{\sqrt{price\ ratio\ change\ \%}}{1 + (price\ ratio\ change\ \%)} - 1.$

Some platforms, such as Aave, Compound, or yearn.finance, automate this process by moving funds between DeFi services to get the highest possible return on capital. In early 2020, it was not unusual to see three-digit (sometimes even four-digit) rates of return in yield farming, which testified to exceptional risk levels. Such yields were only possible through significant leverage and investments in high-risk projects. In the bear market of 2022, yields were more humble, typically single-digit to low-double-digit rates of return, as processes became more established and less risky.

Airdrops

In the cryptoasset context, airdrops are a marketing strategy for new cryptoassets to gain popularity and increase usage. One can think of an airdrop as the crypto equivalent of a free sample offered in a retail shop. While many variations exist, airdrops typically consist of users receiving a small amount of a new cryptoasset for free or in return for small services.[8] These services can be retweeting a post of the cryptoasset issuing company, joining the crypto project's newsletter, following the cryptoasset page on social media, or answering basic questions on how the cryptoasset works, thereby testifying to the user spent time understanding its purpose. Sometimes, services include the usage of the cryptoasset: for example, holding at least a certain amount of it or using a service offered by the issuing company. Airdrops can be crucial to generate network effects through widespread usage of the cryptoasset.

Historically, some airdrops have returned sizable amounts, such as the Uniswap airdrop yielding $15,000 for each recipient. However, airdrop returns are typically tiny (worth a few dollars at most) and often do not even deliver the promised token. In addition, airdrops are typically for crypto projects in their infancy, where the airdropped cryptoasset often becomes worthless. For many cryptoasset investors, whether airdrops are even worth the time necessary to complete the registration process is questionable.

---

[8] Technically, when the cryptoasset is received for free, then the scheme is an *airdrop*, while a service delivered makes the scheme a *bounty*. However, such schemes are almost always referred to as *airdrops* in practice.

Transaction Routing

Some cryptoassets enable opportunities to benefit from transaction routing. A widespread example is Helium mining. In this context, Helium is not a noble gas from the periodic table of elements but a cryptoasset powering the People's Network, a decentralized wireless network. Helium nodes enable smart devices to send data online through a low-power, long-range wireless protocol. As a result, Helium miners can receive sizable rewards based on their coverage. IoT devices connecting to the network include, for example, dogs' smart collars or Lime electric scooters available in many cities. High returns to miners are possible because the model is not scalable for any individual miner. Indeed, two Helium mining devices close to each other provide the same coverage as a single device. Therefore, miners are incentivized to own only one device (per location).

Figure 8-7. *Helium miner from Linxdot*

Another example of routing transactions is through the Lightning Network. The Lightning Network increases the usability of Bitcoin by building infrastructure on top of the Bitcoin blockchain so that transactions can happen instantly and with negligible transaction fees. This feature is critical to address the comparatively slow settlement time of Bitcoin transactions, moving it from minutes to milliseconds. By design, the Lightning Network relies on decentralized nodes to route transactions. Anybody can operate such a node and benefit from a share of the small transaction fees. Running a dedicated node full-time consumes less than 10 watts per hour, corresponding to an electricity cost of roughly $1 per month in a city like New York in 2023. The benefits of running such a node depend on several criteria, including the quantity and size of transactions routed and Bitcoin's price. As of 2023, running such a node is not lucrative: it takes many months to break even in best-case scenarios. However, Bitcoin advocates use it to help decentralize the network and benefit from other services, such as offering Lightning payments and issuing Lightning invoices. As the number of payments on the Lightning Network increases, operating a router node may become a potential additional revenue source.

Figure 8-8. *Bitcoin full node and Lightning Node running on a RaspiBlitz*

Key Concepts

Some investors may not be mandated or regulated to invest directly in cryptoassets. However, they can still benefit from this new asset class through indirect investments, such as ETFs or companies owning, developing, or mining cryptoassets. In addition, one can also choose to directly mine cryptoassets or contribute to blockchain projects oneself.

Investors can benefit from cryptoassets through capital gains and passive income opportunities, such as staking, lending, or liquidity mining. They can also use yield farming to automatically move funds toward the most lucrative options in the DeFi world, though these options often come with additional risks (e.g., leverage).

Another high-risk, high-reward direct investment strategy is investing in ICOs, STOs, or their alternative early cryptoasset offerings to take advantage of possible price increases in brand-new cryptoassets.

Extension Questions

Since most cryptoassets are fundamentally securities (see Chapter 7), ICOs constitute a security offering. And since most ICO issuers are not registered, such offerings would be illegal in many jurisdictions (even if they are often not explicitly forbidden by law enforcement authorities). What are the real regulatory risks for investors in ICOs?

Why aren't there more companies holding Bitcoin on their balance sheet as of 2023?

What are the risks behind staking and lending?

PART III

When Is a Good Time to Invest?

CHAPTER 9

Crypto Trends

With a good perspective on history, we can have a better understanding of the past and present, and thus a clear vision of the future.

—Carlos Slim Helu

Timing is critical for any investor, in cryptoassets or otherwise. While timing an investment well is difficult, it helps to understand macroeconomic cycles, cryptoasset-specific cycles, and ad-hoc calendar adjustments. This chapter investigates these cycles and other cryptoasset trends. Not only will this knowledge reassure investors facing the naturally wild fluctuations of their investments, but it will also contribute to some valuation methods investigated later in the book.

Bitcoin Price

Let us begin by analyzing the historical trend of Bitcoin because it is by far the largest cryptoasset and, as of 2023, still drives the price of most other cryptoassets. While historical data is not predictive of the future, it can provide insights into what has driven price swings in the past. As the philosopher Santayana puts it: "Those who do not remember the past are condemned to repeat it."

Using a standard scale for metrics growing exponentially, as in Figure 9-1, offers limited insight.

T. Jeegers, *Understanding Crypto Fundamentals*, https://doi.org/10.1007/978-1-4842-9309-6_9

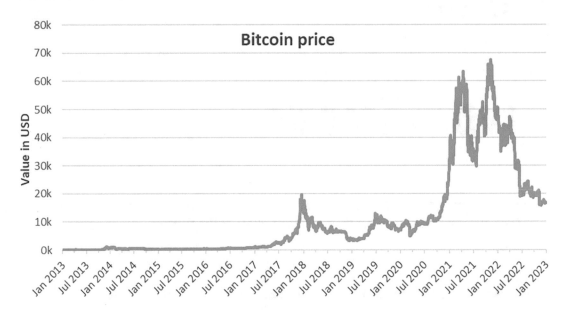

Figure 9-1. *Bitcoin price in USD, January 2013 to January 2023, standard scale*

A logarithmic scale for the same data provides a more helpful analysis of Bitcoin's historical trend. With such a scale, each vertical mark represents ten times the size of the previous one. Figure 9-2 presents the last ten years of data with a logarithmic trend line.[1]

---

[1] The trendline follows the equation $10^{a + b \log_{10}(d)}$, where d is the number of days since Bitcoin's inception (January 3, 2009) and a and b are fixed coefficients selected to optimally fit the daily price data (i.e., –14.39 and 5.16, respectively). The website *Look Into Bitcoin* provides up-to-date data on Bitcoin's price with logarithmic growth curves [84].

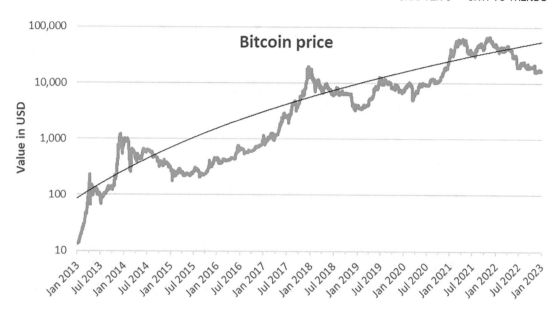

Figure 9-2. *Bitcoin price in USD from January 2013 to January 2023, logarithmic scale, with a logarithmic trend*

The first patterns to identify from this data are the spikes in price in 2013, 2017, and 2021. The careful reader may remember that these years follow the Bitcoin halving event years (i.e., the years in which the number of new bitcoins rewarded per block was divided by two as part of Bitcoin's supply schedule). Specifically, in November 2012, the number of bitcoins rewarded per block decreased from 50 to 25. Similarly, in July 2016, it went from 25 to 12.5 and from 12.5 to 6.25 in May 2020. These spikes brought the price of Bitcoin about two standard deviations above its logarithmic trend before collapsing. From top to bottom, Bitcoin's largest drops were 93% (2011), 86% (2015), 83% (2018), and 77% (2022). Such drops are comparable to technology stocks during their growth phase. For example, Amazon plunged 80% in 2000 and Apple 91% from 2000 to 2002 (including a 51% drop in a single day, on September 29, 2000).

Bitcoin's ups and downs follow a four-year cyclical pattern that gave rise to several theories on how they could evolve.

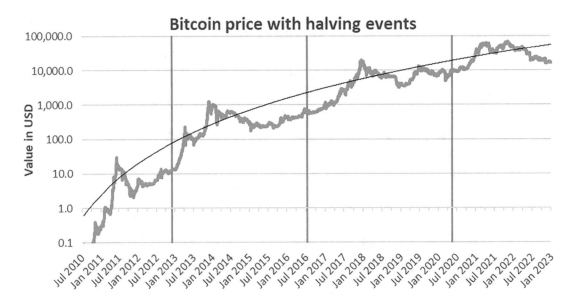

Figure 9-3. *Bitcoin price in USD from July 2010 to January 2023, logarithmic scale, with halving events on November 28, 2012, July 9, 2016, and May 11, 2020*

Bitcoin "Halving" Cycles

The four-year Bitcoin cycles driven by the halving of the new supply are unreliable for future price movements but can hint at what other market participants may expect. Besides, the mere fact that other market participants may expect these cycles to continue could turn them into a self-fulfilling prophecy.

Halving events occur every 210,000 blocks on Bitcoin's blockchain. With a block created every 10 minutes, this rounds up to roughly once every four years. However, Bitcoin's code adjusts the difficulty of mining blocks every two weeks based on the network's hash rate. This adjustment's goal is that it should always take about 10 minutes to mine a block, regardless of the network's total computing power. If the hash rate increases between adjustments, the time to mine a block decreases to below 10 minutes on average until the next adjustment. In the past, halving events occurred faster than every four years because the total hash rate increased with adoption.

As the hash rate increases steadily, this pattern will likely continue, at least in the short term. The last three periods between halving events lasted 3 years, 10 months, and 19 days; 3 years, 7 months, and 11 days; and 3 years, 10 months, and 2 days. As the hash rate grows since the last halving, 3 years and 10 months for the upcoming periods seem a reasonable estimate. Therefore, the next two Bitcoin halving events will likely happen in March 2024 and January 2028.

The underlying fundamental behind increases in value around a halving lies in the change in Bitcoin's stock-to-flow ratio, as explained in Chapter 1. With a halving event, the number of new bitcoins mined per unit of time (the flow) suddenly becomes much smaller as a fraction of the existing quantity of bitcoins available (the stock). In other words, the supply expansion abruptly slows down, making each existing bitcoin more challenging to obtain and thus more valuable. Since the impact of future halving events on this ratio will be smaller, its importance will likely not be as prominent in the future as it was in the past.

Bitcoin Golden Bull Ratio

Bitcoin price patterns after its second cycle (2018) gave rise to the *Bitcoin Golden Bull Ratio* theory. This ratio suggests that the period between the market's bottom and the halving event represents 50% of the time from bottom to peak, and the period from the halving event to the peak represents 50% of the time from bottom to peak. For the first two cycles, this ratio was 50.3%–49.7% and 50.8%–49.2%, respectively. Despite this theory being widespread in 2021, the third cycle fits the pattern almost perfectly, with a 48.4%–51.6% ratio, as shown in Figure 9-4.

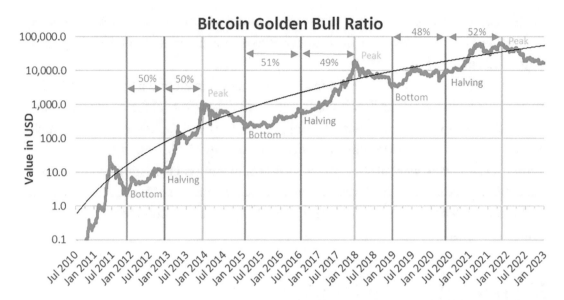

Figure 9-4. *Bitcoin price in USD from July 2010 to January 2023, logarithmic scale. The three cycles are depicted with their key milestones: bottom, halving, and peak*

Some market participants may expect (perhaps irrationally) that this pattern will continue for the next cycle. Based on this 50%/50% pattern, the most recent market bottom (November 21, 2022), and the next expected halving event date (March 12, 2024, assuming 3 years and 10 months between halving events), the next market top would occur on July 2, 2025. Of course, this is only a theoretical date based on the preceding assumptions and is highly unlikely to happen accurately in practice. Regulation changes, market dynamics, or even hash rate growth will impact the next Bitcoin price peak date much more than historical patterns. Nevertheless, the data underlying this theoretical date is provided in Table 9-1.

Table 9-1. *Milestone Bitcoin Price Dates of the Past Cycles: Bottoms, Halving Events, and Peaks, with Their Ratio per Cycle (Bottom to Peak)*

	Bottom	Halving	Peak	Days	Ratio
Pre-cycle 1			June 9, 2011		
Cycle 1	November 19, 2011			163	
		November 28, 2012		375	50.3%
			December 4, 2013	371	49.7%
Cycle 2	January 14, 2015			406	
		July 9, 2016		542	50.8%
			December 16, 2017	525	49.2%
Cycle 3	December 15, 2018			364	
		May 11, 2020		513	48.4%
			November 8, 2021	546	51.6%
Cycle 4	November 21, 2022			378	
		(March 12, 2024)		(477)	(50.0%)
			(July 2, 2025)	(477)	(50.0%)

Bitcoin Cycles Rallies

The next thing to identify from Figure 9-4 is that the post-halving rallies have been much bigger than the pre-halving rallies. In particular, the periods between halving events and peak dates have yielded price increases of 101x (+10,044%), 30x, and 8x for the three instances, respectively. In contrast, the periods between bottoms and halving events "only" yielded 6x, 3.7x, and 2.7x, as shown in Table 9-2.

Table 9-2. *Milestone Bitcoin Price Dates of the Past Cycles, Including Price in USD and Relative Changes Compared to Previous Milestones*

	Bottom	Halving	Peak	Price	Change
Pre-cycle 1			June 9, 2011	29.60	
Cycle 1	November 19, 2011			2.05	−93%
		November 28, 2012		12.20	6.0x
			December 4, 2013	1,237.60	101.4x
Cycle 2	January 14, 2015			178.10	−86%
		July 9, 2016		650.96	3.7x
			December 16, 2017	19,497.40	30.0x
Cycle 3	December 15, 2018			3,236.76	−83%
		May 11, 2020		8,601.80	2.7x
			November 8, 2021	67,566.83	7.9x
Cycle 4	November 21, 2022			15,787.28	−77%
		n.a.		n.a.	n.a.
			n.a.	n.a.	n.a.

Bitcoin Cycles Duration

Another related theory widely discussed in 2021 (before reaching the third cycle's bottom) is that of *Bitcoin's lengthening cycles*. In Bitcoin's first cycle, the period from bottom to peak lasted 746 days, while during its second cycle, it lasted 1,067 days, which gave rise to the theory.[2] The third cycle, however, was eight days shorter than the second at 1,059 days. A similar duration for the fourth cycle would place the next peak in mid-October 2025 (contrasting with the July 2025 peak date suggested by a continuation of the Golden Bull Ratio).

---

[2] The exact number of days may vary slightly depending on which exchange is used as data provider.

Of course, the mere facts that these widespread theories exist imply that some actors are likely to time their transactions to take advantage of the pattern. A sufficiently high number of actors trading accordingly would at least bias these patterns and possibly invalidate them completely.

Another widely discussed theory is that Bitcoin would enter a so-called *supercycle*. In a supercycle, the four-year pattern would fade away with cryptoasset mass adoption, and Bitcoin would enter an extended period of increasing prices.

Relative Market Dominance

Another significant trend is the relative dominance within cryptoassets. Since Bitcoin started as the first cryptoasset, it used to have 100% dominance (i.e., Bitcoin had 100% of the market capitalization of the cryptoasset space). As other cryptoassets entered the space, Bitcoin's dominance decreased. During the 2017 peak of the market, Bitcoin's dominance dropped from 86% to 32%, mostly leaving place to Ethereum and XRP. Bitcoin never lost its number 1 spot, though. Over the following cycle (2018–2022), Bitcoin mainly oscillated between one-third and two-thirds of the total crypto market, while Ethereum fluctuated between 7% and 22% of market dominance. In the meantime, XRP dropped from its 19% high to below 3%, and no other cryptoasset ever broke the 6% dominance threshold.

An up-to-date overview of relative market dominance is available on the website CoinMarketCap.com.[3]

---

[3] https://coinmarketcap.com/charts/

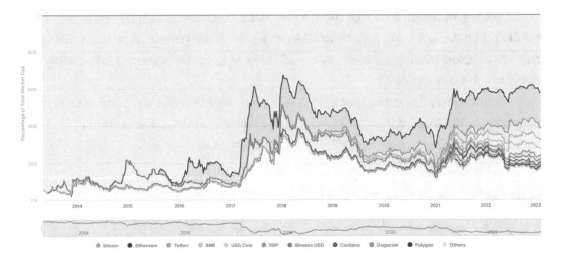

Figure 9-5. *The relative market dominance of key cryptoassets, May 2013 to January 2023, based on their market capitalization (Source: CoinMarketCap.com)*

Bitcoin Lead

The next critical historical pattern in the crypto market is that Bitcoin's price action tends to be a leading indicator for altcoins' price. When Bitcoin's price surges, it is typically rapidly followed by increases in other cryptoassets prices. The same happens when Bitcoin's price drops, inducing price decreases in the rest of the crypto market.

While this pattern is evident from historical price data, it is irrational. What makes Bitcoin valuable is very different from what makes Ethereum, Chainlink, or Stellar Lumen valuable. As the fundamentals behind these assets differ, their price journeys should have little correlation. The historically high correlation between these assets confirms the market's relatively low maturity level. As of this writing, investors still view all cryptoassets as "risk assets" (like technology stocks) without more profound thoughts on what differentiates them.

Macrocycles and Correlations

Beyond the realm of cryptoassets, macroeconomic trends drive the economy up and down in cyclical patterns. These cycles have a material impact on all asset classes, including cryptoassets. As was introduced in Chapter 2, long-term cycles last many decades, and within them, shorter-term cycles last only a few years, typically less than a decade.

The long-term cycles are also called the "long-term debt and capital market cycles" (lasting roughly 50 to 75 years),[4] Kondratiev waves (lasting 45 to 60 years), or the secular trend. They all refer to the same pattern of expansion and then contraction of the economy. Important macro variables such as demographics, debt, and technologies drive the secular trend. Technologies, in particular, tend to be catalysts for changes in the secular trend, sparking a restart after a trough.

Shorter-term or business cycles depend on central bank policies such as quantitative easing or rate hikes. Different assets and sectors are not typically at the same point within the cycle. For example, some sectors are more cyclical (e.g., energy, construction material, and consumer discretionary) and tend to overperform in the cycle's expansion phase. In contrast, other sectors (e.g., healthcare or utilities) are more stable and much less affected by the phase of the cycle. Within business cycles, there are even shorter trends (tactical trends) which can be a few months long but can also be as short as days.

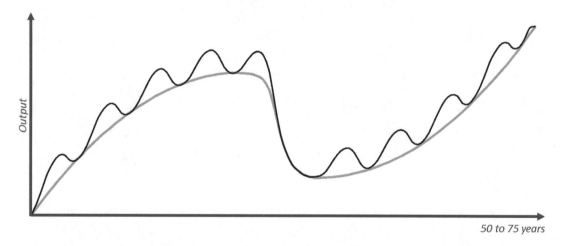

50 to 75 years

Figure 9-6. *Representation of economic cycles, with short-term cycles on top of a long-term cycle*

---

[4] Ray Dalio, *Principles for Dealing with the Changing World Order: Why Nations Succeed and Fail* [60].

Cryptoassets follow a similar cyclical pattern: first, a comparatively long trend of growing value that aligns with the global level of adoption of cryptoassets. Second, short cycles are driven by regulations, policies, and significant events, such as a Bitcoin halving event or Ethereum's "The Merge" event of mid-September 2022.[5]

The low correlation of cryptoassets with traditional investments was highlighted in Chapter 4. However, correlations between asset classes tend to increase in cyclical recessionary phases. Indeed, when business becomes difficult, and the economy slows down, investors in need of cash tend to sell all types of assets. These selloffs happen throughout all asset classes and bring all prices down. It happened, for example, with gold in 2008 or with cryptoassets in 2022: correlation with equities materially increased as part of a global selloff. Higher correlations are reducing diversification's benefits when investors need them most. This financial phenomenon is called *contagion*.

Figure 9-7. *Bitcoin (left axis) and S&P500 (right axis) prices over August 2020 to January 2023, showing higher correlation during the selloff of 2022 (i.e., spikes and drops tend to happen simultaneously when correlations between assets are high)*

As the cryptoasset market evolves, it will decouple from Bitcoin halving cycles because they will proportionally have an increasingly smaller effect. As it does so, the cryptoasset market may align more with traditional cycles, which reflect capital invested

---

[5] The Merge was the highly scrutinized switch of Ethereum's blockchain from PoW to PoS.

(when capital is scarce, investors tend to sell all types of assets). Moreover, in the medium term, many cryptoassets are likely to continue being treated like risk assets due to their high level of volatility. Understanding where we are in the macroeconomic cycles and how other investors perceive asset classes will likely become increasingly relevant for cryptoasset investors.

Yet, the value proposition of cryptoassets is fundamentally different from traditional asset classes. This value proposition can also be very different between cryptoassets. It would be reasonable to assume that diversification benefits will be sustained among asset classes and within the crypto asset class.

For example, this diversification benefit was already visible in mid-March 2023 during the collapses of multiple traditional banks. While financial markets dropped, Bitcoin's price climbed 40% in a week—from $20,000 to more than $28,000. This episode testifies that the narrative around Bitcoin becoming a "safe-haven asset" starts to settle.

Other Crypto Cycles

Cryptoasset cycles can be defined not only by prices but also by other metrics. For example, block space is one such metric, which is the quantity of information that can be put in a block. Depending on the blockchain, block space is used, expressed, and valued differently. On the Ethereum blockchain, for example, users pay a fee of a few gwei (a gwei is one billionth of an ether) to be included in the next block. As the crypto business cycle evolves, the demand for block space and the corresponding fees vary. In some cases, block space fees can even be an early indicator of future price movements.

Similarly, many other on-chain metrics offer insights on possible future price movements through their position in their cycle. Future chapters include a discussion on such metrics.

Charts in Technical Analysis

The crypto community sometimes relies on charts such as price patterns or transaction volume to indicate future possible price movements. This approach moves away from fundamental analysis and enters the dangerous territory of technical analysis.

This territory is dangerous because charts alone do not predict future prices and provide insufficient information to make long-term trades. Nevertheless, they can help choose the timing of a trade based on fundamentals. For example, they can inform on the presence of support and resistance levels. A support level is a price below the current asset price and at which many investors are willing to buy. Breaking through the support level would need enormous downward pressure on the price (i.e., even more sellers than buyers at that level). A resistance level is the opposite: a price above the current market price and at which many investors want to sell.

Charts complement an investment thesis but do not replace it. They can confirm or challenge a theory, but charts alone cannot be the theory itself.

Understanding Gartner's Hype Cycles

The technological research and consulting firm Gartner provides a valuable framework to navigate the hype around technological innovations.[6] Most innovations follow a similar pattern, first going through high enthusiasm and expectations before crashing through disillusionment and only afterward stabilizing at a reasonable level of productivity during mainstream adoption. In particular, the hype cycle is divided into five phases, as shown in Figure 9-8.

---

[6] Gartner and Hype Cycles™ are registered trademarks of Gartner, Inc. and/or its affiliates in the U.S. and internationally and are used herein with permission. All rights reserved.

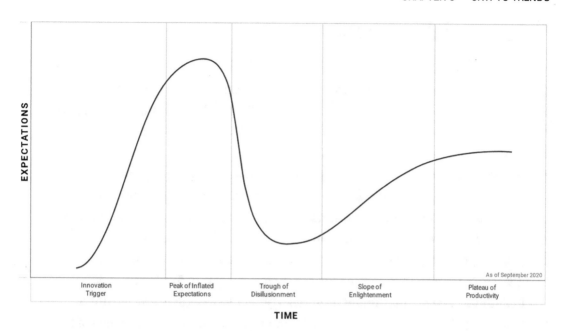

Figure 9-8. *Gartner, Understanding Gartner's Hype Cycles, Frances Karamouzis, Jan-Martin Lowendahl, September 27, 2022*

Identifying where the crypto space as a whole is in this cycle is challenging. Different sub-innovations within the space are likely at different cycle stages. For example, the market peak of 2013 and the crash of 2014 are likely the "inflated expectations" and "disillusionment" of the original innovation, Bitcoin. Once smart contracts entered the game with Ethereum in 2015, a new cycle began for this innovation. Again, a peak of inflated expectations took place in 2017, and a trough of disillusionment in the following year. Then, further innovations such as Web 3.0 and NFTs created similar ups and downs over 2020–2022. In particular, the market capitalization of NFT projects grew over 100 times in 2021 alone, to over $40 billion, before collapsing by more than 75% in the next year.[7]

---

[7] CoinGecko, https://www.coingecko.com/.

Calendar Adjustments

Specific calendar dates drive some investors' behaviors, directly affecting cryptoasset prices. At the end of each calendar year, many investment funds close their profit and loss statements. The gains accumulated over the financial year appear in the financial statements and may define the fund's future. In anticipation of this critical year-end close event, funds may want to lock in some of the unrealized gains of the year to show more green figures on their statements. As a result, these funds may induce an over-proportional selling pressure when markets are largely up in December.

To a smaller extent, calendar quarter ends also tend to show irregular patterns compared to other days. The expiration date of options (financial derivative products) happens mostly at quarter-end dates, which induces this trend. The large market for cryptoasset options makes quarter closes especially relevant for this asset class.

In addition to that, investment funds also often follow a quarterly portfolio rebalancing cycle. At quarter end, portfolio managers reassess the relevance of their assets and rebalance their portfolio. This trend materially increases the volumes traded for all assets, including cryptoassets.

Fear & Greed Index

Long-term and medium-term crypto cycles have been discussed, but when is the optimal time to buy within a cycle? To answer this question, one must understand that the market often acts irrationally. Specifically, it regularly overreacts to news that should have little to no impact on asset prices. This irrationality creates excellent opportunities for those able to see through it. For example, when things are bad in other financial markets, particularly equity (stocks), many investors move away from high-volatility assets, such as cryptoassets. These occasional flights to safety temporarily bring the price of volatile assets lower than their trend would predict. All other things equal, this is a favorable time to buy. As the business magnate John D. Rockefeller eloquently phrased it: "The way to make money is to buy when blood is running in the streets."

The Fear & Greed Index can measure the metaphorical "blood running in the streets." The software comparator company alternative.me created this index based on sentiment changes on social media, surveys, and market metrics such as momentum, dominance, and trends. It is updated daily on the webpage `https://alternative.me/crypto/fear-and-greed-index/`. The index outputs a metric ranging from 0 to 100. A lower score indicates extreme fear (the market emotionally overreacting negatively), and a higher score indicates extreme greed (the market emotionally overreacting positively). Therefore, this index may be helpful for timing purchases and sales of cryptoassets.

Figure 9-9. *Fear & Greed Index from alternative.me per May 7, 2023*

Adoption

It is 1990, and you go to work at the local post office. As you get your morning coffee, your technology-enthusiastic colleague rambles on about a new trend that is supposed to change everything. All you hear is incomprehensible jargon and unknown acronyms. *What is this TCP/IP thing, anyway? Nobody will ever use this.* Actually, it was the birth of the modern Internet. In the following decades, only a few people could describe what TCP/IP was, but almost everybody learned to use the Internet daily.

Thirty years later, we are in a similar situation. Just replace TCP/IP with blockchain and the Internet with cryptoassets. Mass adoption does not require everybody to understand the intricacies of blockchain technology, consensus mechanisms, and the meaning of hard forks. Instead, mass adoption is about using cryptos for payments or savings, the same way people use emails or instant messaging for communication without understanding the underlying protocols.

The number of Internet users in the late-1990s is similar to the number of cryptoasset users in the early 2020s: about 300 million. However, there is a major difference between the adoption of crypto today and the adoption of the Internet 25 years ago: crypto adoption is happening much faster than Internet adoption at the time. Specifically,

Chapter 16 of this book analyzes data on usage growth, which is particularly relevant in the context of cryptoasset valuation. The blockchain data platform Chainalysis reveals that worldwide crypto adoption is driven by English-speaking countries and developing economies, especially younger generations (under 34 years of age).[8]

The high adoption pace of crypto and decentralized finance and their transformative potential could start a new secular trend—the era of cryptoassets. The next chapter investigates what it will take for crypto to be the catalyst for the next secular trend.

Key Concepts

Bitcoin's price has grown exponentially since its inception and has driven the growth of the crypto market. It went through three four-year cycles, prompted by its halving events. In particular, the steepest price increases happened after every halving, for a duration (from halving to peak) equivalent to the duration from the cycle's bottom to its halving. Bitcoin remained the largest cryptoasset throughout its existence, though its dominance decreased over time as more cryptoassets emerged. While the cryptoasset market went through high peaks followed by sharp price drops, it follows Gartner's hype cycle for emerging technologies for each subinnovation in this asset class (e.g., Bitcoin, smart contracts, Web 3.0/NFTs). Besides, specific calendar dates are likely to significantly impact prices, especially year-ends and quarter-ends, as investment funds rebalance their portfolios or lock in gains by selling. A useful metric to identify market sentiment at purchase or sale dates is alternative.me's Fear & Greed Index.

Finally, cryptoasset adoption in 2023 is similar to Internet adoption in the late 1990s in terms of the number of users; however, crypto adoption is happening much faster than the adoption of the Internet at the time.

Extension Question

What is likely to happen to Bitcoin's 4-year cycle for the coming two cycles, regarding size and duration?

What would cause Bitcoin to enter a supercycle?

Which fundamentals explain the very similar price pattern experienced in each of the previous three Bitcoin cycles and will this pattern continue?

---

[8] https://blog.chainalysis.com/reports/2021-global-crypto-adoption-index/ and https://blog.chainalysis.com/reports/2022-global-crypto-adoption-index/

CHAPTER 10

Prime Time

> *The individual investor should act consistently as an investor and not as a speculator.*
>
> —Benjamin Graham

As of this writing, the cryptoasset market is not mature yet. Nevertheless, trends indicate that the sector's maturity is rapidly improving as the market evolves. This chapter identifies characteristics temporarily holding cryptoassets back. Improvements in any of these characteristics increase the fundamental value of cryptoassets. In particular, cryptoasset prime time will only happen once these characteristics reach a sufficient maturity level.

Liquidity

In finance, liquidity is the ability of investors, big or small, to buy or sell an asset quickly at a fair market price without impacting the price of that asset. As of 2023, the liquidity of the cryptoasset market is well below that of large asset classes.

The foreign exchange market for major currency pairs, say EUR/USD for example, is highly liquid. Major organizations can buy or sell billions of EUR for USD with a negligible impact on the price. The equivalent of several trillion USD changes hands daily in the foreign exchange market as a whole.

In comparison, Bitcoin's average daily volume was "only" around $26 billion in early 2023[1] or less than 1% of the foreign exchange market's liquidity.

---

[1] Historical data coming from CoinMarketCap, https://coinmarketcap.com/currencies/bitcoin/historical-data/

© Thomas Jeegers 2023
T. Jeegers, *Understanding Crypto Fundamentals*, https://doi.org/10.1007/978-1-4842-9309-6_10

However, cryptoasset liquidity is rapidly growing with adoption. Over the last ten years, on average, transaction volume (in USD) more than doubled every year. For example, Bitcoin's liquidity has grown three orders of magnitude since October 2014.

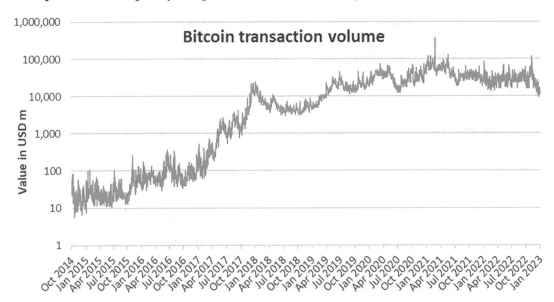

Figure 10-1. *Bitcoin transaction volume in USD millions (log chart) from October 2014 to January 2023*

DEX Accessibility

While the promises of decentralized exchanges (DEX) are manifold, they are not broadly usable by the public yet. They are technically accessible, but as of this writing, they are very complex. In the same way the Internet in the 1990s was nowhere near user-friendly, DEX usage requires extensive user knowledge. Users must thoroughly understand what they are doing and have the grit to go through convoluted processes, often looking shady and untested.

However, developers are working toward simplifying DEX platforms and reducing underlying risks. Ultimately, using a DEX should be as simple as sending an email, but we are not there yet.

Layer 1s Interoperability

As of 2022, bridges between layer 1s (e.g., Ethereum, Cardano, Solana, Polkadot) are limited. Continuing the parallel to the Internet, it is as if one could not surf from one website to another. Properly tested and functional interoperability bridges are under development but not widespread yet.

Exchange-Traded Funds (ETF) Availability

The absence of spot crypto ETFs in many countries (especially the United States)[2] limits many institutional investors from investing in the crypto asset class. This limitation induces less attention given to the asset class than would be the case otherwise and, therefore, less effort provided to growing the ecosystem. A spot ETF approval for a major cryptoasset (Bitcoin and Ethereum will likely be the first ones to get such an approval) in the United States (and in other countries that currently lack it) would open the door to many more investors, which would increase scrutiny and decrease regulatory uncertainty for the industry.

Formal Taxonomy

As covered in Chapter 7, formal taxonomies have been introduced recently, such as the DACS in December 2021. These taxonomies enable funds to allocate their investments according to a formal structure, facilitating portfolio attribution and reporting. However, investors worldwide have not adopted a single taxonomy yet.

In contrast, the Global Industry Classification Standard (GICS) is a worldwide benchmark for equities. Cryptoassets need something similar. A broadly recognized single taxonomy backed by authorities (e.g., the SEC) brings higher transparency and clarity to the market. Specifically, it reduces uncertainty about how specific cryptoassets will be regulated in the future, particularly whether they will be treated as securities. It also contributes to increased comparability across funds and, ultimately, it would likely justify more investments in cryptoassets.

---

[2] See Chapter 8 for more on this.

Regulation

Perhaps the most critical obstacle to cryptoasset market maturity is its lack of consistent regulation. While excessive regulation is clearly not conducive to effective financial markets, no regulation is not either. The first decade of the existence of cryptoassets was the equivalent of the wild west in terms of regulation. Countries treated cryptoasset trades differently, with different classifications and tax rates. They allowed disparate levels of access to cryptoassets, even with some countries banning access altogether. In most jurisdictions, there were neither rules nor oversight, leaving the door open to market manipulations (e.g., "pump-and-dump" schemes) and hazardous projects hiding as safe investments.

Here again, material changes happened in the early 2020s. For example, the proposed regulation Markets in Crypto Assets (MiCA) in EU law forms the cryptoasset equivalent of the corresponding regulation for securities, investment intermediaries, and trading venues (i.e., the Markets in Financial Instruments Directive (MiFID)). Under Biden's administration, the US Treasury also developed a framework for international crypto regulation. These pieces of regulation aim to increase investors' protection and level the regulatory playing field across jurisdictions. If these upcoming regulations achieve their aims without materially distorting the market, significant benefits for the crypto sector will ensue.

Historical Data

Compared to other financial assets, cryptoassets have relatively few historical data points. In addition, the exceptional pace of growth of the market makes a large quantity of these data points irrelevant. Every year, the market is substantially different than in any previous year, so data points are quickly outdated. Furthermore, scaling solutions, crypto platforms, and other crypto services are still mainly in the development and implementation phases but not at the broad adoption phase yet. The longer the relevant history of cryptoassets, the more confidence the market has in the technology and its future, which drives further adoption.

Awareness on Privacy

When social media became mainstream in the late 2000s, privacy was barely on the radar of users and companies. Countless scandals, data breaches, and hacks exposed the importance of privacy and progressively increased the general public's awareness of it. This process is still ongoing. With large companies collecting more personal data points on users at an ever-accelerating pace, users increasingly seek solutions to keep data confidential and secure. As privacy awareness grows, the privacy benefits of blockchain technology are likely to become increasingly desirable, providing additional appeal to cryptoassets offering higher levels of security for private data.

Adoption As Means of Payment

For cryptoassets to become means of payment, buyers must be willing to pay with cryptoassets, sellers must be willing to accept cryptoassets as payment, and easy-to-use technology must exist to match them. Though it sounds simple, these conditions are interdependent, as in a chicken-and-egg problem. For instance, buyers will only request to pay with cryptoassets if a sufficient number of sellers accept them and have the technology. Similarly, sellers will only acquire the technology if a sufficient number of buyers request to pay with cryptoassets.

In the same way that Uber had to reach sufficient drivers and riders to give each group incentives to use their platform, the cryptoasset market must reach a critical mass of buyers and sellers before blooming. Only once a critical mass of each group exists will the market take on the feature of means of payment.

Crypto Ecosystem

The criteria discussed in this chapter do not evolve consecutively but in parallel. They are not independent from each other but intertwined. Indeed, every improvement in any characteristic impacts all others, in most cases, positively. For instance, higher liquidity is likely to increase adoption and the other way around, which are both likely to increase the need for regulation. At the same time, clearer and more consistent regulation will likely attract more crypto actors, increasing liquidity and the likelihood of ETF approvals. A whole ecosystem binds them together, with each filling specific functions to make the new asset class complete.

In terms of actors, the ecosystem includes innovators (coders and developers), venture capitalists such as Andreessen Horowitz, institutions such as VISA or Goldman Sachs, NGOs such as the Chamber of Digital Commerce, academics, governments, regulators, and users. Each actor increases the acceptance of the whole crypto sector, which benefits all others.

Crypto prime time will not happen when one specific event occurs. Instead, it is a continuous process relying on a set of characteristics and actors, all evolving in parallel and feeding on each other's improvements. The crypto market fundamentals will improve on many fronts in parallel.

Nevertheless, for the bullish cryptoasset investment thesis to materialize, there must be a catalyst: A specific event changing the game. For example, the burst of the housing market bubble in 2008 was the catalyst for the subsequent economic collapse. It uncovered an overheated market with many precarious and highly leveraged positions. Not only was the market unsustainable, but it needed something to spark the correction.

A cryptoasset catalyst in the past was Tesla accepting Bitcoin as payment and adding it to its treasury in early 2021. These events sparked the subsequent upward movement of the crypto market. Similarly, while prime time does not depend on any specific event, one or a few catalysts will likely spark the market's next leg up.

Key Concepts

As of early 2023, the cryptoasset market is not mature yet. However, major ongoing developments are improving this level of maturity quickly. Many characteristics evolve in parallel, each impacting others and contributing to a more developed, sustainable, and safer crypto market. These characteristics include market liquidity, platform accessibility, interoperability, investment vehicle availability, formal taxonomy, and regulation. Cryptoassets will only reach their prime time through mass adoption once these characteristics achieve a sufficient state of development for most users.

Extension Questions

What are possible catalysts for the next crypto bull run (the start of the next uptrend market)?

What catalysts would delay crypto prime time? Can they invalidate the bullish crypto thesis altogether?

What characteristics of the upcoming crypto market regulation will the United States and the European Union likely adopt, and how will they affect cryptoasset prime time?

Given the current level of maturity and pace of development of the crypto industry, what level of adoption will it reach in 2025 and 2030 in terms of the number of active users?

PART IV

Where Should One Invest?

CHAPTER 11

Investment Vehicles

> *It is not how much money you make, but how much money you keep, how hard it works for you, and how many generations you keep it for.*
>
> —Robert Kiyosaki

Investors in cryptoassets need to choose where to invest. Options are available, from pure investment on the blockchain to custodians investing on one's behalf. This chapter investigates these options and the benefits they provide.

Keys and Addresses

Going back to the mechanics of blockchain presented in Chapter 6, a private key enables access to cryptoassets sent to the corresponding public address on the blockchain. A public key is generated from the private key, and the public address is generated from the public key. This generation takes place through cryptographic algorithms. It is straightforward to obtain the output from the input but almost impossible to guess the input from the output (with current technology, at least).

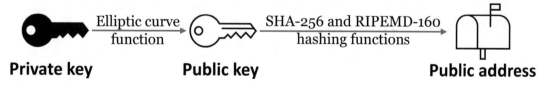

Figure 11-1. The public address (where senders send cryptoassets) is a function of the public key, which is itself a function of the private key. The functions depicted are the ones for Bitcoin to get from a private key to a public address

T. Jeegers, *Understanding Crypto Fundamentals*, https://doi.org/10.1007/978-1-4842-9309-6_11

These keys are only a long string of random characters stored in a "digital wallet" by analogy to the physical wallet used to store cash and physical credit cards.

Losing one's private key means losing access to the content of one's public address. For this reason, safely securing keys is of paramount importance. Counterintuitively, a wallet does not hold the underlying coins. For example, a Bitcoin wallet does not hold the user's bitcoins. The ownership of these bitcoins is recorded on the Bitcoin blockchain, while the wallet only holds the keys enabling the movement of the corresponding bitcoins. A better analogy for a cryptoasset wallet would therefore be a keychain. As per industry standards, however, we will continue using the word *wallet*.

Different wallet types exhibit different risk profiles. In particular, crypto investors need to weigh the benefits of easy access to their funds with the increased risk they run for this comfort.

Hot Wallets and Cold Wallets

Wallets having private keys stored online or on devices connected to the Internet are called *hot storage wallets* or simply *hot wallets*. In contrast, wallets storing private keys offline are called *cold storage wallets* or *cold wallets*.

Investments made with a hot wallet run a higher risk of theft, as a successful hacker could access one's private key and steal one's funds. For example, a hacker could send spyware to access your confidential data or use a malicious app to fool you into giving away your private key. On the other hand, since cold wallets are offline and only occasionally connected to the Internet for transactions, they are comparatively safer.

Hot wallets include desktop, mobile, and web-based wallets, while cold wallets include hardware and paper wallets. Of course, both hot and cold wallets can receive cryptoassets anytime, regardless of whether online. Again, the cryptoassets are not sent to the wallet but to an address on the blockchain. The wallets simply contain the key giving access to the content of that address.

Hot wallets	**Cold wallets**
• Connected to the internet • Easy access to funds • Comparatively more risky • Includes desktop, mobile, and web wallets	• Not connected to the internet • Cumbersome access to funds • Comparatively safer • Includes hardware and paper wallets

Figure 11-2. Summary of main differences between hot and cold wallets

In a way, hot and cold wallets are similar to checking and savings accounts, respectively. A hot wallet is similar to a checking account in that it facilitates regular currency usage through easy access. A cold wallet is similar to a savings account as it supports long-term storage of wealth, though with more cumbersome access.

A paper wallet is a specific form of cold wallet. It is a printed document containing two pieces of information: the public address to receive a specific cryptoasset and a private key to access the content of that address. When created with the highest level of security, they are generated from a computer or smartphone that has never been connected to the Internet.[1] This complete isolation from the Internet makes such wallets safer against hacking attacks. In addition, they typically include QR codes corresponding to the strings of characters representing the public address and private key to ease their usage through an app.

---

[1] Technically, you download the software to generate a public address from a private key on a reliable, open source platform, upload that software on a physical USB key or disk, then plug that device into a clean computer that has never been connected to the Internet.

Figure 11-3. *Example of a paper wallet (i.e., a piece of paper including two strings of seemingly random characters: the public address and the private key), represented by a QR code to facilitate usage*

The distinction between wallet types sometimes also takes different names (i.e., software wallets (hot) and web wallets (hot) vs. hardware wallets (cold)). Indeed, these names are more intuitive as they suggest that hot wallets run through software like an app downloaded on a desktop or mobile device or accessed online.

For higher safety, software wallets typically partition online and offline sections. A pending transaction first moves offline, where the signature with the private key occurs. The software then only broadcasts the hash of that signature online. This way, it never exposes the private key directly online.

Figure 11-4. *Ledger Nano S hardware (cold) wallet. Such wallets have a user interface via a desktop app, enabling to sign transactions offline and only submit the hash of the signature online*

Custodial and Non-Custodial Wallets

Wallets are also different in a meaningful way based on whether they are custodial. Custody refers to whether the end user owns the keys to the wallet. In particular, a custodial wallet is one in which a third party holds your keys on your behalf. To get access to your funds, you must trust a custodian and register via a traditional login and password on a website or an app. It is, for example, the model that many online exchanges use. Your investment is, therefore, directly dependent on the security infrastructure of the third party. As a result, if the custodian is corrupt, hacked, or forced by authorities to stop its activities, you may lose your funds. On the other hand, if you lose your password, there may be ways to recover it by proving your identity to a third party.

In contrast, wallets can be non-custodial, also known as self-custodial. In such cases, users own their private keys. No trust in any third party is necessary as users genuinely own their funds. This distinction substantiates an important motto used by the crypto community.

Not your keys, not your coins.

Non-custodial wallets are the preferred option of users living by the cryptoassets' trustless value proposition. They can also provide users a higher degree of privacy, as KYC (Know Your Customer) processes are not always required, contrary to most custodial exchanges. However, they are generally less user-friendly for holding one's fund than going through a custodian. Furthermore, the risk profile of this option is also different: if the user loses the private key, the corresponding funds are irretrievably lost forever.

Centralized and Decentralized Platforms

Custodial wallets are typically automatically set up via centralized platforms when a user joins. In particular, about 99% of transactions in cryptoassets in 2021 were made through centralized platforms.[2] Such platforms function like a traditional online stock exchange: a user sends money to a private platform (e.g., with a credit or debit card) and can invest it online. Their user-friendliness likely drives their market dominance. Transacting via such platforms is indeed much easier and more similar to familiar platforms for average users.

Furthermore, centralized platforms differ based on whether they are *exchanges* or *brokerage services*. An exchange enables users to trade directly with each other on an open exchange. In contrast, a brokerage service platform is the counterparty to all trades on that platform. Famous centralized cryptoasset exchanges include Binance, Kraken, and Bitstamp. Famous cryptoasset brokerage services include Coinbase[3], eToro, and Robinhood.

In contrast to centralized platforms, decentralized exchanges also exist and enable purer peer-to-peer transactions, though they remain the exception as of 2023. Decentralized exchanges (DEXs) resemble their decentralized cryptoasset counterpart in that there is no central authority on the other side of the trade, nor even facilitating the trade. They are typically open source projects matching buyers with sellers and lenders with borrowers via smart contracts without unique omnipotent supervision. Following the original cryptoasset philosophy, they are trustless.

In some cases, DEXs rely on user-generated liquidity pools, where users are incentivized through rewards to provide liquidity. This way, the platforms can become automated market makers (AMM). In other words, they no longer need to rely on an order book. With an AMM, prices are driven by mathematical formulas rather than specific buy and sell orders, increasing the liquidity of countless tokens. One of the first DEXs, Uniswap, was instrumental in growing the DEX industry through its AMM

---

[2] D-Core, *2021 Institutional Blockchain Investment Guide* [38].

[3] While Coinbase is mainly a brokerage service, Coinbase Pro is also an exchange.

feature. Though its first version launched in 2018, the second version changed the game in 2020 by enabling direct swaps of any token via Ethereum. Any cryptoasset could be decentrally exchanged for any other cryptoasset. Quick followers of Uniswap also grew among the biggest dApps in the ecosystem.

While they better suit the decentralized value proposition of cryptoassets, DEXs are more challenging to use and prone to scams than centralized exchanges. They require more knowledge of the processes and more time to get familiar with. On the other hand, they forgo some of the fees, KYC, and AML[4] processes that centralized exchanges impose, thereby offering higher privacy. They also offer higher security as funds are split among many wallets, making them less attractive to hackers than centralized exchanges. However, while DEXs may be the preferred trading forum for cryptoassets in the future, they are hardly mature yet and require users to proceed with caution. The much larger usage of centralized platforms compared to decentralized exchanges proves that many users currently value the custodian service's ease of use more than they value the extra benefits of decentralization.

DEXs differ from one another based on the underlying protocol on which they are built (e.g., Ethereum or Binance Smart Chain), their focus (e.g., ERC-20 tokens), and specific features they offer (e.g., cold storage and two-factor authentication).

Beyond centralized and decentralized exchanges, hybrid exchanges combine the best of both worlds. In particular, they provide the ease, speed, and high liquidity of centralized exchanges but with decentralized exchanges' peer-to-peer and privacy features. They typically have both an on-chain section (like DEX) and an off-chain section (like CEX). Hybrid cryptoasset exchanges include BitMax and CEX.IO, each providing centralized and decentralized trading options.

While selecting an exchange, one should consider the following characteristics among the available options. As for wallets, many websites rank crypto exchanges based on some or all of these characteristics.

1. Custodial status
2. Transaction costs
3. Withdrawal costs
4. Volume traded
5. Possibility to earn passive income
6. Possibility to use derivative products, such as futures or options

---

[4] Know Your Customer and Anti-Money Laundering.

7. Redeemability of funds into fiat currencies

8. Transaction limits (daily deposit/withdrawal limit)

9. Level of privacy (presence of KYC and AML processes)

10. Ease of use

User Interfaces and Exchanges

While exchanges sometimes include wallets as part of their service, wallets and exchanges are very different concepts. In particular, one can set up a wallet in many different ways and independently choose an exchange to which to connect this wallet. For example, one can set up a web or hardware wallet and connect it to either a centralized or decentralized exchange or not to any exchange.

The user interface of software wallets (e.g., Electrum, Mycelium, Exodus), web wallets (e.g., Metamask, MyEtherWallet, Bitcoin.com Wallet, Trust Wallet, Coinbase Wallet), or hardware wallets (e.g., Ledger, Trezor, KeepKey, Coldcard) is independent of any exchange. For example, even Trust Wallet is independent of the exchange Binance, even though Binance Holdings Limited has owned it since its acquisition in 2018. Similarly, Coinbase Wallet is independent of the Coinbase exchange, even though the same parent company, Coinbase, Inc, owns them. They remain standalone products, not directly linked to the corresponding exchange. Therefore, these wallets' user interface should not be misunderstood as an exchange. By extension, the user interface of a self-custodial wallet does not imply the same third-party risks as a brokerage service (e.g., risk of corruption, fraud, or intervention by authorities).

Deterministic and Non-Deterministic Wallets

Another distinction in wallets is whether they are deterministic, which only applies to wallets containing multiple key pairs (private and public keys). Each key pair has its own public address. This way, a single user can use multiple addresses on the blockchain, much like a single user can have different bank accounts at the same bank.

In a deterministic wallet, a single master key creates multiple key pairs. The master key is typically a seed phrase (explained in the next section) and can produce, for example, a hundred key pairs. In such a wallet, the user only needs one backup: for the master key. Once he has the master key, he has access to all key pairs and to all cryptoassets on the corresponding addresses.

In a non-deterministic wallet, each key pair is independent. Therefore, the user must create separate backups for each wallet key.

Additional subcategories of deterministic wallets exist. For example, hierarchical deterministic (HD) wallets enable a set of private keys based on another private key in a hierarchy. Each private key created by the master key is also a master key in its own right. It may be helpful for corporate structures with several layers of hierarchy, each in charge of multiple addresses.

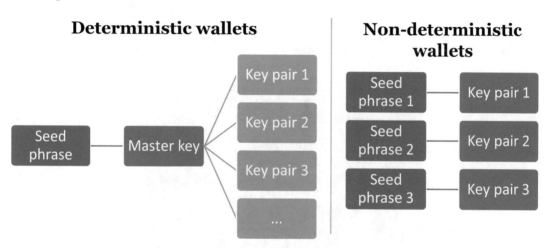

Figure 11-5. *Illustration of deterministic vs. non-deterministic wallets*

Seed Phrases

The *seed phrase*, also known as *seed words, recovery phrase,* or *mnemonic phrase,* is a list of random words (typically 12 or 24 simple words) written in a specific order. They are given as input in a mnemonic phrase converter, which is an algorithm that converts them into a private key for a specific cryptoasset, as shown in Figure 11-7.[5] Each blockchain has a specific format for its private keys, such as the character it starts with or the number of bytes with which it is written. Therefore, sending bitcoins to an Ethereum address, for example, will either not work or the funds will be lost forever.

---

[5] For Bitcoin, for example, the seed words are converted into a private key of 256 bits or 64 hexadecimal numbers, which is how private keys are typically presented. The number of possible private keys (2^{256}) is about as large as the number of atoms in the observable universe.

A seed phrase may look like the following 24-word list.

1. bless	9. figure	17. dolphin
2. sun	10. year	18. salad
3. moral	11. romance	19. panel
4. farm	12. purpose	20. rich
5. saddle	13. glad	21. honey
6. good	14. satoshi	22. board
7. live	15. point	23. success
8. sphere	16. novel	24. swap

Figure 11-6. *Aluminum case designed for 24-word seed phrase recovery with engraving pen and anti-tamper seals. The case is fireproof, waterproof, shockproof, and corrosion-resistant. It is a type of paper (cold) wallet (in this case, not made of paper)*

The Bitcoin community agreed on an official list of 2048 (i.e., 2^{11}) words as the base for Bitcoin private keys to ease their storage. A similar list also exists in languages other than English. A set of rules make the words simple and unmistakable. For example, the list does not include words with multiple spellings or words existing in other languages' corresponding lists. Also, no two words start with the same first four letters, so knowing the first four letters of each (12 or 24) seed word is enough to recover one's private key. In addition, the final word is a checksum dependent on all other words to ensure the validity of the seed phrase. Each word is also linked to a number of the 2048-word list, so knowing one's list of (12 or 24) numbers (and the list selected, i.e., language) is an alternative to knowing one's seed words. For this reason, some hardware wallets simply list numbers corresponding to the seed words that can reinstate the user's private key.

Mnemonic

You can enter an existing BIP39 mnemonic, or generate a new random one. Typing your own twelve words will probably not work how you expect, since the words require a particular structure (the last word contains a checksum).

For more info see the BIP39 spec.

Generate a random mnemonic: **GENERATE**   [24 ⌄] words, or enter your own below.

☐ Show entropy details

☐ Hide all private info

☑ Auto compute

Mnemonic Language	English 日本語 Español 中文(简体) 中文(繁體) Français Italiano 한국어 Čeština Português
BIP39 Mnemonic	bless sun moral farm saddle good live sphere figure year romance purpose glad satoshi point novel dolphin salad panel rich honey board success swap
	☐ Show split mnemonic cards
BIP39 Passphrase (optional)	
BIP39 Seed	16b24665552578867a7d494265a186766b4f36594f9c5a69b5455784fcbadb54c467a198047ac5157ab91fdaf832b27e1e22b10763968f7fdbc608a34d71a59c
Coin	BTC - Bitcoin
BIP32 Root Key	xprv9s21ZrQH143K4PjMMeEYjnMkjZmhqWBM9x327iFRRhLJn6QtQgvXXH8pkAURUo7KGsN58pvy4qd3W1o7QFXUhHj6ybvQyXYXbApQ8TfNGKL

Figure 11-7. *Bitcoin mnemonics, seed phrases, and private keys generator. (Source:* `https://iancoleman.io/bip39/`*)*

Additional Wallet Features

Another possible feature in blockchain wallets is a master public key, which provides access to all public keys in a wallet but without access to their corresponding private keys. Holders of the master public key see the balance of all addresses in a wallet but cannot move the corresponding assets. It is useful, for example, for accounting and audit, as one can share the master public key with auditors without risks to one's funds, just to one's privacy.

A MultiSig wallet is another useful security feature. It requires multiple signatures from different private keys to submit a transaction. It is a form of two-factor authentication, like a locker with multiple locks and keys held by different people. Each person needs the others' approval to open the locker. For example, the crypto wallet of a company could require all board members to sign a transaction before submitting it. Alternatively, several but not all signatures can be required, such as three out of five. MultiSig wallets have a higher level of security since different private keys reside in different locations, thereby avoiding a single point of failure.

Bitcoin Core

One specific wallet type deserves a dedicated mention. In 2009, Satoshi Nakamoto released the first crypto wallet, Bitcoin-Qt, as open source code. Now known as Bitcoin Core (or Satoshi Client), it is the "official" code of the Bitcoin network, maintained, developed, and promoted by the Bitcoin Foundation. Essentially, Bitcoin Core is a desktop wallet that is also a *full Bitcoin client*, or *full node*.

A full node downloads the entire Bitcoin blockchain[6] on one's computer and permanently synchronizes it with the rest of the network. Thereby, it helps the network to increase its decentralization. However, having a full Bitcoin client is unnecessary to run a Bitcoin node. Unlike a full node, a *thin client* (or *lightweight* client or *simple-payment-verification* client) downloads only the last few blocks from the blockchain. The more blocks it downloads (the *deeper* the client), the more trustworthy the client. Full nodes and thin clients are a tradeoff between storage space and trust in the integrity of the underlying blockchain.

Furthermore, Bitcoin Core has multiple levels of security and is continuously improved by the Bitcoin Foundation to keep its safety at a state-of-the-art level.

Wallet Safety

It is paramount for the security of one's funds to ensure that the wallet provider is trustworthy. Several resources help to choose wallets carefully. For example, the not-for-profit website Bitcoin.org provides a list of trustworthy Bitcoin wallets, filterable by essential and desirable features (e.g., hardware wallets, MultiSig wallets).[7] In addition, countless other online resources list the pros and cons of other cryptoasset wallets.

Storing Private Keys Safely

Another essential safety measure for the self-custody of cryptoassets is storing one's private key wisely and reliably. On the one hand, you may be tempted to keep multiple

---

[6] The full Bitcoin blockchain contains about 0.5 terabyte of information as of 2023 and increases by about 5GB per month. In other words, it can be held on a traditional computer's hard drive and should remain so for the foreseeable future because hard drives capacity grow rapidly.

[7] See in particular https://bitcoin.org/en/choose-your-wallet.

copies of your private key to minimize the risk of loss (which would imply losing all your funds). However, on the other hand, the more copies you keep, the higher the risk that one of them is stolen (which would also imply losing all of your funds).

One way to mitigate this dilemma is through sharding. Instead of keeping the entire private key in one piece, you could split (or "shard") it into two (or more) pieces. This way, should anybody steal one shard of your private key, your funds are still not at risk. The thief would need all shards to reconstruct the private key and get access to your funds.

Private key:

0xD388C6EC98E4643915d1C4Ba4856DB1183A71da4

Private key's shard #1:   **Private key's shard #2:**

0xD388C6EC98E4643915d   1C4Ba4856DB1183A71da4

Figure 11-8. *Splitting a private key into two shards*

For example, you could have three copies of each of the two shards, locked or hidden at six different locations (one location for each copy of each shard). This way, neither the theft nor the loss of any single copy would put your funds at risk.

Of course, you could do the same with your seed words instead of the raw private key. Alternatively, or on top of this approach, you could also choose to memorize a part of your key or seed words to protect them from theft.

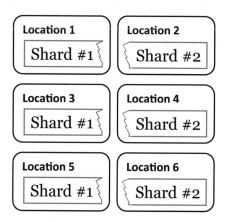

Figure 11-9. *Spreading copies of shards in multiple locations mitigates both the risk of theft and the risk of loss of one's private key*

Key Concepts

There are different ways to invest in cryptoassets. In particular, one can use a third party (a custodian) or set up one's own wallet. While most transactions rely on the former, the latter aligns more with the decentralized, trustless philosophy behind cryptoassets. Custodial wallets rely on a third party to hold users' private keys. In contrast, non-custodial (or self-custodial) wallets enable users to genuinely own their funds by making them inaccessible to anyone else.

There are different types of wallets: hot wallets are connected to the Internet, easing frequent transactions, while cold wallets are offline, offering higher security to users. Many recent developments in the industry enable new features, such as deterministic wallets, multiple signatures, and master public keys. These features enable the industry to grow by responding to corporate and institutional needs.

Selecting a wallet or an exchange should be a careful endeavor to ensure optimal fit and high security. Similarly, storing one's keys safely is of utmost importance.

Extension Questions

Which wallet type is most appropriate for a private investor, a private trader, a professional individual investor, an individual professional trader, a Bitcoin mining company, a traditional corporation active in a non-crypto sector for its internal treasury, a traditional corporation active in a non-crypto sector but enabling payment in cryptoassets?

Which creative method could investors use to secure their private key against loss and theft?

What is the safest way to set up a private key?

PART V

How Should One Invest?

CHAPTER 12

Investment Strategies

The best way to measure your investing success is not by whether you're beating the market but by whether you've put in place a financial plan and a behavioral discipline that are likely to get you where you want to go.

—Benjamin Graham

Literature on investing is abundant, wildly diverse, and sometimes even self-contradicting. In any case, presenting a complete investing framework is well beyond the scope of this book. Instead, this chapter only briefly highlights fundamental principles for new investors in cryptoassets and reminds some words of caution especially relevant to this asset class. This chapter will likely fall short of the expectations of advanced investors, which are thus invited to skip it.

First, investing is a highly personal endeavor. Investors have different time horizons, return objectives, abilities to take risks, willingness to take risks, legal obligations, tax rates, preferences (e.g., ESG), and other unique characteristics. Insights from this chapter, or even from this book, should therefore not be seen as a recommendation for any investor. Instead, they aim solely to contribute to investors' education on cryptoassets. Potential investors should carefully assess where they lie on these characteristics and consider referring to professional portfolio managers to help them craft an investment strategy.

Secondly, markets are in perpetual motion. The relationship between asset classes, such as bonds, stocks, currencies, and commodities, is not fixed but changes over time. Besides, their valuation depends on the perception and judgment of other market players, not on specific formulas or models. In particular, cryptoassets are evolving faster than any other asset class and are especially subject to other players' perceptions. The content of this chapter should be considered with caution and challenged for its relevance in time and in the face of changing conditions in the market.

© Thomas Jeegers 2023
T. Jeegers, *Understanding Crypto Fundamentals*, https://doi.org/10.1007/978-1-4842-9309-6_12

Nevertheless, developing an investment strategy is essential. Especially for an asset class that is still volatile and subject to market changes, an investment strategy can help investors focus on the long term and prevent them from reacting emotionally to news or market swings.

Buy Low, Sell High

Many new investors decide to enter their first position at the worst possible time. It is especially the case in the cryptoasset market because news tends to share extensively about a market asset after major increases in its price. For example, Bitcoin tends to make the headlines when its price increases by an order of magnitude or another cryptoasset soars even more. As a result, potential investors fear missing out. They are often drawn to the market when prices are materially above their long-term trend, which is typically quickly followed by a downward correction. In particular, many newcomers joined just before the price spikes experienced in 2013, 2017, and 2021 (presented in Chapter 9).

At the risk of stating the obvious, realizing capital gains through investments consists in buying when prices are low and selling when prices are high. As evident as it sounds, many new investors do not manage to do so. Specifically, market entry is typically inappropriate when prices are significantly above their long-term trend. Buy low, sell high.

This simple objective sometimes involves adopting a contrarian approach: invest when the market sentiment is down and withdraw when it is irrationally exuberant. For example, the Fear & Greed index introduced in Chapter 9 helps assess the general euphory level around the crypto market. In addition, the *relative strength index* (RSI), although a short-term instrument, is a momentum indicator that also provides valuable information on whether an asset is currently overbought (possibly a good time to sell) or oversold (possibly a good time to buy). These indicators tended to make valuable suggestions about the timing of purchases and sales of cryptoassets in the past. However, these suggestions were not consistently accurate. They should, therefore, not be the sole basis for any investment decision.

Timing the Market

While financial analyzes, trends, models, and news are helpful tools to inform where one is in the business cycle, timing the market accurately is impossible. Due to inherent uncertainties, nobody knows when the market has reached its bottom or peak. Striving to buy at the absolute lowest price and sell at the exact market peak may therefore be a counterproductive endeavor. An alternative would be dollar-cost averaging.

Dollar-Cost Averaging

Conscious of the impossibility of timing the optimal entry and exit points, investors can rely on multiple entries and exits. For example, an investor could invest 1% of the available capital or a fixed amount every month. This process, called "dollar-cost averaging," is a sort of temporal diversification. It limits the likelihood of investing a material amount at the wrong time. Dollar-cost averaging is already prescribed on page 2 of Benjamin Graham's 1934 value-investing book *The Intelligent Investor*, which became a reference for the industry [42].

In addition, dollar-cost averaging limits the risks implied by emotional trading. The cryptoasset market is more emotional than others because cryptoasset fundamentals are less understood than those of traditional asset classes. Also, the comparatively lower level of liquidity makes large trades more impactful on price. Spreading purchases and sales over time seems the more prudent and recommendable approach, especially for cryptoassets.

Note, however, that from a purely mathematical perspective, dollar-cost averaging is not superior to a large one-off purchase (assuming sufficient liquidity to absorb the purchase without a material impact on price).

Filter the Noise

The exceptional growth of the cryptoasset industry created hype around investments in this new asset class. As a result, more information is available on the industry than anybody could process. This information comes from all sources, from academic research to public figures and corporations to regulators. Traditional news media, in particular, like to comment on the cryptoasset industry, even when they do not understand its fundamentals. It is, for example, how the narrative of Bitcoin mining being bad for the environment spread. As covered in Chapter 3, this narrative is inaccurate and biased; considering everything, the opposite is more likely to be true.

In the face of a rapidly growing and misunderstood industry, it is essential to filter useful information from abundant noise. The careful investor should ensure to select high-quality, informed sources.

In addition, conscientiously searching for information contradicting one's views is paramount. Diligent investors should actively search for knowledgeable people disagreeing with their investment thesis. The ground-breaking potential of the industry gathered vocal followers whose devotion to promoting cryptoassets is nothing short of religious fervor. Similarly, the industry has strong opponents flagging the whole industry as a scam. Listening exclusively to missionaries either for or against cryptoassets is dangerous, as it would bias one's opinion in a single direction. As a result, either the potential returns or the risks of cryptoassets would be underestimated.

The ultimate objective is not to prove to anybody that any opinion is correct but to reach the highest possible level of market understanding to make wise investment decisions. Filtering the noise implies ignoring short-term price movements and cheap or biased media highlights and focusing on the long game based on high-quality, independently researched information.

Taxation

Taxation differs wildly depending on the jurisdiction. Familiarizing oneself with local tax regulations (and in other jurisdictions where one may need to pay taxes) is essential to decide whether and how to trade. Cryptoasset taxes may include income, capital gain, and wealth taxes. Typically, cryptoassets are classified as commodities, securities (like stocks and bonds), digital property, or foreign currencies. This local treatment for tax purposes fundamentally affects how to treat the asset.

Besides, the tax treatment may differ based on the holding period. For example, in some jurisdictions, cryptoassets sold within one year can be considered speculation and therefore taxed, while beyond one year, they would be considered an investment and therefore not taxed. In addition, some sales may trigger tax events while others do not. For instance, selling a cryptoasset like Bitcoin for a stablecoin like USDC may not trigger a tax event, while selling it for a fiat currency would. Many other local tax specificities may suggest trading differently due to their implications. Furthermore, rules also evolve quickly. The diligent investor should remain current on local regulations to decide how to manage a cryptoasset portfolio optimally.

Dealing with assets as volatile as cryptoasset can be dangerous if fiscal aspects are not considered. For example, a careless investor could sell a cryptoasset in December and make a large capital gain through this sale. Reinvesting all proceeds immediately in another cryptoasset could put him at risk. Suppose the other cryptoasset loses most of its value, as occasionally happens in this industry. In that case, the investor may not have enough liquid funds to pay the taxes due on the original large capital gain. When taxes come due in the next year, he may have to sell assets at a very unfortunate time to pay taxes due.

Readers interested in the taxation of cryptoassets can refer to the extensive book *Taxation of Crypto Assets* by Schmidt, Bernstein, Richter, and Zarlenga, second edition (2023), covering tax law for cryptoassets in over 40 countries [3].

Borrowing As an Alternative to Sale

An investor in need of immediate liquidity faces alternatives to selling cryptoassets. For example, instead of selling a cryptoasset at an unfortunate time, one can borrow against it. As long as the interest rate on the loan is below the rate of appreciation of the cryptoasset, the investor is better off by borrowing. Also, a higher inflation rate in the currency in which one borrows is better for the borrower. It is the case because the money owed will be worth less in terms of real goods and services in the future.

Behavioral and Mental Biases

While traditional investing already requires emotional self-discipline and knowledge of one's limitations, cryptoasset investing brings these requirements to a new level. Indeed, rapid and often irrational price moves in either direction regularly test investors' temperament. To face such volatility, emotional detachment is essential. For better or worse, it is not a skill mastered by anybody, and it can have drastic consequences for those who ignore its necessity. Beyond emotional self-control, awareness of one's mental biases is especially important to manage a volatile portfolio in a dynamic industry.

The father of economics puts it as follows.

If you don't know who you are, the stock market is an expensive place to find out.

—Adam Smith

This section covers some common emotional biases and cognitive errors that diligent investors should consider while making investment decisions. These biases and errors justify, in part, how otherwise rational investors can make inappropriate investment decisions, leading to opportunities for those on the other side of the trade.

Confirmation Bias

If you believe there are more gray cats than black cats, every time you see a gray cat, it strengthens your belief, regardless of its accuracy. This tendency is called a *confirmation bias*, to which most of us are naturally subject, though often unknowingly. Unsurprisingly, this bias also manifests in investing.

For example, looking to prove one's theory for or against a specific asset (class) can cause investors to only consider some of the available information. In contrast, information conflicting with one's investment thesis would be ignored even if it contains essential elements of data the investor should consider.

Our natural confirmation bias can be mitigated by seeking diverse information from various sources and actively looking for information against one's investment thesis. In particular, it involves critically thinking about why and how one could be wrong rather than striving to prove why one must be right.

Loss Aversion

Another bias extensively supported by social science research is loss aversion. In particular, research establishes that for most people, the pain they suffer from a loss is disproportionally more intense than the satisfaction they get from a gain of the same amount. In other words, the pleasure of gaining $100 is smaller than the pain of losing $100.

This simple fact has significant consequences for portfolio management. In particular, it supports the value investment thesis that an investment price may be lower than its economic value. For instance, investors facing highly volatile investments tend to shun them, a tendency referred to as *myopic loss aversion*. Indeed, when faced with an investment in two highly volatile securities, one of which will likely collapse to zero, most investors prefer not to invest. That is, even if the outsized gains on the other investment may still make the total a highly attractive opportunity. Loss aversion has been part of human behavior since as far as our history goes and is likely here to stay [43].

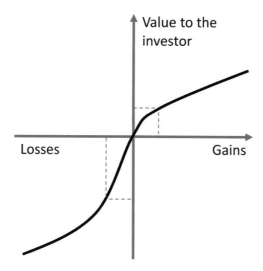

Figure 12-1. *Visual representation of the loss aversion effect, where a loss has a much more significant impact in the eyes of the investor than a gain of the same value*

This bias is especially relevant for small and less liquid asset classes, such as cryptoassets, since they are more volatile than established asset classes. To mitigate this bias, it can be helpful to consider the entire portfolio and focus on the potential long-term benefits of an investment rather than the short-term risks of any specific part of a portfolio.

Endowment Effects

Another bias is the *endowment effect*, which is similar to the status-quo bias in this context. It suggests that we value something we already own more highly than something we do not yet own. For example, one would be ready to sell a specific mug for $5 but not ready to buy it for more than $2. Rationality would suggest that the threshold for both buying and selling would be the same: at a price corresponding to the utility derived by the object. However, empirical evidence from social science suggests that owning something makes it more valuable to the owner.

In investing, this bias has important consequences. For example, just because you bought a cryptoasset in the past does not mean it is still the optimal investment in your portfolio if the situation has changed. Nevertheless, people tend to prefer to stay in their current position, even though it may be an inadequate asset allocation.

Conservatism Bias

Among others, conservatism bias is one possible cause for the endowment effect. When an investor forms a view on something, changing that view takes disproportionally more effort. For example, when an investor concludes based on initial information that an asset will rise in price, updating this conclusion will likely require more signals and information than was needed for the original conclusion. This bias is directly relevant for cryptoassets, as most traditional investors are unwilling to put the entire monetary model (based on fiat currencies) into question, as it has been the backbone of the investment profession for the last half-century.

Anchoring Effect

Anchors (specific prices reached in the past) often become a reference point for future developments, even when irrational. For example, when Bitcoin broke the $69,000 barrier, any subsequent price was compared to that peak: "Bitcoin went down that much percent," "Bitcoin lost that much value", etc. However, few mentioned that Bitcoin's price was below $4,000 just 18 months before. Regardless of the fundamental value of an asset, it is easier to anchor a price to a historical level, which is why many investors do so.

The diligent investor should not primarily consider what price an asset reached in the past but what fundamental value it is worth. Thereby, one should detach from any anchor, which may be and often is caused by irrational reactions from the market.

Overfitting Bias

While data is helpful for financial analysis, it may also be misused, purposefully or not. In particular, analysts have an overfitting bias if they find patterns and relationships that do not exist. For example, they may force a model or theory to fit a particular dataset, even though data would not naturally back that model or theory.

Data-mining Bias

Previous findings from data may also bias any new analysis. For example, data analysis can be biased if new research is based on previously reported evidence or if many analyses use the same database. If data in an overused dataset indicated by chance a specific pattern, this pattern may be excessively relied on because many studies highlight it.

Sample Selection Bias

In contrast, some pieces of data may be systematically excluded, for example, due to lack of availability or difficulty in extracting this information. Something easily obtainable is not more important than something difficult to obtain.

To mitigate these data-based biases, diligent investors should strive to gather complete sets of raw data from an objective, independent, and original source (e.g., gathering data directly from a blockchain rather than using data reported by third parties) and reach their own conclusion.

Survivorship Bias

Another crucial bias related to data and highly relevant in the context of cryptoassets is survivorship bias. Looking back at historical data may create a biased view if one only considers current survivors. For example, one may regret not investing in a cryptoasset whose price was recently multiplied by 10. However, when making that investment was possible, there may have been 100 cryptoassets with a similar risk profile to invest in. If 99 were worthless and only one became successful, it does not mean the original investment was worth it. At the very least, investing in this asset was not as attractive as an analysis focusing exclusively on survivors may suggest. Therefore, a proper analysis should include the assets that survived and those that did not.

In this sense, survivorship bias is closely related to hindsight bias, suggesting that people tend to selectively recollect facts to justify how obvious an outcome is after it happened. For example, many investors regret not investing in Bitcoin 10 years ago. However, Bitcoin's riskiness was much higher than today, even though many risks did not materialize. In addition, most investors would have used a centralized platform to invest at the time (because it was even less user-friendly to invest directly on the blockchain than today), many of which have been hacked. Most of these investments would have ended up lost or stolen.

Therefore, a proper analysis of past investments should consider what was known at the time rather than what is known today. Extensively documenting one's investment thesis and reasons for every trade helps limit the tendency to recollect facts selectively and to be subject to survivorship or hindsight biases.

Framing Bias

People are often biased depending on how information is framed, even when the underlying information is the same. For example, investors could make different decisions based on the taxonomy they are using or the number of investment alternatives they have. For example, if you have $100,000 to invest and you identified ten cryptoassets of high interest, you may tend to split your portfolio equally, with $10,000 in each asset. However, it may be more recommendable to have over 50% in one asset, less than 1% in seven of the ten assets, and the rest split among the last two. While it is often more rational not to split investments equally among the options available, many investors do so for simplicity reasons. They thereby ignore the relative size of the investment opportunities. It is especially relevant in the case of Bitcoin, which has roughly the same market capitalization as all other cryptoassets combined. Specifically, Bitcoin should not be considered as one cryptoasset among many but, as a particular case very different from any other cryptoasset.

Herd behavior bias

Herd behavior refers to the tendency to follow the opinions or actions of other investors, even when they may not align with their own opinion. People are subject to herd behavior (also called the *momentum effect*) by fear of missing out and due to media sharing extensively about the benefits of an asset when it goes up and its collapse when it goes down. Consequently, herd behavior reinforces cycles and may lead to market bubbles, as many investors follow a trend much beyond what underlying fundamentals suggest.

To mitigate the likelihood of being subject to herd behavior bias, investors should conduct their own analyses and stick to their investment strategy despite short-term market fluctuations.

Prediction Overconfidence Bias

Another bias is prediction overconfidence. In particular, investors tend to overestimate the accuracy of future price predictions. Financial models amplify this bias because they typically provide an exact output for the future price of a security (e.g., $123,456.78). In contrast, a wide range of possible prices is more reasonable to assume given the uncertainty of the future. It is also related to the illusion of knowledge, suggesting that analysts typically overestimate themselves and the quality of their analyses.

Size and ESG Biases

Another type of investment bias is due to the mandates of large investment firms. For example, take an investment firm willing to split equally $1 billion of capital into no more than 20 investment projects. As part of its mandate, the firm may also want to own at most 10% of the project in order not to obtain a controlling interest in it. Each selected project will benefit from an investment of $50 million but must have a market capitalization of at least $500 million to be considered. As of this writing, less than 100 cryptoassets can claim this minimum market capitalization. With a sufficient number of firms restrained by similar limits, high-value cryptoassets benefit from more investments, while smaller-value ones suffer from underinvestment. All other things being equal, smaller-value projects are frequently undervalued simply because large investment firms shy away from investing in them.

An additional bias based on the mandate of investment firms is related to corporate responsibility or environmental, social, and governance (ESG) practices of investment targets. In particular, the growing pressure to find investments that respond to specific corporate responsibility criteria may leave otherwise financially attractive investments underfunded. For example, large investors may be restricted in their mandate to only invest in cryptoassets that are not based on proof-of-work mechanisms, as some may argue that they are a net negative for the environment. It is not the lack of fundamentals but arbitrary restrictions in large investors' mandates that would create a downward bias to the market price of these targets.

Key Concepts

Selecting the optimal investment depends on many criteria. Among others, it depends on the risk appetite of the investor as well as his time horizon, needs for liquidity, tax status, and legal considerations. No unique investment or strategy is optimal for all investors. Nevertheless, some approaches may be recommendable for most investors. For example, investing smaller amounts in waves rather than a large amount at once enables to spread the risk of investing at an unfortunate time. Also, all investors are subject to mental biases that can interfere with rational investment strategies. Being aware of these possible flaws can help mitigate them.

Extension Questions

How do you research the cryptoasset industry to maximize the likelihood of making unbiased investment decisions?

Which taxation rules would prevent a cryptoasset from being used as a medium of exchange?

Which additional psychological bias are you subject to that could impair your ability to invest effectively?

CHAPTER 13

Non-Financial Risk Management

Successful investing is about managing risk, not avoiding it.

—Benjamin Graham

To make effective decisions, responsible investors should thoroughly understand financial and non-financial risks related to their investments. These two risk categories are different and likely higher for cryptoasset investments than traditional investments, making risk management even more critical. This chapter covers non-financial risks, and Chapter 14 covers financial risks. Besides describing the risks, these chapters also provide tools to mitigate them.

Non-financial risks are high in cryptoassets because the industry is still maturing and rapidly changing. Also, the short span of historical data points does not enable assessing all risks the industry faces. Even these data points are in many respects of limited value, as the industry in the last cycle was materially different from its state in the current cycle, making older data of little relevance.

Let us start with risks that are often mentioned but do not represent any material threat.

"51% Attack" Risk

The abstract of Bitcoin's white paper specifies an important assumption for the functioning of its blockchain [21].

> *As long as a majority of CPU power is controlled by nodes that are not cooperating to attack the network, they'll generate the longest chain and outpace attackers.*

T. Jeegers, *Understanding Crypto Fundamentals*, https://doi.org/10.1007/978-1-4842-9309-6_13

This "as long as" condition refers to what is commonly known as a *51% attack* or a *double-spend attack*. By design, in a proof-of-work (PoW) blockchain, if the majority of nodes (in terms of computing power) use a blockchain on which a specific transaction is not included, then this transaction officially never happened. Also, there is no recourse unless the rest of the network decides to hard fork from the main chain (as happened to Ethereum following the DAOsaster, as covered in Chapter 6).

Technically, the risk of a 51% attack is a situation where a pool of miners controls most of the hash-generation power in a PoW consensus setting. This pool could validate fraudulent blocks faster than honest nodes mine valid blocks. As a result, the fraudulent blocks could, for example, exclude a transaction for which the sender already received benefits. The sender would be able to spend this amount anew, which gave its name to this fraudulent behavior: a *double-spend* attack.

However, in the case of the Bitcoin blockchain, the possibility of a 51% attack is arguably non-existent. Indeed, the network's security is directly proportional to the hash rate. The higher the hash rate, the more power the attackers must gather to outpace honest nodes in block creation. A higher hash rate means higher security. However, the hash rate on Bitcoin's blockchain is so high that the probability of a consortium gathering 51% of the network's computing power is next to zero. Even if all big tech companies combined their global computing power and coordinated to use it exclusively to attack Bitcoin's blockchain, they would still not come close to 51% of the global Bitcoin hash rate. For instance, "the combined power of AWS, Azure, and Google Cloud would be less than 1% of Bitcoin" (as of end of 2022) [44].

The security of the Bitcoin network is over 100 times higher than the security of all other PoW blockchains combined. Consequently, investors may conclude that, while the Bitcoin blockchain is safe, this risk is still relevant for smaller PoW blockchains. However, a 51% attack is unlikely even for such chains. It is due to incentives inherent to the blockchain mining process: any potential attacker has little incentive to act deceitfully, while the participating nodes have a strong incentive to act honestly, as per the functioning of the blockchain. The bigger the cryptoasset at hand, the stronger the incentives for nodes to act honestly and the higher the network's security. Regardless of their size, PoW blockchains are always unattractive for possible attackers: the cost of attacking the chain is higher than the potential gain. This consensus method makes misbehaving an ineffective strategy, implying that even enemies abide by the same rules since it is clearly in their interest to do so.

Nevertheless, some sort of 51% attack has occurred in the past. For example, in April 2018, the Verge (XVG) blockchain suffered a 51% attack after a hacker identified a bug in the code, enabling him to mine blocks much faster than expected. Note, however, that the root cause of this attack was a bug in the code and not incorrect incentives. Moreover, for more established cryptoassets, security experts have reviewed and tested the corresponding blockchain's code many times. In fact, anybody can do so at any time since the code of such blockchains is open source, available for anybody to view and review. The existence of major bugs for large cryptoassets would therefore have likely already been identified.

Not only is the risk of a 51% attack highly unlikely to materialize, but it is also not a material risk. A common misconception is that a 51% attack would allow a hacker to seize funds from any address by sending them to himself. It is incorrect. Even if the hacker managed to get the large majority of the hash power on a blockchain, he would still need the digital signature of the address owner to transfer funds to himself. Therefore, his ability to hack the blockchain would still be limited even if such a scenario happened.

The only thing a hacker could manage to do is to reverse a transaction he made. For example, he could spend the coins for a tangible or digital good and mine blocks that exclude this transaction afterward. According to the blockchain's records, he would still have the funds and be able to spend them again. However, before many such transactions would happen, it would become evident that the corresponding blockchain lost integrity. As a result, other users would likely hard-fork it from before the attack.

In summary, though it is often mentioned in the community and theoretical settings, a 51% attack would be virtually harmless, and its likelihood is nearly non-existent.

Quantum Computing

Another risk that is often mentioned for cryptoassets but that is actually not substantial is the threat coming from the emergence of quantum computing.

Over the past 70 years or so, computing power has increased exponentially while computers shrunk in size at the same time. This process is driven by the continuous reduction of transistors' dimensions in a computer chip. Transistors are simply gates enabling a bit to change from 0 to 1 or inversely. However, we are now approaching the physical limits of this reduction process, as the size of transistors (ca. 5 nm) is nearing the size of a few atoms. In comparison, a red blood cell is about 1000 times larger than today's typical transistor.

Due to the nanoscopic size of transistors, particles could move through a blocked gate via quantum tunneling. Specifically, as the probability waves associated with the particles can extend beyond the barrier, there is a non-zero probability that the particle will be found on the other side. A theoretically blocked gate (a bit set on 0) would not be effectively blocked (it would act like a 1). Unfortunately, this possibility limits the power of traditional computers. To circumvent this issue, scientists are working on engineering quantum computers.

In quantum computing, instead of having the smallest bit of information taking a value of either 0 or 1, values can range anywhere between these two extremes. A quantum bit is in a state of either 0 or 1, with a certain probability changing over time. When measured, however, the quantum bit subsides to either 0 or 1, as in traditional computers. One consequence of quantum computers is that fewer bits are required to produce a similar output, enabling computing to be exponentially more efficient than with traditional computers.

Especially for large sets of information, quantum computing requires much less computing power and time to reach a similar output. For example, Google claims that its Sycamore processor (its attempt at building a quantum computer) takes about 200 seconds to perform a specific task that would require about 10,000 years for a classical supercomputer [45]. One crucial area of application of this property is IT security. By extension, quantum computers challenge traditional cryptographic security in most cryptoassets.

In particular, while it is currently impractical, or rather next to impossible, to guess a private key based on a public address, quantum computers could make it possible, at least in theory. A quantum computer could use the brute force method to guess many possible private keys until breaking the one that enables to move cryptoassets on a blockchain.

Nevertheless, it would still not be straightforward. For the Bitcoin network, for example, getting the private key from the public address is especially difficult because it uses multiple cryptographic algorithms. As a reminder, the public address is a function of the public key, and the public key is a function of the private key. Figure 11-1 illustrates this. In particular, an Elliptic Curve Digital Signature Algorithm (ECDSA) defines a public key from any private key on the Bitcoin network. Next, the two hashing algorithms, SHA-256 and RIPEMD160, define a public address from a public key. ECDSA is likely the first algorithm that quantum computers will crack, while the ulterior algorithms require more advancements. Quantum computers might be able to break the system by identifying a private key from a public key because the only cryptographic algorithm necessary to break is ECDSA.

However, it is easily possible to protect oneself against the risk of quantum computers reverse-engineering the ECDSA for a specific public key. The public key is made public when a user digitally signs a transaction. A highly risk-aware user (e.g., the main account of a large crypto exchange or institutional fund) could use one account to transfer all funds to a new address. As the new address would never have published its public key, the corresponding private key would be safe even in the theoretical presence of quantum computers able to break ECDSA.

Another solution to protect against that risk is to use hierarchical deterministic (HD) wallets.[1] HD wallets create a new public-private key pair based on a seed phrase for each transaction. Using HD wallets enables users to have multiple IDs on the same blockchain. As before, even if quantum computers managed to break the algorithm, the user's assets would still be safe.

In addition, this risk will not be relevant any time soon. At best, such a scenario is decades away. Furthermore, even if quantum computers ever become feasible, they will not become broadly available at once. Instead, there will be a transition period. During this period, cryptoasset communities would undoubtedly work to change the cryptographic algorithms to become quantum resistant. Quantum resistance is, for example, already identified as one step in the existing development roadmap of Ethereum. Therefore, this entire risk would be made irrelevant as quantum computers could not break the new cryptographic algorithms.

Nevertheless, a smaller related risk remains for the network. By changing the cryptographic algorithm to a quantum-resistant one, all active wallets update to a new standard, implying a different method to sign transactions and possibly different key pairs. Any active users download the new code and continue business unbothered, now safe from quantum risk. However, all wallets with lost private keys do not update to the new algorithm. Therefore, if quantum computers break the cryptographic algorithms protecting private keys, non-updated wallets could be hacked. The consequence is that lost coins would suddenly become retrievable. Nevertheless, the consequences are not drastic: they only imply that the effective supply of the cryptoasset would increase by the amount of the retrieved coins. No active wallet would be compromised.

In conclusion, risks coming from the emergence of quantum computers are unlikely, far in the future, and can easily be mitigated.

---

[1] Many modern wallet providers offer the HD feature by default, regardless of whether they are for hot or cold wallets. For example, Ledger, Trezor, KeepKey, Mycelium, and Electrum all offer HD features for their wallet.

Governmental Risk

One criticism regularly expressed toward cryptoassets is that governments would never let an alternative to their currency become too big. Indeed, an established, global, and independent currency such as Bitcoin would remove governments' monopoly on money. Their control of money flows would fade away, and so would their ability to ban specific transactions from happening. It would be the end of governments' monetary hegemony.

Even worse for governments, citizens could realize that Bitcoin, for example, offers a superior case for money (explained in Chapter 1), as it is a provably scarce asset that will ultimately enable them to maintain purchasing power over time. They would notice that many of the desirable characteristics of money are missing from fiat currencies. Once this becomes obvious to many, citizens will shift their savings from the local fiat currency toward Bitcoin, and the value of the local fiat currency will drop as a result. Governments would likely want to avoid such a scenario and do everything they can to prevent it. For example, they could ban transacting in Bitcoin or even ban Bitcoin ownership.

Such a ban, however, is unrealistic for at least three reasons. First, it ignores the incentives that it would create. Banning Bitcoin would strengthen Bitcoin's value proposition. A Bitcoin ban would make the abusive governmental monopoly on money even more evident. More than ever, it would spotlight the need for people to look for an alternative to government-issued currencies.

Second, such a ban is not applicable in practice. From a technological standpoint, Bitcoin is straightforward: it is a network broadcasting a small amount of data (typically 1 MB to 2 MB) every ten minutes to the rest of the network. As long as two computers are connected, the Internet survives, and the propagation of the Bitcoin blockchain can continue. It is difficult to imagine governments able to apply such a ban in practice when seeing how ineffective they have been at enforcing another ban: the war on drugs. Drugs going from production to end customers involve highly complex processes, much more complicated than Bitcoin mining. They start with significant upfront investments, specialized farming, a complex international supply chain, and even some marketing to create awareness of availability to end customers. Hindering any step of the process from happening would reduce the availability of drugs. Nevertheless, anybody can easily obtain drugs in any major city in the world. As governments have never been able to prevent drugs from reaching customers anywhere, it is delusional to imagine they would have any success in preventing Bitcoin from spreading.

Major real-world Bitcoin ban cases have already happened in China. As early as December 2013, the Chinese central bank and several Chinese financial regulatory institutions jointly issued a statement preventing local commercial banks from handling Bitcoin-related transactions. After little success with this prohibition, further bans occurred in the country: ICOs in 2017 and Bitcoin mining in 2019. The Chinese government strengthened its stance on these bans in 2020 and reiterated it more firmly in 2021. This last reiteration occurred while two-thirds of worldwide Bitcoin mining power came from China.

In addition, China made all cryptoasset transactions illegal, and all jobs for international crypto exchanges were subject to prosecution. As a result of this latest ban, Bitcoin mining in China halted for a few months, bringing the worldwide hash rate down 50%. With a lower hash rate, mining Bitcoin suddenly became much more profitable for remaining miners. As a result, many Chinese miners relocated to other countries, and many more miners joined the race elsewhere. Bitcoin's hash rate was back to a new all-time high only a few months later. One year after the 2021 ban in China, the country was back to the number 2 spot worldwide for hash power generation, accounting for about 20% of the global hash rate. In other words, despite its best efforts, the Chinese authorities did not manage to prevent Chinese citizens and corporations from mining and holding Bitcoin. This example testifies that a Bitcoin ban is not applicable in practice.

Governmental risk is, therefore, not likely to kill Bitcoin or cryptoassets. At best, it will delay adoption but not stop it. Satoshi Nakamoto was already discussing this issue on the original forum of the Cryptography Mailing List before Bitcoin was even launched. In the first week of the Bitcoin white paper's publication, he argues against this risk based on peer-to-peer logic [20, p. 44].

> *Governments are good at cutting off the heads of a centrally controlled network like Napster, but pure P2P networks like Gnutella and Tor seem to be holding their own.*

Finally, it is also not in the interest of governments to ban Bitcoin because doing so would be a national strategic security mistake. In his MIT thesis "Softwar" (2023), US Air Force Major Jason Lowery provides a lucid account of the vital national strategic interest in stockpiling Bitcoin reserves and encourages Bitcoin adoption [46]. In the same way the military preserves freedom through armies, naval, air, and space forces, it is essential for governments to gather sufficient power in cyberspace to prevent potential enemies from inflicting physical costs or imposing any sort of limitations. Bitcoin has become the most secure way (by far) to store and exchange digital information. Through its globally leading open source PoW protocol, it imposes exceptionally high costs (via the necessary use of electricity) to any attacker willing to tamper with this information.

It does so without resorting to nuclear threats accompanied by mutually assured destruction. Maintaining the ability to own and control valuable digital information should be at the forefront of the agenda of governments willing to maintain the freedom of people within their jurisdiction. In this sense, Bitcoin extends beyond its original monetary role and encompasses the function of national security tool to maintain the freedom to use and integrity of valuable digital information for individuals, corporations, and institutions.

Therefore, as for the 51%-attack and quantum computing risks, the risk of governments banning cryptoassets is often mentioned in media and online communities but, upon further analysis, inconsequential.

Developer Risk

In contrast, some risks are rarely discussed in cryptoasset communities but are the weakest links. For example, developer risk could be both very harmful and conceivably likely.

The protocol's code of a blockchain is typically not fixed. For all major blockchains, developers maintain and upgrade the code to improve the blockchain. While this continuous improvement addresses existing weaknesses, it also represents a significant risk. Should a new upgrade contain bugs, it could be exploited by malicious third parties or even the developers themselves at the expense of all ecosystem members.

Assessing a cryptoasset, therefore, requires understanding how the development and upgrading of the code take place. For example, best practices suggest using a testnet, where beta versions of upgrades run before their implementation on the blockchain's mainnet. They also suggest having transparent easy-to-understand code (for example, precisely and extensively commented) reviewed by many independent developers and security experts. Such transparency and reviews minimize the likelihood of a bug and back-doors purposefully implemented in the code. Using standard, well-known, and open source cryptographic libraries also limits these risks.

A bug in a critical area of the code, say in the encryption mechanism, could mean the end of the cryptoasset. If the bug can be exploited, the encryption could be cracked, and a hacker could, for example, obtain a private key from a public key. The hacker would gain access to all corresponding funds, and the blockchain would lose its integrity. Admittedly, upon identification of the bug, the community could agree to a hard fork from before the attack, correct the weakness, and continue operating. Nevertheless, some users could have lost funds in the process, and the asset's reputation would be forever stained by its past failure.

Also, the diligent investor should identify how the blockchain development of a specific cryptoasset is financed. Where financing is weak, developers are more subject to pressure from external stakeholders (bribes or blackmail). As a consequence, the risk of the underlying cryptoasset increases. One possible step to mitigate this risk is to ensure that the development team comprises trustworthy individuals with a strong track record of ethical behavior. Another step is implementing robust internal controls to prevent and detect potential bribery or blackmail attempts. It could include regular audits and reviews of the team's activities and policies and procedures for reporting and addressing any potential issues. Overall, while it is not possible to completely eliminate the risk of developers being subject to bribery or blackmail, taking these steps can help to reduce the likelihood of these threats and protect the integrity of the cryptoasset.

Risk of Community Disagreement

Another often ignored risk is a possible disagreement within a community, splitting support for a cryptoasset. One particularly meaningful historical conflict best illustrates this risk.

From mid-2015 to the end of 2017, fierce debates took place around the size of Bitcoin's blocks on the blockchain. Two opposing camps, the "small blockers" and the "large blockers," argued whether the Bitcoin protocol should increase its 1 MB blocksize limit. Small blockers were in favor of keeping the status quo. Their justification revolved around the possible slippery slope that a fundamental change in Bitcoin's protocol would create. If an important feature like the block size were changeable without overwhelming consensus from the community, then nothing in Bitcoin would be permanent. For example, the hard cap at 21 million bitcoins could also change.

On the other hand, large blockers wanted to address the Bitcoin scalability problem immediately. While many agreed it could have damaging consequences in the longer term, large blockers argued that short-term benefits justified this risk. For instance, increasing Bitcoin's block size would enable more transactions to be included per block, thereby keeping fees low. More transactions per block would, in turn, enable billions of unbanked people to access essential banking services (via Bitcoin) without requiring further technological developments.

While it may sound like ancient history today, this conflict has been extraordinarily intense and particularly meaningful for the industry. Jonathan Bier reports a fascinating account of the hostilities in his book *The Blocksize War* [46]. During this period, Bitcoin as it is known today came exceptionally close to dying. Its main threat was not hostile attackers or governments trying to ban the technology. Instead, it came from well-meaning bitcoiners who disagreed on the vision for this new technology. Respected and leading figures in the crypto space (such as Gavin Andresen and Mike Hearn) became loud advocates for changes in Bitcoin's protocol. They even threatened to apply changes by pressuring miners rather than reaching a broad consensus. Effectively, it would have permanently eroded the decentralized spirit of Bitcoin and its unalterable features. If any private party could materially influence how Bitcoin's protocol evolves without having a broad community agreement, Bitcoin would have lost its main value proposition: decentralization.

While Bitcoin barely survived the repeated attacks on its essence, it became much stronger from this conflict. *The Blocksize War* highlighted that the community had not yet agreed on what Bitcoin meant. Developers and miners were divided, and individual parties had too much influence compared to the network size. Post-2017, the likelihood of such a threat decreased radically. If Bitcoin survived this, it would most likely endure any crypto winter. There is now much more clarity among the community on what Bitcoin stands for. Also, there are now so many more miners on the network that coercing any specific group is highly unlikely ever to gather a majority share of the network. Of course, there will always be healthy arguments for Bitcoin Improvement Proposals (BIPs), but none would threaten Bitcoin's existence like this again.

For other cryptoassets, however, internal disagreements among the community are a risk to consider. The stakeholders are many, each with different goals and incentives—developers, miners, merchants, users, regulators, and more. Any stakeholder who disagrees with how a cryptoasset evolves could try to influence its future, perhaps at investors' expense. Internal risks, possibly more than external risks, should therefore stay on the radar of any diligent investor. One factor that can help mitigate the risk of community disagreement is the governance structure of the cryptoasset. Assets with clear and transparent governance mechanisms, such as voting or decision-making processes, may better manage community disagreement and avoid potential conflicts. Additionally, the level of decentralization of the cryptoasset can also impact the risk of community disagreement. Highly decentralized assets may be more resistant to community disagreement, as no single authority or small group could unilaterally make decisions lacking consensus.

Mining Concentration Risk

If too much mining power is concentrated in the hands of a few miners or mining pools, the concept of decentralization might fade away. As decentralization is a crucial value proposition of cryptoassets, this risk threatens their meaningfulness and fundamental value. In a 2017 Medium article, Vitalik Buterin explained the meaning of decentralization and different types of decentralization [47]. In particular, we refer here to "political (de)centralization" (in his words), which is how few individuals or groups control the computers making up the network.

In the case of Bitcoin, China was posing an existential mining centralization risk until mid-2021. With two third of the miners based in the same country, the possibility of a cartel emerging was growing. It could have, for example, implied most miners pushing for a specific upgrade of the network's code in favor of a specific group of people. Nevertheless, China's Bitcoin ban of 2021 effectively mitigated this risk by discouraging many Chinese miners and indirectly incentivizing miners everywhere else in the world to join the network. Moreover, the Chinese ban in the summer of 2021 also showed the resilience of Bitcoin's security. Even with most miners suddenly dropping out of the network, the impact was only a blip on the graph, and the hash rate quickly recovered to a new all-time high. Bitcoin's mining concentration risk is, therefore, very low.

In contrast, mining concentration risk remains a possible threat for altcoins on a PoW consensus mechanism, especially for those not ASIC-resistant. Specifically, large Bitcoin miners could choose to switch from Bitcoin to altcoin mining and thereby have a significant share of that altcoin's total hash rate.

Ownership Concentration Risk

Not only the concentration of miners is a potential risk, but also the concentration of funds. First, for PoS-based cryptoassets, ownership implies influence on the protocol's output through the likelihood of being selected as a validator. In a standard proof-of-stake (PoS) setting, the more coins one owns, the higher the likelihood of being selected as a validator for the next block. This system could lead to a few people with disproportionate influence over the network. Such a scenario could create network risks, such as the potential for wealthy users to collude and manipulate the outcome of block validation. A single user could also fake identities (known as *sybils*) to gain disproportionate influence over the network, known as a *Sybil attack*. It is therefore questionable whether PoS cryptoassets provide incentives for decentralization. However, variants to the original PoS aim to address this risk. For example, the automatic slashing mechanism is a penalty for users trying to collude or manipulate the network. Such users would have their funds slashed or permanently frozen.

However, all tradable cryptoassets (PoS-based or not) are indirectly exposed to a risk of ownership concentration because wealthy owners could suddenly sell most or all of their possession in the asset. In this case, it is liquidity risk the issue: the inability of the market to absorb such a large sale quickly without having a substantial downward impact on the price. Diligent investors should analyze the concentration of funds for any cryptoasset and the liquidity for the corresponding asset. High concentration and low liquidity are red flags indicating a higher risk of sudden downward drops in price. It is, for example, a high risk for Dogecoin, ZCash, and Ethereum Classic, each of which indicates that less than 100 participants control more than half of the wealth in their corresponding ecosystem (as of 2021) [48].

The Gini coefficient and the Nakamoto index can measure wealth inequality or ownership concentration risk. The Gini coefficient measures how wealth is spread for a population on a ratio from 0 to 1. A Gini coefficient of 0 indicates a perfectly equal distribution among all individuals, while a coefficient of 1 indicates that a single individual owns all the existing wealth. The country of Ireland, for example, has a coefficient of 0.67.[2] In comparison, Ethereum's coefficient is 0.64, and Bitcoin's

---

[2] Ireland is used as example because it is where the cited study has been conducted (i.e., *Characterizing Wealth Inequality in Cryptocurrencies* by Sai, Buckley, and Le Gear (December 2021)).

coefficient (on a consistently decreasing trend since 2010) is below 0.50 as of 2021, which suggests a lower concentration of wealth. Dogecoin, in contrast, has a coefficient above 0.80 and has been on an increasing trend since 2015 [48].

The Nakamoto index measures how many individuals ("addresses" in the case of cryptoassets) are needed to reach 51% of the asset's existing supply. For fiat currencies overall and worldwide, this index is 388, meaning that the wealthiest 388 individuals on the planet have more wealth than the rest of the world's population. As of 2020, this value was 4,652 for Bitcoin, on a trend toward a more equal distribution of wealth over time. These figures suggest that Bitcoin is spread much more equally than traditional fiat currencies. In contrast, Dogecoin is highly concentrated, with only seven addresses owning 44% of all coins and trending toward even more concentration. Ethereum lies between the two, as the top 100 addresses own 35% of all wealth in ethers [48]. Diligent investors should systematically analyze the concentration of wealth in cryptoassets and attribute a higher investment risk to more concentrated assets.

Regulatory Risk

As a recent and quickly-evolving asset class, cryptoassets face high regulatory uncertainty. This uncertainty creates a risk that the environment for cryptoassets may change, which could impact their value or viability. For example, regulation could limit the ability of a cryptoasset to operate as intended. Privacy features or certain types of transactions could become prohibited in some jurisdictions, potentially making some cryptoassets irrelevant in these places. In a more extreme case, regulation could force an exchange to close, implying the possible liquidation of many assets at historically low prices.

As a concrete example, the Digital Commodities Consumer Protection Act (DCCPA) bill has been heavily debated in the last quarter of 2022 in the United States. Had it passed, it would have been a de-facto ban on decentralized finance, essentially killing a nascent and promising industry. The bill would have required compliance and reporting requirements that could technologically neither be met by a decentralized platform nor make sense in this context. For example, it would have required designating a Chief Compliance Officer, a questionable requirement for open source and self-executing smart contracts auditable by anyone in real time. Also, it would have required DEXs to register with the CFTC, thus challenging their permissionlessness. It later became clear that FTX CEO Sam Bankman-Fried had heavily lobbied the bill before the historic collapse of his fraudulent empire, as it would have benefited FTX extensively.

However, all cryptoassets do not face the same type of regulatory uncertainty. For example, while Bitcoin's accounting treatment is generally agreed upon (treated as a commodity or digital property), other cryptoassets face much higher uncertainty (especially their potential status as security). For example, it is still not broadly agreed whether all PoS-based cryptoassets should be considered securities and treated very differently from Bitcoin. In any case, diligent investors should remain constantly informed of regulatory changes and consider their potential impact on investments.

Platform Risk

Many cryptoasset investors hold their crypto funds on either centralized or decentralized platforms. However, history has shown that neither of these alternatives is safe. Famous examples include the collapse of Mt. Gox (centralized) and the DAOsaster (decentralized).

In the early days of crypto, Mt. Gox was the biggest cryptoexchange. This Tokyo-based platform started operating in 2010 and grew to become the chosen intermediary for over 70% of Bitcoin transactions at its peak. However, the rapid rise in the value of Bitcoin put Mt. Gox under increasing focus of hackers. In 2014, a successful hack stole 840,000 bitcoins (worth $460 million at the time and $23 billion as of May 2023) and caused the exchange to file for bankruptcy [49] A few years later, a similar story happened to the decentralized The DAO, as explained in Chapter 6.

Unfortunately, these infamous events are not isolated. Several other security breaches caused investors to lose their cryptoassets in the past. Not only could hacks threaten the stability and reliability of a platform, but they could also affect its reputation. While the frequency of these events is likely related to the low level of maturity of the cryptoasset space, one should still consider platform risk as a reasonably likely and material risk as of 2023.

To mitigate this risk, one should thoroughly research the platforms one uses and diversify among several of them. For example, the diligent investor would review the platform's size (volume of transactions), history of hacks, recurrence of independent audits, and reputation. In addition, one may consider splitting funds over multiple platforms or skipping intermediaries altogether. See Chapter 11 for information on investment vehicles and options available to investors.

Custody Risk

If you have a $100 bill in your pocket, you risk losing it or somebody stealing it from you. With a private key, you run the same two risks. Losing your private key implies that the funds in the corresponding wallet would become permanently inaccessible. No central authority can restore your funds or cancel a transaction on a decentralized network. Therefore, if you decide not to use a centralized exchange or a custodial service to manage keys on your behalf, losing them may be the most likely and the most material risk (complete loss of your investment). To mitigate it, using back-ups or recovery mechanisms is strongly recommended.

In addition, private keys can also be lost through theft. In particular, hackers could try to lure you into providing private keys. While the most attractive targets would typically be large users or exchanges with significant funds, the average investor is not safe from such a risk either. Some hackers operate through the use of malware. They include malicious software like a keylogger retrieving private keys from your computer and sending them to the attacker. Other types of malware act on the clipboard of the victim's computer: when the user copies his wallet address to indicate it on a website, the malware replaces this address with another one. The victim then copies the wrong address, sending funds to the fraudulent public address.

To mitigate this risk, users should have a clean, up-to-date operating system and state-of-the-art antivirus software. In addition, downloads should only ever take place from trusted sources, and regular clean-ups are advised.

Overall, investors should weigh custody risk with platform risk and choose the most appropriate strategy. For example, splitting funds so that not all are subject to the same type of risk may be an advisable strategy for most investors.

Oracle Risk

Hackers can also attack investors indirectly. For example, they can manipulate an oracle's output that flows into a smart contract. This risk is especially relevant in DeFi and prediction markets.

For example, imagine a smart contract including a payment conditional on the result of a sports match (information provided by an oracle), where the attacker could manipulate the data source. The security of the smart contract is directly dependent on the security of the underlying oracle. Even if the oracle is technologically sound, corruption through bribes or blackmail should also be considered.

One way to mitigate this risk is to use multiple data sources in a contract. Alternatively, oracles could be selected based on reputation mechanisms or incentive schemes nudging oracles to provide accurate and reliable data consistently.

DDoS Attacks

Distributed denial of service (DDoS) attacks are cyberattacks that can disrupt the operations of a network by flooding it with traffic to prevent it from functioning correctly. The risk of DDoS attacks is relevant for cryptoassets that rely on partially centralized networks to function, for example, to process transactions.

Cryptoassets with a low risk of DDoS attacks use robust and resilient network infrastructure. They could include, for example, load balancing and traffic filtering to distribute traffic across multiple servers and prevent a single server from being overwhelmed. Effectively decentralized network architectures mitigate this risk as the network's operations are spread on many computers. Their design with multiple redundancies makes it more difficult for attackers to target and overwhelm specific parts of the network. For this reason, low decentralization of nodes processing information flows increases risks for a cryptoasset.

Scams and Market Manipulation

As the cryptoasset industry is still relatively young and known to have provided exceptional returns in the past decade, unscrupulous groups may seek to take advantage of greedy investors through deceptive practices. One traditional type of scam is the Ponzi scheme, where investors are offered high rates of returns but paid with funds from new investors. While such schemes may go undetected during their growth phase, they eventually collapse when a sufficient number of investors withdraw their money and notice insufficient assets back the claims. Countless other scam practices exist, from unsolicited investment offers to fraudulent marketing of non-existent projects.

Market manipulation happens through pump-and-dump schemes, where a wealthy group heavily promotes a specific cryptoasset and possibly even buys much of it to pump the price. Then, as speculators join the exuberance, the price continues to rise until the wealthy group sells all of its holdings, pocketing a significant profit and leaving most other investors with a loss and the pumped token worthless.

Of course, these practices are illegal, but they are present in the cryptoasset industry nonetheless. The fall of the FTX empire in the last months of 2022 illustrates this well. Not only was FTX committing fraud through Ponzi schemes and market manipulation, but also accounting fraud, equity fraud, and multiple other illegal practices. As a result, the empire went from a $32 billion valuation at the beginning of the year to bankruptcy in November, bringing countless other companies down in its wake.

While the collapse of one of the largest cryptoasset exchanges is a hit to the industry's reputation and ruined innumerable investors, there may be a silver lining to this debacle. In the following months, an unprecedented number of centralized-exchange investors embraced the decentralized spirit of cryptoassets and moved their funds toward self-custody. Indeed, the collapse of FTX was not a problem underlying the cryptoasset industry but a problem of centralization; ironically, it is precisely the problem that cryptoassets are solving. In addition, all other exchanges became much more heavily scrutinized, required to provide their proof of reserve, and held to much higher regulatory and transparency standards.

Despite these developments, FTX is undoubtedly not the last scam to hit the finance and cryptoasset industries. Therefore, researching companies, platforms, and protocols is of utmost importance, as well as diversifying funds to spread risks to the extent possible.

Decentralized Insurance

One way to minimize several risks mentioned above is to subscribe to centralized or decentralized insurance. While centralized insurance is not new, the decentralized model provides different incentives to the other side of the trade. Decentralized insurance, or *blockchain-based insurance*, can be smart contracts, where the terms are triggered upon the occurrence of an insured event. Alternatively, a decentralized insurance platform can pool funds via smart contracts, then let users who contributed to the pool vote on claims. Insurances can cover, for example, exchange hacks or exploited weaknesses in a poorly coded smart contract. Decentralized insurance platforms include Etherisc and Nexus Mutual.

Key Concepts

Diligent investors should understand the risks related to cryptoassets. As of 2023, the market typically misidentifies and misunderstands many such risks. For example, a 51%-attack risk or double-spend risk is often mentioned in cryptoasset articles but is actually close to non-existent and harmless. The same applies to the risks implied by the emergence of quantum computers. Similarly, one argument put forward by cryptoasset skeptics is that governments would not allow cryptoassets to eclipse their own fiat currencies; however, it is not in a government's interest to fight cryptoasset head-on, and they likely do not even have the technical capacity to prevent such assets to spread. This risk is, therefore, also not as crucial as some literature may suggest. Other risks, in contrast, are not much discussed but are far more likely and could cause much more harm to investors; for example, the risk of a developer's mistake or purposeful sabotaging.

Nevertheless, most risks can be mitigated or even fully insured against. The diligent investor's first step is acknowledging these risks and then managing them appropriately. Where relevant, such risks should also be considered while valuing cryptoassets.

Extension Questions

Which risks are you facing for your own investments?

What can you do to mitigate these risks?

How can risks be incorporated in cryptoasset valuations?

Are ordinals inscriptions a risk for the functioning of the Bitcoin blockchain?

Can a PoS consensus mechanism genuinely incentivize decentralization?

CHAPTER 14

Financial Risk Management

Risk is a function of how poorly a strategy will perform if the "wrong" scenario occurs.

—Michael Porter

Similar to non-financial risk, financial risk is higher for cryptoassets than traditional investments. For example, as introduced in Chapter 4, the most traditional measure of financial risk is volatility, expressed as the standard deviation of returns. Downward volatility is another helpful metric used as an input to compute the Sortino ratio, which was introduced in the same chapter. Both metrics indicate risk levels much higher for cryptoassets than stocks, for instance. These increased risks are only acceptable for investors because the level of expected return is correspondingly higher for cryptoassets. In any case, other metrics are necessary to fully understand the risk profile of cryptoassets; where possible, forward-looking metrics are especially beneficial.

Responsible investors should understand not only an investment's risk profile but also their personal situation. Indeed, the perceived risk of an investment depends critically on the investor's circumstances. For example, a young investor with a long-term horizon will not perceive risk the same way as a seasoned investor with a time horizon of only a few years or months. Also, an investor with a stable income and promising career opportunities will not give the same importance to financial risk as an investor whose living standards depend on capital gains. This chapter defines multiple types of financial risks (e.g., credit, liquidity, and market risks), then introduces some metrics to assess them and approaches to mitigate them (e.g., value at risk, shortfall risk, expected shortfall, stress testing). Admittedly, this chapter is aimed toward more

T. Jeegers, *Understanding Crypto Fundamentals*, https://doi.org/10.1007/978-1-4842-9309-6_14

finance-affine readers, such as institutional investors considering large investments in cryptoassets. Still, it gives all readers a base to understand how financial risks can be measured for cryptoassets.

Credit Risk

Credit risk refers to the risk that a counterparty cannot meet its debt or contractual obligations. An extreme scenario refers to a counterparty not making the required debt payment altogether (known as *jump-to-default risk*). However, credit risk also includes the possibility that the counterparty's debt has to be restructured in a way that is unfavorable to stakeholders.

One of the points of decentralization behind cryptoassets is to circumvent this risk altogether by not having any counterparty to deal with. However, credit risk is still relevant for users of centralized platforms, as the platform is the counterparty that could get into trouble. It is also relevant in some cases of decentralized finance, where payments rely on a counterparty's creditworthiness. It would be impossible to make a complete list of all possible cases involving credit risk. Nevertheless, diligent investors should understand the nature of any deal they enter and whether future cash flows depend on any counterparty's ability to service their debt obligations.

Liquidity Risk

Liquidity risk refers to the possibility that an investor may not be able to buy or sell an asset when needed due to a lack of market liquidity. As a reminder, liquidity is the capacity of the market to absorb large purchases or sales without affecting the price of an asset. Cryptoassets are particularly susceptible to liquidity risk due to their comparatively small trading volume and low levels of institutional participation. While this risk is irrelevant for small investors focusing on the largest cryptoassets, it becomes relevant for adventurous investors considering assets with a small market capitalization and for large investors. For example, individual investors trading a couple of bitcoins or ethers will not impact these assets' market prices. However, large investment funds considering sizable investments (e.g., tens of thousands of bitcoins) or investors considering cryptoassets with a small market capitalization should be mindful that liquidity may be insufficient to maintain the market price intact.

One solution to address this issue is to split a significant transaction into many smaller transactions spread over time to give the market the ability to absorb it. This is, for example, the strategy used by the company MicroStrategy when it made large Bitcoin purchases in the past.

Market Risk

In the context of portfolio management, market risk refers to changes in portfolio value implied by changes in market metrics such as interest rates and other economic indicators. Specifically, it refers to the systematic risk that cannot be eliminated through diversification by opposition to the unsystematic risk (or idiosyncratic risk) that is asset-specific or firm-specific, and that can be diversified away. The following sections introduce several metrics to measure this risk. Limiting exposure to market risk is possible through different forms of hedging. However, most hedging strategies come at a cost; therefore, reducing risk is not usually free for investors.

Value at Risk (VaR)

People non-versed in traditional finance often intuitively understand risk as "the probability of losing one's money."[1] This concept is represented formally by the *value at risk* (VaR) metric, which JPMorgan introduced in the 1990s. It subsequently became widely used by the industry and became a standard for senior management to understand the full risk of any investment. In particular, the VaR aims to measure the expected loss on an investment at a particular level of likelihood and over a specific period. So, for example, it would answer the question, "How much would I lose on my investment over one year if the worst 5% of scenarios happened?". In other words, it enables investors to establish that they are P percent certain that they will not lose more than D dollars over a time period T.

There are three methods to compute VaR: analytical, historical, and Monte Carlo.

---

[1] Contrary to finance professionals, who traditionally define it as the standard deviation of returns, by industry standard.

Analytical VaR

The analytical method uses statistics to compute a theoretical value. It first establishes the portfolio's expected return and standard deviation[2] over the considered time horizon. Then, assuming a specific probability distribution, it identifies the factor to use at a specific level of significance (e.g., "worst 5%"), as shown in Figure 14-1.

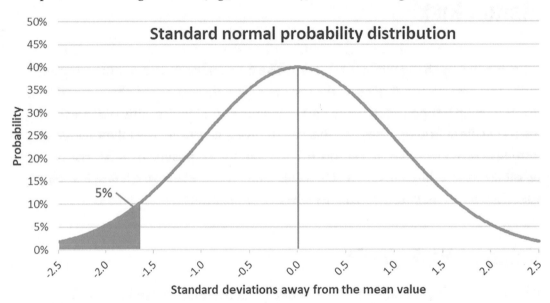

Figure 14-1. *Backward-looking worst 5% of events with a standard normal probability distribution (i.e., events with a value below 1.645 standard deviations below the mean)*

To illustrate this, assume that a cryptoasset portfolio worth $100,000 has an expected return of +50% over a four-year horizon, with a standard deviation of 40%, and that returns follow a standard normal probability distribution. The investor would like to know the expected loss at the 5th percentile (i.e., the worst 5% scenario). Algebraically, it looks as follows: where $\widehat{R}_p$ is the expected return of the portfolio, z is the number of standard deviations away from the mean value for a specific probability distribution and at a specific likelihood (it can be obtained via distribution tables), σ is the standard deviation, and V_p is the value of the portfolio.

---

[2] Advanced analysts should consider diversification benefits via a variance-covariance or delta-normal method.

$$VaR = \left[\widehat{R_p} - (z)(\sigma) \right] V_p = \left[0.50 - 1.65(0.40) \right]($100{,}000) = -$16{,}000$$

Given these assumptions, the expected loss at this probability level is –$16,000. In other words, the investment will do better than "lose $16,000" (i.e., either lose less or gain) over a four-year horizon with a 95% probability.

Of course, the output ultimately depends on the quality of the assumptions. For example, one could challenge whether a standard normal distribution is the most appropriate probability distribution in the case of portfolio returns, especially for cryptoassets. Realistically, a probability distribution assuming fatter tails (a higher likelihood of extreme outcomes) would be more appropriate for financial returns.[3] Also, estimating the standard deviation of returns of a maturing financial asset is challenging because this standard deviation is likely not to be constant. Instead, it could decrease as the market evolves or be dependent on other criteria, such as the state of the overall market.[4]

Finally, given the presence of crypto cycles described in Chapter 9, taking a horizon shorter than four years is unlikely to be meaningful since cryptoasset returns in a bull market (uptrend) are very different from returns in a bear market (downtrend). All in all, the analytical VaR approach depends on many assumptions.

Historical VaR

Instead of using theoretical values, one could reduce the number of assumptions in the computation and use historical values. It is precisely what the historical VaR does.

Specifically, one could, for example, gather the last 200 weekly returns for Bitcoin and identify that in 90% of the cases (180 observations), the return for that asset is better than –10.1%.[5] Given the data sample gathered, the weekly historical VaR would suggest an expected loss of that value at the 90% probability level.

A yearly (instead of weekly) historical VaR is less reliable for cryptoassets because of the much lower number of observations available and given the pace of development of the assets (Bitcoin 10 years ago had a materially different risk-return profile than five

---

[3] In statistical jargon, the distribution should have excess kurtosis.

[4] In statistical jargon, when returns have non-constant volatility, they are said to be (conditionally) heteroskedastic.

[5] Taking the last 200 weeks ending on December 31, 2022.

years ago, which was again very different from today). Nevertheless, a similar analysis is also possible. For example, Bitcoin's yearly historical VaR yields a value of +60% at the 50th percentile. In other words, half of the last ten observations for Bitcoin indicate a yearly gain of at least 60%.

An approach to address the outdatedness of data is to give a weight to each historical data point, where older observations have a lower weight and more recent observations have a higher weight. Richardson et al. suggested this approach in 1997 to consider more heavily the current macroeconomic conditions and volatilities while at the same time not ignoring older data completely.[6] Given the high pace of development of the cryptoasset industry, a similar approach is recommended. One possible way of applying this method is by having weights decline exponentially with recency.

Monte Carlo VaR

The Monte Carlo method[7] is a statistical approach to model the probability of a specific outcome in a process that considers many variables. A computer runs thousands of simulations for input variables (e.g., inflation, interest rates, GDP growth, cryptoasset adoption growth, and other market conditions). Since these variables impact one another, their combined effect is much less straightforward to understand than analyzing them independently. The many simulations output a specific portfolio value at a certain likelihood (e.g., 10th percentile).

Monte Carlo simulations are a valuable tool for risk management because they allow investors to understand the potential impact of many scenarios where variables interact in a complex way.

Characteristics of VaR Metrics

On the one hand, VaR metrics are helpful because they can compare likes-for-likes regardless of the asset class under consideration. On the other hand, they are also limited because they do not consider extreme cases. For example, a VaR of –10% at the 5th percentile does not reveal whether the last five percent of cases would yield

---

[6] Richardson, Boudoukh, and Whitelaw, *The Best of Both Worlds: A Hybrid Approach to Calculating Value at Risk* (November 1997) [80].

[7] Its name comes from the city of Monte Carlo in Monaco, which is known for its famous casinos and the many probability-based games of chance played there.

returns between –10% and –15% or would yield returns close to –100%. In other words, these metrics do not consider extreme moves (or *black-swan events*), which are not uncommon in the cryptoasset industry.

Another limitation of the historical VaR is that it is, by definition, a backward-looking metric, not considering recent developments or likely future developments. The analytical VaR, in contrast, is highly dependent on assumptions. For these reasons, none of these metrics alone can establish an investment's complete financial risk profile. Instead, they should be considered together to give investors a better understanding of the type and level of risk they face.

Regulators extensively use VaR metrics to define the level of risks banks are allowed to take and the level of capital they need to hold to cover that risk.[8] While it is not yet broadly present in the cryptoasset industry, it is reasonable to assume VaR metrics will play a role in future cryptoasset regulation. In particular, cryptoasset funds and centralized exchanges could be subject to VaR measurement and reporting in the future. One can also speculate whether decentralized platforms holding cryptoassets may face similar regulatory requirements in the future.

Roy's Safety-First Criterion

One of the most cited measures of downside risk is Roy's safety-first criterion, proposed by André Roy in 1952 as a metric to optimize portfolio selection under risk constraints. Fundamentally, it is an optimization problem aiming to maximize the expected return of a portfolio under the constraint that the probability of a loss of a certain amount is not superior to a specific value.

For example, it would maximize a portfolio's expected return under the constraint that the expected loss is not bigger than –5% at a 95% probability. Alternatively, it could target at least a return of +1% at a 90% probability. Roy's safety-first ratio is computed as follows.

$$Safety\ First\ Ratio = \frac{expected\ return - minimum\ return}{standard\ deviation\ of\ return}$$

[8] See, for example, the multiple Basel regulations.

In this equation, "minimum return" is the minimum acceptable return by the investor. It is very similar to the Sharpe ratio introduced in Chapter 4. The only difference is that the minimum acceptable level of return for the investor replaces the risk-free rate of return from the Sharpe ratio. Investors worried about cryptoasset volatility can consider using a similar approach to define the share of their total portfolio to allocate to cryptoassets. Since adding cryptoassets to a traditional portfolio will likely increase expected return and (after all diversification benefits are factored in) increase the standard deviation of return of the total portfolio, optimizing for this equation could provide an "optimal" allocation in cryptoassets (e.g., 10%) given the investor's arbitrary constraints.

Shortfall Risk

Roy's safety-first criterion approach draws parallels to a target of minimizing shortfall risk (i.e., the risk that a portfolio does not meet a target return over a specific period). It is especially relevant for portfolios with long-term investment horizons or for portfolios necessary to maintain a specific lifestyle, such as retirement portfolios. However, given the "higher risk, higher return" characteristics of cryptoasset investments, minimizing shortfall risk suggests a lower allocation to cryptoassets than Roy's safety-first criterion because minimizing shortfall risk ignores the benefits of having a return possibly much higher than the target.

Expected Shortfall

The next shortfall risk measure is assessing how bad things get if the wrong scenario occurs. It is referred to as *expected shortfall* (or *conditional value at risk, conditional tail expectation,* or *expected tail loss*) and addresses one limitation of traditional VaR metrics. While VaR metrics do not consider how bad things are beyond a certain probability level, expected shortfall measures precisely this scenario. It is the expected loss on a portfolio over a specific time horizon if the portfolio ends beyond a specific percentile of the probability distribution (e.g., worst 10% of scenarios).[9]

---

[9] Interested readers may refer to literature on *extreme value theory*, especially Gnedenko (1943) [81].

Backtesting

Regardless of the specific metric used, investors should backtest their approach. Backtesting is a reality check to assess the quality of a risk metric. For example, investors could compute what the VaR would have been had it been measured a year ago. Then, they should compare it to how reality played out to assess the robustness of this risk metric.

For instance, they could analyze how often a cryptoasset's weekly returns in the past year were lower than the 90% weekly VaR that would have been measured a year ago. The VaR metric seems to hold well if returns were only about 10% of the time beyond this range. However, if many more observations fall beyond the threshold, the backtest indicates that the risk metric may not have been conservative enough.

For example, the 90% weekly Bitcoin VaR measured with 200 weeks of data ending on 31 December 2021 is –11.0%. In 2022, only six weeks yielded a return below this threshold. Therefore, six weeks out of 52 in the year (11.5% of the weeks) were beyond the 10th percentile as computed with this VaR approach. Since 11.5% is reasonably close to 10%, this VaR approach and this sample seem to be appropriate. A similar approach for Ethereum also yields six observations in 2022 and, therefore, a similar conclusion. However, unprecedented events are ignored in this analysis. This is where stress testing is a useful complement for managing possible future risks.

Stress Testing

A meaningful approach to challenge traditional risk metrics consists of running imaginary scenarios, a method called *stress testing*. Typically, the scenarios considered are bleak but plausible to assess how poorly an investment would perform under adverse circumstances. If, even under pessimistic conditions, a scenario plays out acceptably, the stress test is passed. Alternatively, one can find out how bad conditions must be for a scenario to become detrimental (an approach called *factor-push analysis*). Stress testing complements previously covered risk management approaches by including scenarios that have not happened before or that are not easily implementable in the assumptions of statistical approaches.

In particular, scenarios including the non-financial risks covered in the previous chapter could be valid examples to be included in a stress test. Alternatively, one could consider scenarios with extreme lack of liquidity or major bankruptcies with contagion across the industry. Of course, stress tests depend on the assumptions used for each scenario and are unlikely to play out precisely as predicted. Nevertheless, they are helpful because they challenge statistical risk metrics and force the analyst to consider the consequences of wildly different scenarios on a portfolio's value.

Key Concepts

Similar to non-financial risks, financial risks are also bigger for cryptoassets than traditional investments. In particular, investors should consider possible defaults of third parties in the cryptoasset ecosystem and, where possible, avoid them through decentralization. Besides, liquidity can also be an issue as cryptoassets have a lower volume exchanged daily than traditional asset classes; large trades can therefore have a material impact on prices. Nevertheless, market risk is given the most attention in the cryptoasset universe because of the rapid price swings it is known for.

The value at risk concept is especially useful as it provides a single standard metric for the expected loss at a given level of likelihood. There are multiple ways to compute it: either by relying on assumptions (analytical method) or past data (historical method). Each has advantages and limitations; investors should therefore rely on a range of metrics rather than any single one.

Regardless, risk metrics should be backtested and complemented with stress tests to challenge their impact and likelihood in this rapidly evolving environment.

Extension Questions

Which past data are relevant to infer the current risk on the market?

How far back can you go to rely on data?

Which stress tests would be especially meaningful for cryptoasset investments?

PART VI

Which Valuation Methods Exist?

CHAPTER 15

Assessment Framework

Success in investing comes not from being right but from being wrong less often than everyone else.

—Aswath Damodaran

Before measuring the value of a cryptoasset, the diligent investor should ask critical questions to identify whether the asset has value in the first place. While the next chapter dives into valuation methods, this chapter covers preliminary questions to filter out candidates for these valuations.

What Problem Is the Asset Solving?

A cryptoasset must address a real, unmet need in the market.

For example, Bitcoin was the first digitally scarce asset that could be exchanged without intermediaries. It addresses the need for a decentralized and secure transfer of value online. Similarly, Ethereum was the first decentralized platform that allows developers to build and deploy smart contracts and dApps. It addresses the need for a secure and transparent way to automate business processes and interactions without a central authority. Likewise, 0x is a decentralized exchange protocol that allows users to trade tokens and other assets securely and transparently. It addresses the need for a decentralized alternative to traditional exchanges, often subject to security breaches. Furthermore, several other cryptoassets uniquely deliver a valuable service that addresses a genuine and unmet need.

In contrast, some projects are copies of existing ones without significant innovation or improvement. For example, Litecoin and Bitcoin Cash are hard forks of Bitcoin without many innovative features but different block times, block sizes, and maximum supply.

© Thomas Jeegers 2023
T. Jeegers, *Understanding Crypto Fundamentals*, https://doi.org/10.1007/978-1-4842-9309-6_15

Besides, other cryptoassets are created for the sole purpose of generating hype (or even as Ponzi schemes) without any real service behind them. Such projects should be filtered out from any fundamental valuation method. Their market price may increase in the short run, but such development would be driven by speculation rather than actual economic value. Dogecoin is, for example, a cryptoasset based chiefly on its potential for creating hype. While it was initially created as a joke and did not offer any unique features, it gained much popularity on social media. It even grew to a market capitalization of over $88 billion in May 2021.

How Important Is the Problem?

It is essential to consider the potential value of solving the problem. A cryptoasset addressing a critical and pressing problem in a large and growing market has a higher potential than a cryptoasset addressing a minor or niche problem in a shrinking market. Metrics that analysts could investigate to assess the problem's importance include the number of people suffering from the problem, how much they would be willing to pay to solve this problem, and for how many years this problem will likely remain relevant.

For example, major and lasting problems affecting many users include high transaction fees and slow transaction times in the international payment industry, data security against breaches and leaks, and censorship of freedom of speech. Some cryptoassets can help mitigate or even solve such problems.

How Is the Asset Solving the Problem?

Analysts should also evaluate the quality of the solution proposed to the problem. They can do so, for example, by exploring the following characteristics of the proposed solution.

First, they should consider its effectiveness. In particular, whether the project can deliver the desired result. It includes, for example, case studies of how the solution is used in the real world.

Second, analysts should consider the efficiency of the solution. For example, solving the problem of high transaction fees should not come at the expense of settlement time.

Third, the solution should be scalable. Even if niche use cases are successful, the solution should be able to meet the needs of a growing user base without materially losing out on efficiency.

Analyzing how the asset is planning to solve a problem in the future should also include a clear roadmap by the developing team and how they execute this roadmap.

Which Candidate Best Solves the Problem in this Market?

Depending on its size and complexity, it may be optimal for a market to have only a few prominent actors (a natural oligopoly) or even a single actor (natural monopoly). For example, large upfront investment costs may make the case for a market to become a natural monopoly. For example, the water and sewage services market is typically a monopoly because pipelines and treatment plants imply high fixed costs while marginal costs are low. The same goes for electricity and telecommunications companies, where only one or a few actors typically operate in a market.

Furthermore, network effects may also limit the number of actors in a market. For example, the number of successful ride-hailing companies active in any particular market is typically not more than a few because each company needs to reach a critical mass of drivers and riders to succeed.

Similarly, in the cryptoasset industry, some markets will likely only have a few successful competitors unless they materially differ. Specifically, there is likely no need for hundreds of smart contract platforms, for example. Instead, successful platforms must gather enough developers and enough users to be convenient for each group. In most cases, developers only learn to code in the platform's programming language if there are enough users, and users only join an ecosystem if enough apps are available.

For these reasons, analysts should identify what competitive advantage each cryptoasset offers against its competitors. For example, the largest proof-of-work cryptoasset benefits from a natural competitive advantage through an effective barrier to entry: the hash rate. While any new cryptoasset could try to compete with Bitcoin, it is unlikely to be able to do so. Indeed, the security of a PoW cryptoasset depends on the ability of the network to repel a 51% attack. Such an attack is only possible if a nefarious actor gathers most of the hash rate for that cryptoasset. Since Bitcoin gathered a hash rate over 100 times higher than all other PoW cryptoassets combined, some individual Bitcoin miners represent a risk for any new PoW cryptoasset.[1] If a new PoW cryptoasset

---

[1] To mitigate this risk, new PoW cryptoassets should be made ASIC-resistant. Bitcoin's ASIC miners would thereby lose their edge over traditional GPUs, making the assets more resilient.

grew to become financially attractive, a prominent Bitcoin miner could redirect its hashing power toward mining this new asset and potentially attack it with more than 51% of the hash rate. While it is likely not in the attacker's interest (Chapter 13 discussed how well-designed incentives can mitigate this risk), it is theoretically possible. For this reason, the security of any PoW cryptoasset that is not Bitcoin is low. Proof-of-work is a winner-takes-all consensus mechanism—a competition that Bitcoin has clearly won.

Assessing whether a cryptoasset project is the best candidate to address a problem implies understanding the dynamics of the market at hand and the characteristics of its competitors. Subsequently, the analyst should identify the candidate's unique advantage over its peers, given this market structure.

How Reliable Is the Team Behind the Asset?

Given the presence of potential scams, investors want to keep a close eye on the development team of the crypto project.

First, investors should ensure that the team has good credentials. For example, after having laid the base of Ethereum, its co-founders split because they could not agree on the future path the platform should take. Some of them moved on to develop their own smart contract platform as an alternative to Ethereum. For instance, Charles Hoskinson founded Cardano, and Gavin Wood created Polkadot. The presence of leading figures in the developing team with credentials as co-founders of Ethereum was seen as a token of credibility. Investors must ensure that developing teams of other cryptoasset projects are similarly capable, trustworthy, and reliable.

Second, investors should ensure that the incentives of the development team are aligned with those of the asset holders. In particular, ICOs sometimes give inappropriate incentives to founders. For example, founders could receive a large share of the cryptoasset (say, over 20%) as funding for the project's development and not be held accountable for what they do with these funds. In many cases, founders left with the funds or did not do the necessary work to ensure the project reached fruition. Understanding the funding structure, each actor's incentives, and legal limitations is essential.

Finally, diligent investors should be on the lookout for whether the development team is doing what it claims to be doing. For example, the team should meet development deadlines and stay aligned with the roadmap.

How Is the Local Regulatory Environment?

As identified in previous chapters, the regulatory environment is among the material risks faced by cryptoassets. Navigating this regulatory complexity and uncertainty is far from straightforward, and cryptoasset projects must ensure they can deal with it appropriately. Therefore, a cryptoasset project with high potential has gathered a competent legal and regulatory team.

Also, a cryptoasset project may be brilliant, with a strong team and scoring high on virtually all desirable metrics but face additional hurdles due to likely regulatory backlashes. For example, Monero has multiple reasons to claim technological superiority over Bitcoin. For instance, it provides users with a much higher level of privacy by using ring signatures to hide the identity of senders and receivers. It also uses stealth addresses, which are one-time use addresses generated for each transaction, thereby further protecting users' privacy. This way, Monero offers cash-like respect for personal privacy, which Bitcoin lacks.

Furthermore, Monero's ASIC resistance makes it more prone to be decentralized, as there are lower incentives for running large mining farms. Finally, Monero's dynamic block size adjusting based on demand has ground to justify better scalability than Bitcoin. Nevertheless, Monero peaked at a market capitalization of only $8.5 billion in September 2021, when Bitcoin was worth over 100 times more. One reason for this difference is that regulation could fight a privacy-driven cryptoasset in the future because it could open the door to untraceable illicit transactions. Investors should consider how upcoming regulations could impact the future value of specific cryptoassets.

Do the Tokenomics Make Sense?

Tokenomics refer to the economic aspects of a cryptoasset's functioning as implemented in its code. Investors in cryptoassets should consider whether the tokenomics of a particular asset make sense with respect to the need that the asset is addressing.

Tokenomics include, among others, the token distribution schedule (is it distributed fairly between founders, developers, investors, and community?), token governance (how are decisions made?), token supply design (is it infinite like fiat currencies or limited like Bitcoin?), token inflation rate, consensus mechanism, and interoperability

(ability to connect and exchange with other blockchains). In particular, a good token has a transparent and fair distribution of tokens between stakeholders, well-designed incentives aligning their interests, a limited supply, and a low or adaptive inflation rate.

How do Rating Agencies Assess the Cryptoasset?

Rating agencies, such as Fitch, S&P, and Moody's, assess the quality of bonds, stocks, derivative products, and other financial instruments. However, as of this writing, there is no major rating agency for the crypto market, even though this is deemed to change. As the market grows, there will be growing interest in a standardized and trusted rating system. There may even be a decentralized system, something the industry needs because of existing rating agencies' recurrent failures and limitations.

Once such a cryptoasset rating industry exists, analysts should compare their analysis with prevalent companies' ratings of these assets. Blindly adopting any rating is not recommended, but standardized analyses may challenge an analyst's assessment and is a view worth considering. In particular, analysts should understand the assumptions made by the rating agencies on the cryptoasset and assess their relevance in the face of changing market conditions.

Cryptoasset Picking

Upon considering these questions, investors may wonder whether it is worth cherry-picking cryptoassets or simply investing in the largest ones. Another argument supports the latter. In equities, as a rule of thumb, about 50% of performance is due to the overall market performance, 30% due to the sector, and maybe 20% due to individual stocks selected. Whether an investment does well is, therefore, not mainly driven by the stock-picking skills of the portfolio manager but rather by market performance. In cryptoassets, the market performance also dominates, as testified by historically high correlations within the asset class. Until now, it may even have been more the case for cryptoassets than equities. In other words, when the cryptoasset market went up, price increases were seen across most cryptoassets and in similar proportions.

Nevertheless, what makes Bitcoin valuable fundamentally differs from what makes Ethereum valuable, for example. Classifying them in the same industry is misleading because they are inherently different. They are arguably more different than stocks of two companies, say one in shipbuilding and the other in food delivery. They could even be considered as distinct as investing in different asset classes. The same goes for many other tokens. Therefore, while cryptoassets have tended to be highly positively correlated in the past, their correlation is poised to decrease eventually. When the market matures enough to distinguish the characteristics of each cryptoasset, they will likely evolve in their own direction. For this reason, it is meaningful for long-term investors to diversify within this new asset class to optimize their total portfolio's risk-return characteristics.

Besides, picking cryptoassets involves choosing which risk the investor is willing to face and which risk-reward features are most appropriate for that investor. For example, some cryptoassets have a much larger upside potential in percentage terms, typically with a much larger risk. For example, prominent crypto protocols (layer 1 solutions) are considered much safer than their competitors, which are a fraction of their market capitalization. However, they could also have a lower probability of multiplying an investment's value by 100 in the coming few years than smaller crypto projects. Therefore, choosing cryptoassets to invest in depends critically on how much return the investor is seeking and how much risk is acceptable.

Key Concepts

Before even attempting to value a cryptoasset, one must identify whether the asset has value in the first place. For this reason, investors should start by filtering out candidates for valuation. In particular, cryptoassets that can be valued should solve a real and unaddressed problem on the market. The bigger this problem, the more important the solution will be. Candidates for valuation should also have reasonable grounds to be the most appropriate asset to solve the problem, given the market dynamics and the existing competitors. In addition, reliable teams should be behind the development of the asset, with especially strong regulatory and legal teams, to address the industry's regulatory uncertainty. Finally, meaningful tokenomics should be the base for the asset; for example, with effective incentives for all stakeholders.

Extension Questions

Which cryptoasset features are red flags that will likely prevent them from ever having genuine fundamental value?

How can you make sure to identify when a cryptoasset project is a scam?

Which are the top assets for each category identified in the cryptoasset taxonomies presented in Chapter 7?

CHAPTER 16

Value Investing in Cryptoassets

In essence, the stock market represents three separate categories of business. They are, adjusted for inflation, those with shrinking intrinsic value, those with approximately stable intrinsic value, and those with steadily growing intrinsic value. The preference, always, would be to buy a long-term franchise at a substantial discount from growing intrinsic value.

—Michael Burry

As introduced at the beginning of this book, value investing, or *fundamental analysis*, focuses on fundamentals. It identifies and measures the pillars giving real economic value to an asset. Value investors compare the asset's value with the asset's price and invest when the latter is significantly lower than the former. Gains materialize for the investor when the price eventually converges toward the underlying value.

Even in traditional finance, value investors face challenges to value assets of different natures. For example, while the traditional discounted cash flow approach is appropriate for some assets (e.g., high-growth companies with expected future cash flows), it is not for others, in which case ratios of value over earnings may be more suitable. With the arrival of cryptoassets as an investable asset class, value investors face additional, new, different challenges. However, value investing is neither confined to one or several methods nor one or several asset classes. It is rather a principle—an approach. Value investing is about betting on an investment's long-term real economic value.

Still, value investing and cryptoassets are terms traditional investors dislike using in the same sentence. Indeed, the Capital Asset Pricing Model, traditionally used to compute an investment's expected return, does not apply directly to cryptoassets, making any subsequent analysis a more adventurous endeavor.

T. Jeegers, *Understanding Crypto Fundamentals*, https://doi.org/10.1007/978-1-4842-9309-6_16

This book's objective has been to dismantle the apparent dichotomy between the terms cryptoassets and value investing. Not only is value investing in cryptoassets possible, but it is also the critical element welding this new asset class and traditional investments together. It is essential to enable the finance and investment industries to evolve to their next level, harnessing the ground-breaking potential of cryptoassets.

From 2020 to 2023, the size of the crypto market (the cumulated market capitalization of all cryptoassets) oscillated between $0.7 trillion and $3 trillion. To know whether it is more or less than it should be, methods to measure the underlying value of cryptoassets are needed. Unfortunately, traditional financial modeling techniques cannot be used directly to value cryptoassets. At the very least, they need to be adapted to provide a meaningful valuation of a cryptoasset. This chapter reviews and adapts traditional valuation methods and introduces additional methods specific to cryptoassets.

Combining Valuation Methods

Diligent investors do not want to rely on a single valuation method, especially for cryptoassets. Instead, combining several valuation approaches and assigning a weight to each would likely provide a more reasonable valuation. For example, assume method A values a specific asset at $7 at the end of the current year while method B values the same asset at $12. If the investor believes that method A is the more reliable and assigns it an 80% weight, leaving a 20% weight for method B, a reasonable asset's valuation would be $8 ($7 × 80 % + $12 × 20 % = $8).

In addition, using different methods provides a range of possible values, suggesting how differently the asset could evolve. This approach would therefore mitigate the illusion of an accurate valuation that could otherwise lead to incorrect financial decisions. Even well-established assets with consistent cash flows are a challenge to value accurately, regardless of the quality of the model, as they are also subject to uncertain events. For example, a US carmaker's stock price is influenced by commodities price expectations, European car emission regulations, and competition from Japan. This reality is nicely encapsulated in a quote from the twentieth-century British statistician George Box.

All models are wrong, but some are useful.

A more reasonable approach for financial valuations is to consider the expected direction of future prices. The real objective is to be directionally correct rather than accurately wrong. In the case of cryptoassets, a 24-month ahead valuation landing in the correct order of magnitude could be considered accurate enough. Given the uncertainty around the future treatment of cryptoassets, even such a broad range seems challenging to predict. Taking Bitcoin as an example, investor valuations for the end of the year 2024 span over at least three orders of magnitude: below $100,000, between $100,000 and $1 million, and above $1 million. The further in the future the target valuation date, the broader the range.

Being directionally correct rather than accurately wrong.

With this objective in mind, best practice suggests keeping valuation models parsimonious. A simple model is often more helpful than a convoluted one, with more room for errors and unappreciated risks.

Net Present Value of Future Cash Flows

A net present value (NPV) approach or discounted cash flow method measures the current value of future cash inflows and outflows. To understand this, one must first acknowledge the time value of money. For example, receiving $100 today is worth more than receiving $100 next year, even if it is with absolute certainty. Indeed, $100 today could be invested so that it is expected to have more value next year. Therefore, the further in the future a cash flow is, the larger it must be to have the same value as a similar cash flow today. In other words, the present value of future cash flows is discounted.

The NPV approach suggests that the value of an asset is the sum of the present values of its future cash flows. To compute it, an analyst estimates future cash flows and a discount rate. This approach has traditionally been central to fundamental analysis. However, a common argument against using it for cryptoassets is that they do not have future cash flows. First, this argument is technically incorrect because some cryptoassets have future cash flows. For example, any proof-of-stake cryptoasset (such as Ethereum) generates future staking rewards that can be used as cash flow in an NPV analysis.

Nevertheless, the difference with a traditional company generating cash flows in US dollars is that the staked cryptoasset provides staking revenues in the cryptoasset itself. For example, staking Cardano provides revenues in its native currency, ADA. It is a chicken-and-egg problem in which the value of the cryptoasset depends on the future inflow of more of that cryptoasset. The same issue would arise if one tried to assess the value of the US dollar in another currency with an NPV analysis. Therefore, even for cryptoassets with future cash flows, the traditional NPV model is, at best, a valuation tool with limitations.

Valuation Based on Multiples

Another central pillar in fundamental value measurement is the use of *multiples*. In particular, analysts using this method measure distributable cash flows generated by a business and multiply them by a specific number to establish the value of the business. The specific number, or *multiple*, can be estimated based on similar businesses in the same industry. Of course, this valuation method ultimately depends on the appropriateness of measuring cash flows (e.g., net income, free cash flows, or operating earnings) and the multiple used. Specifically, multiple analysis suffers predominantly from the difficulty of finding comparable businesses. Every business has characteristics making it different from any other. For example, a levered company (one that uses leverage—i.e., debt) can hardly be compared to a non-levered one because the underlying risks are vastly different. Therefore, the stability and predictability of future cash flows can be very dissimilar.

For these reasons, even in traditional finance, analysts must arbitrarily adjust their valuations, regardless of whether they use a multiples approach or an NPV one. These adjustments are already controversial for traditional investments and would be even more so for cryptoassets, which are new and unknown to most analysts. In addition, valuations using multiples suffer from the same limitation as NPV analyses for valuing an asset with cash flows expressed in this asset. Multiples are, therefore, also an imperfect tool for valuing cryptoassets.

Asset Value, Earnings Power and Value of Growth

Traditional value investors such as Benjamin Graham and David Dodd accept the aforementioned limitations of NPV analyses and valuations based on multiples for traditional investments. In addition, they list several additional shortcomings of these methods beyond the scope of this book. To address these limitations, however, they offer an alternative approach, consisting in measuring the real net asset value, the earnings power of a business, and the value of growth separately. This is important because the last of these three terms, the value of growth, is highly subject to an analyst's arbitrary estimates and much less tangible than the other two. This approach enables tangible value to be measured independently from the rest [43].

Again, however, even the more tangible parts of the equation—asset value and earnings power—are not directly applicable to cryptoassets. At best, only by adapting these metrics and their underlying fundaments can one reasonably use this approach. The following sections cover these adaptations.

Asset Value Based on Replacement Costs

The first of the terms is *asset value*, typically assessed based on the net book value of the assets on a company's balance sheet. However, a fully digital asset typically lacks traditional book value. In particular, the book value of a proof-of-stake cryptoasset is non-existent, which makes this term irrelevant for such assets. However, the book value of a proof-of-work cryptoasset (in particular Bitcoin, because it is much larger than all other PoW assets combined) could be interpreted as the value of the electricity that was required to mine the asset, which corresponds to *historical costs*.

More reasonably, it could be based on the value of the electricity required to mine the asset at the current electricity price and hash rate (i.e., *replacement costs*). Indeed, Bitcoin's costly production costs are precisely what give it a basis for value.

A traditional supply and demand argument makes a case for the validity of this approach. In the eighteenth century, the father of economics, Adam Smith, described the process of supply and demand as the *invisible hand of the market*. As per this fundamental economic insight, if there are more sellers than buyers of an asset (supply is higher than demand), then the price drops. A lower price attracts more buyers and discourages some sellers, stabilizing prices where supply matches demand.

This insight can be extended to price PoW cryptoassets. Since mining blocks on the blockchain of a proof-of-work cryptoasset requires electricity, the price of the electricity necessary to mine a new block can be used as an indication of demand. Indeed, miners would not spend the electricity necessary to mine the asset if it had less value to them than the price of this electricity.[1]

As in the supply and demand example, the invisible hand of the market pushes the asset price to where it matches the price of the electricity necessary to mine that cryptoasset. Should the electricity price be higher than the expected mining rewards, miners redirect their energy toward another purpose, such as selling energy to the grid. Conversely, should the electricity price be lower than the expected mining rewards, miners upscale their operations, and more miners join the race. As a result, the hash rate adjusts until the equilibrium is restored. The hash rate is a leading indicator of miners' expectations of the future price of a proof-of-work cryptoasset.

Investors pursuing their self-interest do the rest of the job. In particular, the price of a PoW cryptoasset in an efficient market eventually follows costs implied by the electricity price and hash rate, as Satoshi Nakamoto was already suggesting in 2010.[2]

> *The price of any commodity tends to gravitate toward production costs. If the price is below costs, then production slows down. If the price is above cost, profit can be made by generating and selling more. At the same time, the increased production would increase the difficulty, pushing the cost of generating toward the price.*

As of this writing in May 2023, the market price of Bitcoin corresponds exactly to the price implied by the average cost of the electricity used by the latest ASIC miners. Detailed computations are shown in the Appendices.

In traditional value investing, liquid assets on a company's balance sheet (current assets such as cash, marketable securities or inventory) have a more reliable value than illiquid assets (property, equipment or intangibles such as goodwill). Nevertheless, valuations in the Graham and Dodd tradition also consider intangible assets such as reputation and quality of customer relationships. Cryptoassets similarly fall in the *intangibles* category. Therefore, they can be valued, but the limitation of this valuation approach for cryptoassets is similar to the limitation of valuing intangibles: they have little to no liquidation value.

---

[1] This approach is not perfect because the necessary purchase costs of ASICS are fixed costs for miners, acting as a barrier to entry and distorting the equilibrium price. Nevertheless, since they are comparatively small in proportion to electricity costs and since they are sunk costs once the purchase is made, electricity costs are still a valid proxy for demand.

[2] Post on the BitcoinTalk forum on February 21, 2010 [89].

A failing business' goodwill loses most, if not all, of its value. Similarly, a failing cryptoasset would quickly lose its value. The underlying assumption for valuing both an intangible and a cryptoasset is, therefore, that they remain going concerns. In other words, they are assumed to continue their activities in the future.

Earnings Power Value Based on Staking Rewards

Contrary to proof-of-work cryptoassets, which have replacement costs but no future cash flows, proof-of-stake cryptoassets have future cash flows but no replacement costs. PoS cryptoassets were, therefore, not the target for asset value (last section) but are so for the upcoming earnings power value (EPV) analysis.

As introduced in the NPV section, future staking rewards can be used as future cash flows—*earnings* in Graham and Dodd's valuation approaches. When valuing EPV for a business, choosing the appropriate measure of earnings is essential. For example, net operating profit after taxes considers the impact of taxes, which is not the case of operating income. Similarly, measuring staking rewards in terms of their real yield is essential. For instance, there may be costs implied with holding a sufficient amount of a PoS cryptoasset to benefit from staking rewards. For example, to activate the validator software and stake ethers directly on the Ethereum blockchain, one must deposit at least 32 ETH (worth over $50,000 as of this writing). In addition, validators need the computer on which they run the software to always be connected to the Internet; otherwise, they face penalties for being offline.

Removing indirect costs from the gross staking yield provides a more accurate measure of earnings, based on which EPV can be computed with a standard NPV approach. Similar to traditional finance models in value investing, EPV is obtained by dividing earnings by the cost of capital for the investor. As the denominator (the cost of capital) is similar for cryptoasset and traditional investments, this book does not cover its details and challenges. A sufficient number of quality resources already exist on the topic.

Valuing Growth

While most traditional value investors focus exclusively on the tangible part of a business, the industry generally evolved toward valuing growth in the last three decades. Indeed, a growing business typically has more value than a stable business, even if the book value of assets is similar. It is one of the reasons why some technology companies are valued in trillions of dollars.

Besides, for most new high-growth businesses (e.g., ambitious technology start-ups), growth represents the lion's share of their valuation. In this respect, cryptoassets share similarities. They are also new, high-growth endeavors whose primary value resides not in their tangible assets but in their growth prospects. Growth, however, is by far the most challenging element to value. In particular, it tends to be systematically and materially overvalued for technology companies. This fact substantiates our recommendation to take cryptoasset valuations, regardless of the method, with a considerable error margin and tilt toward the more conservative end of the valuation range. It does not mean that valuation is impossible, just that any valuation method is inaccurate and an overvaluation bias likely.

Moreover, growth for a cryptoasset is very different from growth for a traditional business. While the value of a traditional business depends on the pace of organic growth of its revenue stream, this is not what is creating value for cryptoassets. In contrast, in the crypto industry, it is rather the usage of an asset that is creating value. In particular, the higher the usage of a currency, network, or cryptoasset, the more it is valuable to all users. This leads us to identify possible metrics for assessing usage.

Measuring and Valuing Usage of a Cryptoasset

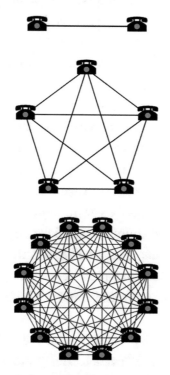

Figure 16-1. *An illustration of Metcalfe's law and the value of a network represented by connections between telephones: the more users on the network, the more this network becomes valuable. (Source: Wikicommons, public domain)*

Metcalfe's law illustrates why usage may be the primary driver for value. Coined by Robert Metcalfe, one of the founders of Ethernet, Metcalfe's law states that the value of a network is proportional to the square of its number of users. In a simple example, if you are the only person in the world with a telephone with no other function than calling, it has little value to you. However, once another user has a telephone, yours becomes valuable because you can call the other user. When a third user joins the network, the original two phones have more value because more people can call. With every new user on the network, all phones become more valuable. Since the value of the network can be represented as the number of connections between nodes, it increases quadratically with the number of nodes. As per Metcalfe's law, the value grows with adoption and much faster than the number of users.

This law is especially relevant when valuing social media networks such as Twitter, Facebook, Instagram, or Weixin/WeChat. Also, companies like Uber, Airbnb, or eBay follow a similar logic. Likewise, a cryptoasset used as a currency also falls in this category. Every buyer on the network adds value to every seller and vice versa. The first metric to measure usage is, therefore, the number of nodes on the network.

The next metric is activity. For instance, active users bring more value to the network than inactive users. Continuing with the telephone example, if most users hardly ever make any call, the network has less value than if they are all regular callers. Among other reasons, regular users are more likely to incentivize non-users to join the network for telephones, social media, or currencies. Activity for cryptoassets can be measured, for example, by the volume of transactions. However, exceptionally low transaction fees for some cryptoassets make this metric easily manipulable. Indeed, a single node could create multiple pseudonymous accounts and make many fake transactions between accounts to simulate activity. Instead, an alternative and less manipulable activity metric is the total transaction costs (or gas fees). Any wealthy buyer could theoretically manipulate the metric, but doing so would come at a high cost, disincentivizing the nefarious behavior.

Alternative metrics for usage depend on the nature of the cryptoasset. For instance, in the case of Defi protocols, the *total value locked* (TVL) is the crypto equivalent of *assets under management* (AUM) of traditional investment funds. In particular, TVL includes all assets locked into a Defi protocol's functions, such as staking, lending, or liquidity pools. Higher TVLs indicate that more value is dedicated to the functions enabled by a Defi protocol. The greater the value of the protocol, the more people rely on its native currency to take advantage of its services. TVL is a reasonable proxy for the usage of the corresponding cryptoasset.

Usage metrics can be adjusted by analysts valuing cryptoassets to reflect the genuine underlying usage. For example, an analyst may want to attribute more value to users living by the industry's decentralization spirit than speculators on centralized exchanges. Indeed, a user going through the necessary hurdles to set up a self-custodial wallet is likely more committed to the underlying asset than users on centralized exchanges are. A usage metric can be weighed based on custodial dominance for the asset (i.e., the ratio of custodial funds over total existing funds). For example, an analyst could define that the more dominant self-custody is for a cryptoasset, the more valuable its users are.

Possible proxies for using a cryptoasset are the number of active addresses, the number of transactions, gas fees, total transaction costs, and total value locked. The transparency enabled by blockchain technology implies that these metrics are directly retrievable from the blockchain in real time. Due to the manipulability of these metrics, using a combination of these proxies is likely a better approach than using exclusively any of them.

Finally, let us highlight that the market capitalization of a cryptoasset is not a measure of usage. Since it is the valuation given by the market, it is not the input in any valuation but the market's average output of all valuations.

Measuring Growth Based on Usage

These metrics enable investors to value the growth portion of a network's valuation. In particular, the growth pace of usage is the technology's diffusion rate. In particular, the global (identity-verified) user base of cryptoassets increased by nearly 190% per year between 2018 and 2020 before accelerating even further in 2021 and 2022.[3] The exact figure depends on which metric is used and how it is measured, but most estimates indicate usage growth of over 100% per year. This rate means that cryptoasset adoption more than doubles every year. For comparison, Internet adoption when it had a similar number of users (300 to 400 million) was approximately half as fast.

Technology adoption is not linear. Typically, it follows an S-curve, with a slow start followed by a steep acceleration punctuated by a slow finish. Everett Rogers' book *Diffusion of Innovations* became a classic in which Figure 16-2 is presented. In this figure, the Bell curve represents the adoption rate at any point over an innovation's life. The S-curve ending at 100% is the cumulated share of the market that the innovation captured until reaching its peak.

---

[3] *Number of identity-verified cryptoasset users from 2016 to November 2022*, Statista [85].

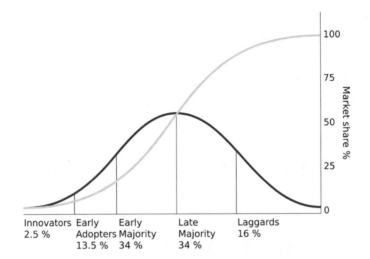

Figure 16-2. *Rate of diffusion of innovations according to Everett Rogers (Source: Wikicommons, public domain [50])*

Based on the accelerating pace of adoption and the potential market available, the cryptoasset industry is in the *early adopter* phase as of 2023. Besides, with a typical S-curve, the time it takes to get from 0 to 10% (2009 to 2022 for cryptoassets) is the same as the time it takes to get from 10% to 90% (suggesting 2022 to 2035). Furthermore, per the GWI market research, worldwide usage of cryptoasset (by Internet users aged 16 to 64) stood at 13% in January 2023.[4] These insights suggest that adoption (usage) will likely increase by a factor of 5 over the coming decade.

Including Supply in Valuations

As mentioned in the introduction, the market price of tradable securities is ultimately determined by the point where supply meets demand. Demand is in many ways similar to usage, as described in the previous sections. In contrast, the supply of a cryptoasset is the total quantity available of it. Many cryptoassets are capped at a fixed amount, with a transparent process on how and at which pace this amount will be reached. For example, the total number of bitcoins that will ever be minted is 21 million. They are issued progressively, with every new block, which is about every 10 minutes. Also, the issue is done at a decreasing pace, as the reward per block is divided by two every 210,000 blocks,

---

[4] GWI data published by Datareportal's *Digital 2022 Global Overview Report* [78].

which is roughly every four years. The Bitcoin supply will continue to follow this pattern until all 21 million bitcoins are issued, around the year 2140, after which no new bitcoin will ever be minted. However, the nature of halving events implies that by the fourth halving event in 2024, 93.75% of the entire supply will have already been mined. Other cryptoassets follow different patterns; while some also have a capped maximum theoretical supply (e.g., Cardano), other cryptoassets' supply is ever-expanding (e.g., Dogecoin), and others still are deflationary (e.g., Ethereum).[5]

Nevertheless, genuine supply is not the total theoretical amount coded in the cryptoasset's feature but the amount of retrievable and tradable coins. In reality, many asset owners have lost their private keys, making all corresponding coins irretrievable and the supply much lower than the theoretical amount suggests. For example, at least 20% of all bitcoins are estimated to be held in wallets whose private keys have been lost. Based on this figure, the total real supply of Bitcoin is not 21 million but below 16.8 million.

Stock-to-flow Model

Supply becomes crucial in the most famous Bitcoin valuation model: the stock-to-flow (S2F) model. Fundamentally, this model values scarcity and is typically applied to natural resources, such as gold. It measures a ratio of the total existing quantity of an asset available for trading (the "stock") over the new quantity of the asset made available per unit of time (the "flow"). The logic behind the value of high stock-to-flow assets was introduced in Chapter 1. The pseudonymous PlanB, a Dutch institutional investor, originally presented the model applied for Bitcoin in a Medium article in March 2019.[6] It relied on Nick Szabo's definition of scarcity as "unforgeable costliness," a feat first achieved in a digital and decentralized way by Bitcoin as its primary value proposition. In other words, producing new gold or bitcoins is hard and expensive, making existing units valuable.

As of 2023, the total global gold supply is around 200,000 tons, with approximately 3,000 tons mined annually.[7] The S2F ratio of gold is 66.7 (computed as 200,000/3,000) and corresponds to the number of years that it would take for the current flow to

---

[5] Since September 2022's *The Merge* event, Ethereum is occasionally deflationary (e.g., a deflation rate of 0.00002% per January 2023), though this rate varies over time.

[6] *Modeling Bitcoin Value with Scarcity*, PlanB, Medium [75].

[7] Rounded data from the World Gold Council, 2022. In addition to the 200,000 tons figure, another 50,000 tons of unmined gold have been identified.

accumulate to the current stock. However, its inverse may be more easily understood: 1.5% (3,000/200,000), which is the fraction of the stock mined in a year. In other words, it is the inflation rate of gold's supply.

In comparison, Bitcoin's stock at its third halving event on May 11, 2020 was 18,375,000 (87.5% of the total 21 million, ignoring lost coins), with a flow of 6.25 bitcoin per block or about 328,725 bitcoins per year. Its S2F ratio was 55.9, just below gold, indicating less scarcity than gold at this point in time in terms of stock-to-flow. This ratio increases slowly between halving events as new bitcoins are added to the stock with every block. In addition, each halving event implies a sudden doubling of the ratio as the flow is halved. Per the fourth halving event, expected around March 2024, the S2F ratio will be 119.8 (computed as 19,687,500/164,362.5), making Bitcoin at that point in time almost twice "scarcer" than gold.

The price prediction of the S2F model uses the value of the S2F ratio over time as input in a formula with other coefficients selected to fit past data. Based on data that best fits past prices and the corresponding S2F ratio, a logarithmic trend can be drawn, and, therefore, future prices can be predicted. For instance, the model solves the following equation, where a and b are constants chosen to fit past price data, and $S2F$ is the aforementioned ratio.

$$Price_{USD} = e^a \times S2F^b$$

This model applied to Bitcoin is presented in Figure 16-3 (with the coefficients a=-1.0 and b=2.9, and the daily flow based on the previous 365 days of data), where one can identify that past data follow closely the theoretical output of the model. However, even though the S2F model has proven exceptionally accurate over the past years, it nevertheless relies heavily on assumptions.

Figure 16-3. *Bitcoin's stock-to-flow model based on the 365-day flow from mid-2010 to January 2028 (expected date of the fifth halving event); Bitcoin price data until March 2023*

In particular, the nature of the formula suggests that prices continually increase in line with the S2F ratio until 2140, when the last new fraction of a bitcoin is minted. In addition, it is questionable why the market capitalization of a commodity (be it gold or Bitcoin) could be derived exclusively from the rate of new supply. Indeed, the model completely ignores factors other than stock, flow, and time. For example, it completely ignores any change in demand (be it due to regulation or business cycles), volatility, or even the supply of the metric in which it is typically expressed: US dollars.

These shortcomings did not prevent much of the Bitcoin community from relying extensively on the model to predict future prices. The main argument is that even though some factors are not considered, the stock-to-flow relationship is the main driver for the market capitalization of scarce assets, not only for Bitcoin but also for precious metals and other commodities. In particular, PlanB rightly points out that this model has an exceptionally high goodness-of-fit[8] for Bitcoin, over eight orders of magnitude.

After the March 2019 publication of the model, Bitcoin's price continued to follow closely the theoretical prediction of the model for three years, including throughout the third halving event in 2020. However, the price lagged behind the model's prediction

---

[8] In statistical terms, it has a coefficient of determination (R^2) over 95%.

during the down market of 2022 and early 2023. Even PlanB admits that Bitcoin's price will eventually decouple from the model's prediction, even though it has been exceptionally accurate so far.

Stock-to-flow Cross Asset (S2FX) Model

To address possible limitations of the S2F model, PlanB published an updated model just over a year after his S2F article. This update removes the time component from the model but adds other commodities, particularly gold and silver. It was coined the Bitcoin Stock-to-Flow Cross Asset (S2FX) model.[9]

In particular, it identifies the different phases through which Bitcoin evolved, from proof-of-concept to payments to e-gold and to a financial asset. In each of these four chronological phases, Bitcoin's S2F ratio and price were materially larger than in the previous phase, as shown in Figure 16-4. Adding silver and gold's market capitalization against their S2F ratio to the model validates the finding, indicating that a higher S2F ratio suggests a higher market value. In fact, the goodness-of-fit of data is almost perfect (R^2 of 99.7%), giving high confidence in the underlying causal relationship. The main weakness of the model is the small number of observations on which it is based: only six (namely, the values for gold, silver, and each of the four chronological phases identified for Bitcoin).

---

[9] *Bitcoin Stock-to-Flow Cross Asset Model*, PlanB, Medium [74].

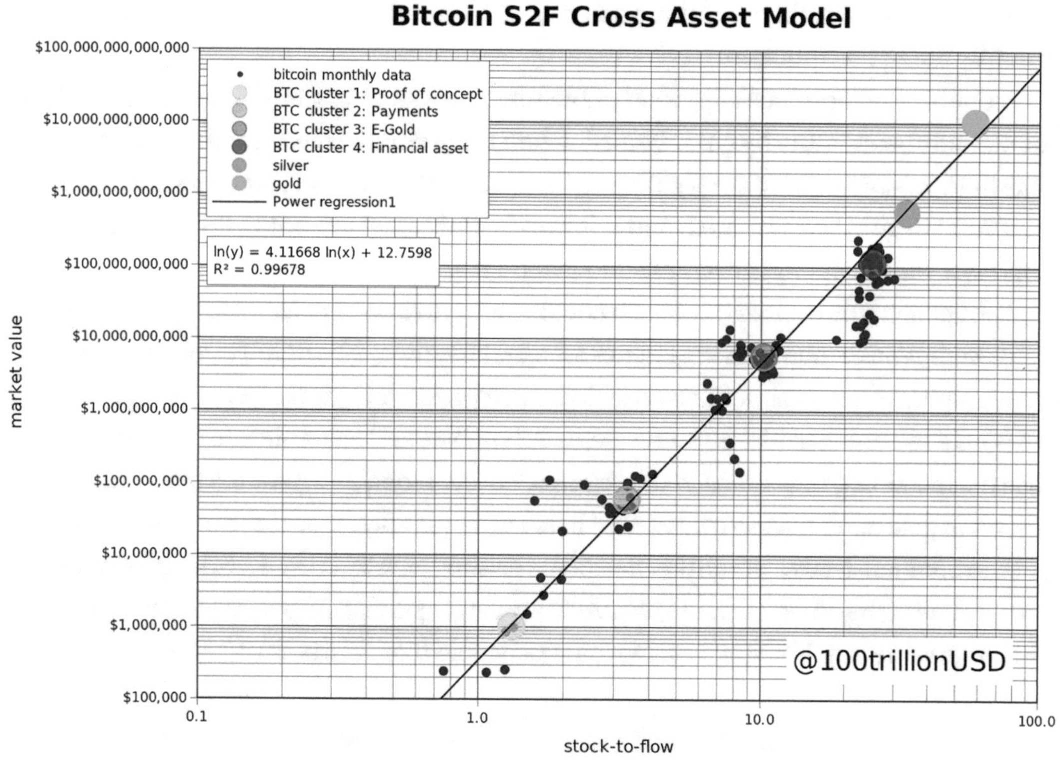

Bitcoin S2F Cross Asset Model

Figure 16-4. *Original S2FX model chart presented by pseudonymous PlanB (@100trillionUSD) in a Medium article (April 27, 2020) [51]*

At the very least, the S2FX model adds more confidence to the S2F model's predictions as it confirms the future trend of Bitcoin's market capitalization by validating this trend against other commodities. In particular, the two models establish that Bitcoin's price per coin will be between $100,000 and $1 million in 2025 (after the fourth halving event is priced in) and well above the $1 million mark by the end of the decade (after the fifth halving event is priced in).

Valuation from Comparables

Using existing commodities' market capitalization to establish Bitcoin's value is also possible more directly, independently from the stock-to-flow ratio. However, the upcoming model (also focused on Bitcoin) relies extensively on arbitrary assumptions. In particular, Bitcoin's comparables method relies on the function that the asset is assumed to hold. It estimates how much it captures market share from other assets currently filling this function.

Arguably the most basic function of Bitcoin is as a store of value, a function that has traditionally been borne by gold. Indeed, when traditional savers aimed to keep the value of their savings over time, gold was the asset class of choice. Of course, it is not the only function gold has assumed, and it is not the only asset assuming this function, but let us start with this simple example and extend it as we go along.

A simplified comparables approach could work as follows. Analysts are invited to refine each assumption to more accurate values for a better estimate. As of 2023, gold has a total market capitalization of about 12 trillion dollars. Approximately 46% of it exists in jewelry, 17% is held by central banks as reserves, and 22% as bars and coins outside of central banks, while the remaining 15% is held in other forms.[10] It is reasonable to assume that central bank reserves in gold and privately owned gold bars and coins fully assume the role of a store of value. In addition, let us assume that half of the existing jewelry is used as a store of value, and so is half of the other forms of gold (arbitrary assumptions). As per these assumptions, the market value of gold's store of value function would therefore be $8.3 trillion.

$$\$12T \times \left(17\% + 22\% + \frac{46\%}{2} + \frac{15\%}{2} \right) = \$8.3T$$

Conservatively assuming that Bitcoin "only" captures 20% of that market by the end of the decade (another arbitrary assumption), in addition to its current market capitalization of about $0.6 trillion, it would grow to a total value of $2.3 trillion based on this function and on the capture of gold's market share alone. Of course, other asset classes such as stocks (ca. $106 trillion), bonds (ca. $124 trillion), and real estate (ca. $327 trillion) are also, in part, stores of value. Conservatively assuming that Bitcoin "only" captures 3% of its total market by the end of the decade, Bitcoin's market capitalization would grow to $19 trillion, or $905,000 per coin.

---

[10] Data per the World Cold Council; *Above-ground stocks* report of 8 February 2023 [76].

Figure 16-5. *The relative market capitalization of different asset classes (Sources: CoinMarketCap for crypto, Savills for gold and real estate, SIMFA Capital Markets Fact Book for stock and bond markets)*

Furthermore, Bitcoin also assumes other functions than only a store of value. For example, it is also valued as an international payment medium, settling transactions permanently in instants. In this sense, it is superior to many existing transaction methods. It will likely also capture a share of the transaction market from incumbents such as Western Union, Visa, or Mastercard.

For example, this valuation can be established based on a comparison with the existing supply of fiat currencies. The total value of fiat currencies is about $50 trillion worldwide as of early 2023. This figure is the narrow definition of currency supply ("M1" in economics terms), which consists of banknotes, coins, and overnight deposits (it excludes other financial assets, such as bonds, stocks, real estate, and gold). Therefore, this definition represents the total wealth used as a medium of exchange and excludes assets meant as a store of value. With an approach similar to the aforementioned valuation for a store of value, one can value Bitcoin based on comparable media of exchange and expected capture of their market share. The medium-of-exchange value resulting from such an estimate should be added to its store-of-value valuation, bringing this comparables-based valuation of Bitcoin well above the $1 million mark per bitcoin by the end of the decade.

Finally, the preceding figures assume that Bitcoin's total market value is divided by 21 million. However, as previously covered, it is more reasonable to assume that many bitcoins (at least 20%) are permanently lost. The price per bitcoin would therefore be correspondingly larger. In conclusion, even using conservative estimates, it is fair to value Bitcoin much higher than its current price level.

Network Value to Transactions Ratio

Moving away from the store-of-value function and focusing on the medium-of-payment function of cryptoassets, it is useful to measure the price-to-transaction relationship of different assets. In the same way that stocks are compared based on their price-to-earnings ratio, cryptoassets can be compared based on their network value-to-transactions (NVT) ratio.

$$NVT = \frac{network\ value}{transaction\ volume}$$

In a 2017 Forbes article, Willy Woo introduced this ratio to assess whether Bitcoin was in a bubble.[11] It identified that the volume of transactions and the market capitalization of Bitcoin were closely related, especially as Bitcoin matured. When the ratio climbs significantly above its normal range, it could indicate a bubble, as was, for example, the case for Bitcoin in 2014. Other cryptoassets can be analyzed with the same metric since the logic is not Bitcoin-specific. However, while the network's value is typically in line with usage, this relationship does not always hold. For example, staking rewards are reflected as transactions but do not represent increased network usage. Also, privacy cryptoassets such as Monero do not enable measuring transactions accurately by design. Nevertheless, the NVT ratio remains a helpful complement to other metrics.

Other Fundamental Metrics Behind Cryptoassets

Beyond the metrics used as inputs in the previous models, countless other metrics can be leveraged to build new models. Among others, analysts could choose to include the following ones in their models: mean block size, block height, exchange deposits,

---

[11] "Is Bitcoin In A Bubble? Check The NVT Ratio," Willy Woo, *Forbes* [77].

exchange withdrawals, supply sold directly by miners/validators, average coin dormancy (the time each coin has remained dormant before being transacted),[12] number of new addresses, and number of active addresses. One could also use the number of addresses with a balance over a certain fraction of the total supply, over a specific amount of the native currency, or a specific dollar amount. In addition, and specifically for PoW cryptoassets, the following metrics are also meaningful: current hash rate, 30-day average hash rate, current difficulty, 30-day average difficulty, or miner revenues from fees. Finally, different decentralization measures (Gini coefficient or Nakamoto index, covered in Chapter 13) could also be valuable additions to valuation models for cryptoassets.

Traditional macroeconomic variables are, of course, also relevant in the context of cryptoassets. In particular, the tendency of cryptoassets (Bitcoin in particular) to absorb the existing liquidity on the market makes a measure of net liquidity especially relevant. The more overall liquidity is available on the market, the more it can flow to capital assets, including cryptoassets.

Fulcrum Index

Another fundamental value method to value Bitcoin is to consider it as portfolio insurance. In particular, and as was presented by Greg Foss in an April 2021 article, Bitcoin insures against fiat governments defaulting on their debt.[13] The value of this insurance can be measured by existing financial tools, which de facto provide a valuation for Bitcoin.

A government defaulting on its debt means it cannot reimburse its contracted loans. Such an event forces it to print more of its currency to devalue its debt until it becomes repayable. As the currency's value collapses, all prices expressed in that currency rise. Users of the currency would be left with savings of much-reduced value and would likely flee to a financial safe haven, one that cannot be manipulated at will by central authorities. Even if governments can print their way out of technical default, it would involve a crisis of confidence in their currency—a de facto default.

---

[12] An increased average coin dormancy indicates that long-term holders sell their position, while low average coin dormancy indicates higher confidence as investors hold their coins longer.

[13] *Why Every Fixed Income Investor Needs to Consider Bitcoin As Portfolio Insurance*, Rock Star Inner Circle [92].

It is reasonable to assume that, if a government cannot repay its fiat-denominated debt, the demand for Bitcoin would rise. Given the fixed Bitcoin supply, the increase in demand would bring prices up with it. The challenge here is to measure the likelihood of such an event and assign a price to it. Fortunately, the finance industry already developed a tool enabling such measurement: credit default swaps.

A credit default swap is a contract that essentially represents insurance against an event of default. The buyer of the swap pays a fixed amount monthly and is entitled to a large payout in a default event. The market defines the price of the swap (the monthly payment) based on the assessed likelihood of the event.

In his article, Greg Foss explains how he constructs the Fulcrum Index. This index measures the cumulated value of credit default swaps on a basket of G20 nations. These nations likely have the most robust fiat currencies of all. Indeed, before a G20 nation currency fails, many other (weaker) fiat currencies will likely have failed already. The index is constructed based on the likelihood of credit default (implied by the market) and the sum of the financial obligations in the corresponding currency (e.g., federal government outstanding debt, Medicare liabilities).

A detailed explanation of the Fulcrum Index is beyond the scope of this book, but the output from Greg Foss' analysis is worth sharing [52]. The valuation of the Fulcrum Index suggests a value of $108,000 to $160,000 per bitcoin (in 2021 dollars).

One useful intuition from this approach is that Bitcoin's price will likely rise with the probability of default of major nations. As the debt-to-GDP ratios of these nations continue to increase to new all-time highs, this intuition suggests that Bitcoin's future price direction is aligned with what previous models suggest.

Valuing Bitcoin As a Cybersecurity Protocol

A breakthrough in Bitcoin literature was the 2023 MIT thesis "Softwar" by US Air Force Major Jason Lowery [46]. While much of the attention around Bitcoin previously focused on its financial and monetary role, Major Lowery took a fundamentally different approach. He analyzed Bitcoin from a military and national strategic defense perspective. His thesis eloquently differentiates abstract, imaginary power from real, physical power and extends the reasoning to the digital world, to software. Contrary to competitors not based on a PoW consensus mechanism, Bitcoin's security relies on real, tangible energy. It can only come into existence through the expenditure of electricity. This physical-world constraint prevents it from being systematically exploited through abstract power, whether from a currency emitter or ruling authority. In other words, its proof-of-work consensus protocol is a new cybersecurity system. In contrast, cryptoassets based on proof-of-stake and fiat currencies rely exclusively on an abstract belief system: imaginary value backed only by trust in the emitting authority.

The most secure blockchain in existence, therefore, extends much beyond its value as a monetary protocol. It can also secure any valuable information, from personal data to national, strategic, and confidential information. In this respect, Bitcoin is completely different from any other cryptoasset and deserves a different categorization—and valuation method. As Major Lowery concludes, the importance of Bitcoin for individuals, corporations, and nations urges to stockpile Bitcoin reserves as a national strategic priority. While this perspective does not provide any specific valuation for Bitcoin, one can infer from this reasoning that Bitcoin's fundamental value should be many times larger than its current level. In other words, it confirms and reinforces the findings from previously presented fundamental valuation methods.

Valuation Methods Not Based on Fundamentals

The previous sections focused on valuation methods based on fundamental value. They rely as little as possible on how other market players assess the asset's value and strive to identify what it is objectively worth.[14] Many methods exist to assess whether a cryptoasset is overpriced, but they rely almost exclusively on other market participants' behavior. It is where valuations drift away from fundamentals and come closer to speculation.

---

[14] Technically, an *objective* valuation is impossible to achieve. All valuations and models rely to some extent on arbitrary assumptions, either by the analyst or by other market players. Even a comparison to electricity costs or gold's market value ultimately depends on what other people think electricity or gold is worth. In this sense, there can be no *objective* valuation, for any asset.

For example, one such approach is to compare an asset's current value to its average acquisition costs. This relationship is called the *market-value-to-realized-value* (MVRV). MVRV indicates to what extent the average asset holder would generate a profit or a loss if it sold its holdings at the current price. Formally, MVRV is computed as follows.

$$MVRV = \frac{market\ value}{realized\ value}$$

While the *market value* is the asset's market capitalization, the *realized value* is the volume held by each holder multiplied by its acquisition costs. A value above 1 indicates that the average holder has an unrealized gain and inversely. The theory behind MVRV predicts that this ratio tends to revert toward its mean. It can be extended by comparing the difference between its terms to the asset's volatility (the MVRV Z-score), another short-term indicator of likely future prices.

Another approach would be dividing market value by a measure of holders' confidence. Such a measure of confidence could be, for example, the average number of days the cryptoasset stays in a wallet. It is, for example, the method of computing the *reserve risk*, a model created by Hans Hauge.[15] Alternative confidence measures include Google search trends, trending tweets, or market surveys. A low ratio of confidence (e.g., when long-term holders sell) compared to the asset's price suggests the asset is overvalued.

Many other short-term indicators exist to assess whether a cryptoasset is currently overpriced but are beyond the scope of this book. The interested reader could look into the Black-Scholes-Merton model applied to cryptoassets, logarithmic growth curves, HODL waves, the RHODL ratio, the Mayer Multiple, and the Puell Multiple. Other metrics should also be considered in assessing shorter-term moves in cryptoasset prices, such as the maximum "pain price" on exchanges (the price that creates the highest total loss to option holders), futures and forward prices (which reflect market participants' expectations), or even debt cycles (in particular, Bitcoin price peaks tend to follow China's debt cycle).

---

[15] Hans Hauge, *Introducing Binary Adjusted BDD, VOCD and Reserve Risk*, May 2019 [82].

Key Concepts

Traditional assessment methods of an asset's economic value need to be adjusted for valuing cryptoassets and differ based on the cryptoasset at hand. In particular, NPV analyses can be used for proof-of-stake cryptoassets, with the limitation that cash flows (staking rewards) are expressed in the assessed asset. In contrast, a proof-of-work cryptoasset can be valued based on replacement costs; that is, the current price of the electricity needed to mine the asset at the current hash rate. Besides, demand for an asset can be measured through usage or adoption, thereby hinting at the value of the growth component in a traditional value investing approach. Supply-based models value scarcity and are especially relevant for scarce assets such as commodities, including Bitcoin. An alternative valuation approach is based on the value of comparable asset classes and the expected market share capture of these asset classes. All valuation models have in common that they suggest that Bitcoin's price should be much higher than its current level as of May 2023. Many variants of these approaches can be based on countless on-chain metrics and can be complemented with short-term indicators.

Extension Questions

Which valuation methods are appropriate to value Bitcoin, and which weight should be given to each method? What about Ethereum, Polygon, Uniswap, and Monero?

How does the appropriateness of valuation methods evolve based on the maturity of the cryptoasset?

How can transaction fees be included in Bitcoin valuation methods?

CHAPTER 17

Concluding Remarks

All rational action is in the first place individual action. Only the individual thinks. Only the individual reasons. Only the individual acts.

—Ludwig von Mises

As we venture into the unchartered territory of the digital revolution, cryptoassets and blockchain technology are bringing about a paradigm shift impacting the global economy, redefining trust, and reshaping industries across the board. This book explored a wide spectrum of topics and disciplines to understand this new paradigm. It covered monetary history, economics, game theory, technological innovations, portfolio management, risk management, and valuation methods. Indeed, valuing cryptoassets requires understanding each of these disciplines, as they all substantially impact ultimate valuations. This final chapter summarizes the key takeaways from the book and sets the stage for what comes next.

Looking Back

Introducing cryptoassets naturally begins with Bitcoin, the first cryptoasset and by far the largest. Capturing about half of the entire asset class value, Bitcoin is a special case with a different purpose, distinct risks, and separate valuation methods from any other asset. It emerged from the ashes of the Great Recession in 2008 and quickly grew into a trillion-dollar asset by putting the meaning of money into question. In particular, Bitcoin reinstated qualities of sound money that the gold standard once enforced, and that were lost in the last century when fiat money became the standard. In addition, it complemented these desirable economic qualities with digitalization, making it more appropriate for the current age.

T. Jeegers, *Understanding Crypto Fundamentals*, https://doi.org/10.1007/978-1-4842-9309-6_17

Furthermore, its main value proposition is unprecedented for a digital asset: combining scarcity and decentralization. By decentralizing a scarce digital asset, Bitcoin gathered the properties needed to solve society's critical problems, such as monetary censorship, savings confiscation through inflation, and the lack of genuine ownership of value and property rights. Moreover, its state-of-the-art use of cryptography solves countless other issues, from privacy intrusions to confidential data breaches. The indirect consequences of these properties include a higher level of financial inclusion, lower fees for international money transfers, quicker settlement of transactions, and higher levels of free speech. Ultimately, Bitcoin is a voluntary, accessible, reliable, hard-to-confiscate, provably scarce, decentralized asset transparently offering finality and immutability of transactions, available at low cost and globally. It is independent of any political agenda and has spread for over a decade without downtime, 24 hours a day, 7 days a week, 365 days a year.

Subsequently, the cryptoasset industry has evolved to offer benefits even beyond these properties. A crucial innovation was the possibility of establishing decentralized agreements of any kind, extending beyond the limits of agreements to be transactions. Such decentralized agreements took the form of smart contracts, first implemented on the Ethereum blockchain. Similar to the Bitcoin innovation, smart contracts opened up countless new possibilities. In this case, they enabled the automation and decentralization of virtually any process to enhance reliability, security, transparency, accessibility, and compliance. They also facilitated new forms of governance for organizations and myriad new business models built on top of one another. In the same way that the Internet revolutionized essentially any business, blockchain-enabled innovations are making revolutionary waves in virtually all industries.

Nevertheless, the path toward greater adoption is not smooth. The novelty of the cryptoasset industry brought challenges, from vocal opponents to hackers and other nefarious actors taking advantage of the industry's publicity. As a result, early systems were hacked, some funds were stolen, others became used for illegitimate purposes, and major players struggled to keep up with the industry's rapid pace of change.

Despite these challenges, the need for decentralization and cryptoassets has never been more critical. Centralized authorities and private organizations collect more data on individuals at an accelerating pace and are increasingly more capable of exploiting this data. They are thereby restraining privacy and the freedom to express opinions without fearing consequences. Traditional institutions are slow, biased, expensive, and corruptible, all of which can be mitigated through a decentralized infrastructure leveraging the potential of cryptoassets.

At the same time, millions of people suffer from sudden devaluations of their life savings due to fiat currency collapses,[1] and billions more experience a steady erosion of their wealth due to rampant inflation. The unnecessary coupling of money and state has had catastrophic consequences for decades, but it can finally be overcome.

Looking Forward

Looking to the future, the promises of cryptoassets are manifold. First, the largest cryptoasset offers a solution to the long-term monetary debasement issue of the past century. Progressively moving toward a Bitcoin standard will restore the position of a hard asset at the heart of the economy and induce governments to live within their means, like everybody else. Monetary authorities will no longer be able to infinitely extend how many resources they have available at the expense of all users of the currency. However, the transition will likely neither be sudden nor complete. The new digital money will rather coexist with fiat ecosystems. It will likely become a complementary currency on a global scale, a concept that has been praised for decades for its expected stabilizing impact on economies.

Second, the carbon footprint outlook of this solution is promising. Specifically, incentives for Bitcoin mining are to use stranded energy that would otherwise be lost rather than consuming electricity from the grid where and when it is most needed. As a result, mining farms often operate next to renewable sources such as hydropower or geothermal energy plants, utilizing excess energy produced by the plant when demand is low. Bitcoin mining operations support grid flexibility and demand response, as they can adjust their energy consumption based on grid conditions and electricity prices. This not only leads to more efficient use of energy resources but also helps stabilize power grids, especially in regions with high shares of intermittent renewable energy. The Bitcoin mining industry thus provides incentives for financing renewable infrastructure by making the expected output of renewable power plants more stable.

Consequently, Bitcoin mining already uses predominantly renewable energy (in a much higher proportion than any country in the world) and is trending toward even greater sustainability. Additionally, new developments enable Bitcoin miners to capture flared methane and other unwanted byproducts of currently polluting processes such

---

[1] As these lines are being written in early 2023, Lebanon is officially devaluing its currency by 90 percent, thereby dividing the wealth of Lebanese citizens by a factor of 10.

as oil drilling, reducing the detrimental results of these processes and contributing positively to the environment. Therefore, if not already the case, Bitcoin mining will soon become a carbon-negative industry.

Third, cryptoassets are automating the entire financial industry and reducing counterparty risks by decentralizing its processes. Not only finance but also most other industries are affected. A whole new world of privacy and data security is made possible virtually everywhere, as information, data, and transactions can be exchanged with the minimum amount of information technically required through zero-knowledge proofs.

In just over a decade, a new asset class was born and grew to over $2 trillion despite many governments persisting in undermining its growth and institutional investors mainly staying away from it. In the early 2020s, multiple milestones were passed as the new reality started to settle. Governments are now trying to understand and work with cryptoassets; many institutions are either joining the game or eager to be allowed to, and retail adoption accelerates.

Furthermore, Bitcoin is becoming the legal tender currency for emerging economies. Talents in the tech and financial industries are leaving the traditional systems to build exciting new use cases with cryptoassets. Awareness of the need for privacy reaches an all-time high. Decentralization takes off as increasingly more activity happens directly on-chain. Capital flows to crypto projects at an astonishing speed. Web 3.0 start-ups are seizing the Internet to make it decentralized. The world of DeFi is becoming usable for the masses. Fiscal and regulatory uncertainty is dropping as legislation is passed to accommodate the unique nature of cryptoassets, giving confidence to investors that they are acting within their mandate. Also, scaling technologies are finally around the corner for both Bitcoin and altcoins.

These developments indicate that the horizon for cryptoasset investors has never been brighter. Specifically, the potential reward compared to the level of risk has never been so attractive. Cryptoassets are an asymmetric trade with probabilities shifting in the right direction: the risk of losing capital decreases as the asset class is accepted as here to stay, and the potential for further exceptional upside is increasingly likely. It is not to say that risks do not exist. On the contrary, one focus of this book was to highlight that many risks remain, some of which are considerable. Proper research and risk mitigation techniques are still essential for cryptoasset investors. Nevertheless, these risks can be managed and seem reasonable compared to the diversification benefits and long-term upside potential of the industry. How cryptoassets will evolve exactly is still unknown, but their pivotal role in reshaping the economy is inevitable.

As a burgeoning asset class, cryptoassets will continue to evolve, and so must our understanding and approach to valuing and investing in them. As seen time and again, those who are well-informed and adaptable will be the ones who thrive in this new era of decentralized finance and digital assets.

Blockchain has become much more than just a new technology. It has transformed into a social ideology that empowers individuals, removes the need for trust in intermediaries, and promotes a secure and transparent digital future. Blockchain is becoming as transformational for society as steam, electricity, and the Internet have been in the past. It is a trigger for the fourth industrial revolution of humanity, a revolution that is still in its early days but has already started.

PART VII

Appendices

APPENDIX A

Precursors of Cryptoassets

Despite being sometimes presented as such, Bitcoin did not emerge in isolation. The first cryptoasset had many precursors that either tried to accomplish the same goal or developed similar technology for other purposes. None of them achieved mainstream adoption like Bitcoin, but they directly influenced how cryptoassets developed, even beyond Bitcoin's conception.

This chapter illustrates how today's cryptoassets are the result of four decades of innovation and development. As such, they result from many trials, errors, and improvements that paved the way for their ultimate success. Moreover, they are a recurring theme for tried innovations in that space because a global digital money independent from third parties is the logical progression in the evolution of the monetary system in a digital age, where self-sovereignty and privacy are becoming increasingly important. This evolution will redefine societies and prove as crucial for developing economies as double-entry accounting has been over the last five centuries.

Anonymous eCash and DigiCash: 1982

Blind signatures are the technology at the base of the electronic payment system *anonymous eCash*, developed by David Chaum as early as 1982 [51].

Blind signatures are an extension to digital signatures that provide anonymity to the user. They enable the signer (e.g., in the case of traditional currencies, a bank) to sign a document without seeing its content. Concretely, if Alice spends money digitally through a blind signature, neither the bank nor the seller knows who spent that money. All parties agree that the money is valid (the bank has a process to verify it) but cannot trace its origin.

© Thomas Jeegers 2023
T. Jeegers, *Understanding Crypto Fundamentals*, https://doi.org/10.1007/978-1-4842-9309-6_18

The blind signature technology can also be used for other purposes, such as electronic voting or any system in which the content of a message of any kind should be kept private. For example, if Bob wants to purchase goods requiring him to be of legal age, he could use a blind signature to convey the piece of information that he is older than a specific age without requiring him to disclose his exact date of birth. Similarly, if an inventor wants to verify whether his invention is patented, he can retrieve specific information from existing patents without needing to reveal his interest in these patents.

David Chaum used *anonymous eCash* as a base for founding the company DigiCash in 1989. The flourishing web environment of the nineties and the growing need for electronic transactions should have set the company in optimal growth conditions. Nevertheless, only a handful of banks in Europe and a single bank in the United States used DigiCash. The company went bankrupt in 1998 and sold its eCash patents to eCash Technologies.

Chaum believes that the lack of interest in privacy at the time caused the doom of DigiCash: "As the Web grew, the average level of sophistication of users dropped. It was hard to explain the importance of privacy to them" [52].

The growing electronic payment environment was seized by credit card companies, which became the preferred online payment method. This was likely driven by the higher importance of convenience compared to privacy at the time.

Secured Chain of Blocks to Timestamp Documents: 1991

In parallel, in the early nineties, Stuart Haber and Scott Stornetta developed a protocol to immutably timestamp documents without requiring a timestamping central authority while maintaining the privacy of the document's content. Fundamentally, their protocol prevents the back-dating and forward-dating of documents and uses a process similar to how a modern blockchain works. They achieved it by using hashes and digital signatures to form what they call a "distributed-trust scheme." [53]

The Eternity Service: 1996

A few years later, Ross Anderson made decentralization possible by replicating data with redundancies across many computers via the Internet, thereby protecting against attacks. In particular, he combined this idea with cryptography to set up an immutable database in much the same way blockchain technology does today. Anderson's 1996 paper, "The Eternity Service," bears in its name the immutable nature of the resulting decentralized data storage. Similar to modern blockchains, it was a service offered to all without any required "proof of identity or other formality." Also, similar to Bitcoin, "there will be no head office which could be coerced or corrupted, and the diversity of ownership and implementation will provide resilience against both error and attack." While it never aimed at creating any tradable and digitally scarce asset, the Eternity Service contained many characteristics that made Bitcoin successful [54].

Hashcash: 1997

The growth of the Internet in the nineties brought new challenges with it. Email spamming spread, enabling denial-of-service attacks. A denial-of-service (DoS) attack is a cyberattack designed to make a computer or network resource connected to the Internet unavailable, typically by flooding the target's resources. In the case of emails, it is achieved by automating the submission of an enormous number of emails briefly to overflow a server. Adam Back suggested a solution to that problem through a proof-of-work mechanism in May 1997, which he formalized in a paper in 2002 [55].

The cryptographic Hashcash algorithm delivers a stamp added to the header of an email, proving that the sender has spent at least a certain amount of CPU time and energy to deliver the email. Human email senders would barely notice this difference, but the automated sending of thousands of emails is made cumbersome. While CPU time and energy are wasted solving a useless computer problem, the objective is to discourage spammers, whose business model relies on sending a vast number of emails. Spammers needing to face this small cost for every email would become unprofitable. In a concrete analogy, the Hashcash algorithm corresponds to having to prove that the sender ran around the neighborhood before delivering a physical piece of mail. It is not too much of a burden to do so once, but one would not do so a thousand times unless necessary.

Hashcash is implemented in the email client Mozilla Thunderbird and inspired major companies such as Microsoft to implement similar spam reduction approaches. It is relevant in cryptoassets because the first cryptoassets also used a proof-of-work algorithm as part of their implementation. However, the usage of proof-of-work in cryptoassets works the other way around: it enables the verification of valid senders rather than deterring undesirable behaviors.

Bit Gold: 1998

Bit gold is a theoretical, decentralized, digital currency created by Nicholas Szabo, better known as Nick Szabo. It was never implemented but resembled Bitcoin in shape and form. In particular, it used a proof-of-work consensus mechanism to solve a cryptographic puzzle. The solved problem would be sent with the public key of the solver to a Byzantine fault-tolerant public database, in which each solution becomes part of the next problem (i.e., effectively a blockchain). Despite Szabo repeatedly denying this statement, bit gold was the closest ancestor to Bitcoin and whose creator is speculated to be Satoshi Nakamoto. Szabo also combined his law and computer science expertise to implement self-executing contracts in computer code. He is namely the one who coined the term "smart contracts," which is central to networks such as Ethereum or Cardano.

B-Money: 1998

A Chinese computer engineer and cryptography expert named Wei Dai described a modern money system based on cryptography in 1998. His publication "B-money, an anonymous, distributed electronic cash system" established how decentralized, digital money and self-executing contracts could function [56]. Most core concepts from that paper, such as a proof-of-work mechanism to update a collective ledger, were later implemented in Bitcoin. This publication is even cited in Bitcoin's white paper.

Wei Dai and Adam Back were the first people contacted by Satoshi Nakamoto during the development of Bitcoin, testifying to their instrumental role in the early development of the concept.

The Ethereum network then took hold of the smart contract idea and implemented it as a main difference from Bitcoin. In the same way that the smallest fraction of Bitcoin has been named a satoshi in honor of Satoshi Nakamoto (100 million satoshis is 1 bitcoin), the smallest fraction of ether has been named wei in honor of Wei Dai (1 million million million wei, or 1 quintillion wei, is 1 ether).

APPENDIX B

Bitcoin's Replacement Cost Valuation

Chapter 16 explained how electricity costs could be used as input for the valuation of a cryptoasset based on a proof-of-work consensus mechanism. To not break that chapter's flow, the following computation-heavy example for Bitcoin's valuation was moved to this appendix.

The valuation of Bitcoin based on its electricity costs is likely the first cryptoasset valuation to ever be established, as it was already used in autumn 2009, when the New Liberty Standard online exchange published the first formal Bitcoin exchange rate. This approach is called Bitcoin's *electricity value*, the *electricity hash valuation,* or *energy-value equivalence.*

Algebraically, the different elements of the following formula establish the implied costs of a bitcoin purely based on the cost of the electricity needed to mine it.

$$BTC\ electricity\ value = \frac{USD}{kWh} \times \frac{kWh}{Joules} \times \frac{Joules}{hash} \times \frac{hash}{block} \times \frac{block}{BTC}$$

See, in particular, how the denominator of each fraction in the formula cancels out with the nominator of the next term, so that only two terms are left.

The first fraction of the formula is the cost per kWh of the electricity used to mine Bitcoin. Even if cheap energy is used, the miner should consider the opportunity cost of that electricity. In our example, let us assume it is $0.11 per kWh.

The second fraction is a constant. A watt is simply a consumption of 1 joule per second. There are 1,000 watts in a kilowatt and 3,600 seconds in 1 hour. Therefore, 1 joule corresponds to 1000×3600 kWh, and 1 kWh corresponds to $\frac{1}{1000 \times 3600}$ joules.

© Thomas Jeegers 2023
T. Jeegers, *Understanding Crypto Fundamentals*, https://doi.org/10.1007/978-1-4842-9309-6_19

The third fraction considers the specificities of the ASIC miner. The number of joules necessary per hash depends on the miner's consumption (in our example, 5,500 watts) and hash efficiency (in our example, 200 trillion hashes per second). These figures correspond to the efficiency of state-of-the-art ASIC miners as of May 2023, when maintained at 25 degrees Celsius. The corresponding value of the third fraction is $\dfrac{5500}{200,000,000,000,000}$ or 27.5 joules per terahash, a unit of measure typically used for ASIC miners.

The fourth fraction is the total hash rate of the network (350 exahashes per second) expressed in the average time necessary to mine a block, 10 minutes. In other words, about 210 zettahashes.

The final fraction is the inverse of the number of bitcoins mined per block: 6.25 BTC since the third halving event of May 11, 2020 and until the next halving event expected in March 2024.

Multiplying these terms with the aforementioned assumptions yields a Bitcoin electricity value of 28,233 USD, the market price of Bitcoin as of this writing. Since its inception, Bitcoin's market price has remained remarkably close (and mean-reverting) to its implied electricity value.

$$BTC \ electricity \ value = \$0.11 \times \frac{1}{3.6E6} \times \frac{27.5}{1.0E11} \times 2.1E23 \times \frac{1}{6.25} = \$28,233$$

This price is a minimum value for Bitcoin, a floor price, for multiple reasons.

First, the most effective ASIC miners in existence were considered in the figures. In reality, most miners are less efficient than in this example. Increasing the number of watts required by the miner and reducing its hash efficiency suggests a higher valuation.

Second, this valuation considers exclusively the electricity cost of mining. However, setting up a Bitcoin mining farm requires many more costs, from purchasing the ASIC miners to setup and maintenance costs.

Third, the hash rate is consistently increasing. This has two consequences: on the one hand, the time necessary to mine a block (the fourth fraction) is, on average, under 10 minutes. On the other hand, it implies that increasingly more miners are joining the race, indicating that they expect future bitcoins mined will be worth more than the current market price.

Also note that the formula can be reworked to isolate the cost of the electricity. Thereby, one can derive the maximum cost of the electricity that will make mining operations profitable for a specific miner, the Bitcoin market price, and the expected hash rate.

Financial Products Applied to Crypto

Since financial concepts are not as digestible for all readers intended for this book, the following sections have been moved to an appendix. They cover approaches that investors may be tempted to use, in cryptoasset or otherwise, to benefit from potential investments, though with a different risk profile than traditional direct investments. Note, in particular, the important words of caution related to these approaches.

Leverage and Margin Trading

To maximize gains, traders in the financial industry often use leverage. Compared to a simple investment (purchase), leverage consists of borrowing funds to invest to benefit even more from price appreciation while running even higher risks if prices drop.

The following example is computation heavy but illustrates the benefits and risks of leverage trading. Assume a trader invested $100 in an asset. If the asset price increases by 10%, the trader has this return: 10% (ignoring transaction costs). However, if the trader borrowed another $100 on top (at a 5% interest rate) and invested it in the same asset before the price appreciation, the return would be much higher. In particular, the trader would have $220 in the asset ($2 \times \$100 \times (1 + 10\%)$), which he can sell. He can repay the loan plus the 5% interest: $105. His return, in this case, would be 15% (computed as $\frac{\$220 - \$105}{\$100} - 1$). In this scenario, the gain with leverage (15%) is much higher than without (10%). However, if the price had dropped (e.g., 10%), then the loss (–25%) would also be bigger than without leverage (–10%). Note that the interest rate on the loan is

© Thomas Jeegers 2023
T. Jeegers, *Understanding Crypto Fundamentals*, https://doi.org/10.1007/978-1-4842-9309-6_20

due no matter what so that potential additional losses are more than proportional to potential additional gains. By borrowing, traders can amplify positions to gain more from price increases while exposing themselves to higher risks if prices fall.

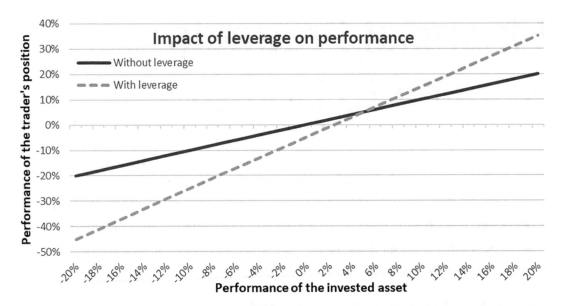

Figure A-1. *Performance of a portfolio with or without leverage (vertically), depending on the performance of an asset (horizontally), assuming a 5% interest rate due on the loan*

Leverage is also possible in cryptoassets and available through many centralized or decentralized platforms. However, the high volatility of cryptoassets makes them much less appropriate for leveraged positions. To understand this, one must be familiar with the concept of *margin trading*.

The trader must typically post collateral for the loan to obtain leveraged positions. The collateral is a sort of security for the lender and is usually the asset the trader invests in. It is the "margin" in "margin trading." The lender can thereby reduce his risk: if the asset's price decreases below a certain point, the lender can sell the borrower's asset on his behalf to reimburse the loan. However, this sale represents a substantial risk for the borrower, especially for volatile assets: the asset is disposed of after losing much of its original value. After the sale, the borrower has nothing left, even if the asset's price rebounds. Not only is the borrowed amount gone, but also the amount initially invested.

Margin trading is, therefore, hazardous for investors in highly volatile assets. Even if the asset price increases eventually, its volatility can "liquidate" many traders on the way.

Cryptoasset sales happening when prices drop (due to the margin of leveraged positions being liquidated) cause prices to drop even further. As the cryptoasset market has traditionally been very leveraged, it constitutes a weighty reason for its volatility.

Derivative Products

Another way to benefit from cryptoassets is through the use of derivative products. A derivative product derives its value from another product (the underlying). For example, the value of a stock option derives its value from the price of a stock.

Call and Put Options

A *call option* on a stock is the right to buy a stock in the future at a specific price. Like all other derivative products, this is a contract. It is similar to a bet on the future price of the underlying over a specific period.

For a numerical example, assume Google's stock price is currently trading at $1,000. I buy a call option on Google's stock, for $50, with a strike price of $1,100 and a maturity of 1 year. In other words, I now pay the premium of $50 to buy a right. The right is that I can (I have the "option" to) purchase Google's stock next year at $1,100, regardless of its trading price. If Google's stock trades next year at $1,250, then I exercise the option. Therefore, the call option seller is obligated to sell me the stock at $1,100, even though it is trading at a higher price. I have made a profit because my purchase price plus the premium ($1,100 + $50 = $1,150) is lower than the current trading price of the underlying ($1,250).

On the other hand, if the stock next year trades at $1,075, I do not exercise the option because I am better off buying the stock at $1,075 on the open market than at $1,100. In this case, I let the option expire worthless and have made a loss (the amount I paid for the right, i.e., $50).

The price of the call option derives its value from the underlying stock's price (among other factors). In other words, if the stock price rises, the option price also rises (all other things equal) because the likelihood of expiring above the strike price increases. A call option can have any product as underlying, from stocks and bonds to commodities, currencies, interest rates, or even other derivative products. Of course, call options also exist with cryptoassets as underlying.

A *put option*, in contrast, is the option to "sell" an underlying in the future at a specific price. A put option is, in some sense, the opposite of a call option. It works like a call option but with the option to sell rather than the option to buy.

One benefit of using put options is to insure oneself against price drops. For instance, a trader unable to afford a cryptoasset dropping below a particular value can buy a put option for that cryptoasset and that value. For example, a trader can buy a $50,000 Bitcoin and insure himself against the price dropping below $40,000 next year. To do so, the trader would buy a put option on Bitcoin with a one-year maturity and a strike price of $40,000. The trader can exercise the option and sell the asset for $40,000, limiting losses if the price drops below that level. Effectively, a put option is an insurance contract. The trader thereby benefits from the upside potential of the investment and, at the same time, limits the potential downside. Such contracts can, of course, be programmed in a smart contract and be traded decentrally.

Futures Contracts

Alternatively, traders can use futures contracts to express views on future price movements. In a futures contract, the buyer agrees to buy an asset for a specific price at a specific future date. This way, he can lock in a price without having to pay it immediately.[1]

Futures often benefit from higher liquidity and lower trading fees than buying the underlying product. Similar to put options, they can provide potentially infinite upside for a limited downside. They can therefore be used to hedge against some risks or for speculation. The cryptoasset trading exchange Binance is among the largest futures exchanges in the world.

Many other derivative products exist for cryptoassets, just like other asset classes. Interested readers should refer to literature on financial derivative products or risk management.

---

[1] Forward contracts are similar to futures contracts, with the difference that they can be customised and are typically exchanged between two parties rather than over an exchange.

Acronyms and Abbreviations

Altcoin	alternative coin
AML	Anti-Money Laundering
AMM	automated market maker
APY	annual percentage yield
AUP	acceptable use policy
BaaS	Blockchain as a Service
BIS	Bank for International Settlements
BTC	Bitcoin
CAGR	compound annual growth rate
CeFi	centralized finance
CEX	centralized exchange
CFTC	Commodity Futures Trading Commission (US)
CPI	Consumer Price Index
CPU	central processing unit
DACS	Digital Asset Classification Standard
DAO	decentralized autonomous organization
dApp	decentralized application
DDoS	distributed denial of service
DeFi	decentralized finance
DEX	decentralized exchange
DLT	distributed ledger technology
ECB	European Central Bank
ECDSA	Elliptic Curve Digital Signature Algorithm

(continued)

© Thomas Jeegers 2023
T. Jeegers, *Understanding Crypto Fundamentals*, https://doi.org/10.1007/978-1-4842-9309-6

EPV	earnings power value
ESG	environmental, social, and governance
ETF	exchange-traded fund
ETH	ether
EU	European Union
EUR	euro
Fed	Federal Reserve (US)
FTP	File Transfer Protocol
GCCS	Global Crypto Classification Standard
GDP	gross domestic product
GDPR	General Data Protection Regulation
GICS	Global Industry Classification Standard
GPU	graphical processing unit
GTCA	General Taxonomy for Cryptographic Assets
HD	hierarchical deterministic
HTTP	Hypertext Transfer Protocol
ICO	initial coin offering
IMF	International Monetary Fund
IoT	Internet of Things
IPFS	InterPlanetary File System
IT	information technology
KYC	Know Your Customer
kWh	kilowatt-hour
LTV	loan-to-value
MB	megabyte
MBA	Master of Business Administration
MiCA	Markets in Crypto Assets

(continued)

MVRV	Market Value to Realized Value
NGO	non-governmental organization
nm	nanometer
NPV	net present value
NVT	network value to transactions
PoS	proof of stake
PoW	proof of work
RIPEMD	RACE Integrity Primitives Evaluation Message Digest
S2F	stock-to-flow
S2FX	stock-to-flow cross-asset
SEC	Securities and Exchange Commission (US)
SHA	Secure Hash Algorithm
SMTP	Simple Mail Transfer Protocol
STO	security token offering
TCP/IP	Transmission Control Protocol / Internet Protocol
TVL	total value locked
USD	United States dollar
VaR	value at risk
VR	virtual reality
XMPP	Extensible Messaging and Presence Protocol
ZKP	zero-knowledge proof

References

[1]   I. Bashir, *Mastering Blockchain*, Birmingham: Packt Publishing, 2020.

[2]   M. Fortnow and Q. Terry, *The NFT Handbook: How to Create, Sell and Buy Non-Fungible Tokens*, 1st ed., Wiley, 2021.

[3]   N. Schmidt, J. Bernstein, S. Richter and L. Zarlenga, *Taxation of Crypto Assets*, 2nd ed., Kluwer Law International, 2023.

[4]   Aristotle, Politics, 350 BCE, The Complete Works of Aristotle, J. Barnes, Princeton University Press, 1984.

[5]   C. Menger, "On the Origin of Money," *The Economic Journal,* vol. 2, no. 6, pp. 239-255, June 1892.

[6]   L. Laeven and F. Valencia, "Systemic Banking Crises Revisited," *IMF working paper,* no. WP/18/206, pp. 1–48, September 14, 2018.

[7]   N. Soto, "Encovi 2021: Venezuela Is The Poorest Country in Latin America," *Caracas Chronicles,* September 30, 2021.

[8]   B. Lietaer and J. Dunne, *Rethinking Money: How New Currencies Turn Scarcity Into Prosperity*, 1st ed., San Francisco, CA: Berrett-Koehler Publishers, Inc., 2013.

[9]   Z. Whittaker, "A new data leak hits Aadhaar, India's national ID database," ZDNet, March 23, 2018. [Online]. Available: `https://www.zdnet.com/article/another-data-leak-hits-india-aadhaar-biometric-database/`. [Accessed May 10, 2023].

[10]   A. Holmes, "533 million Facebook users' phone numbers and personal data have been leaked online," *Business Insider*, April 3, 2021. [Online]. Available: `https://www.businessinsider.com/stolen-data-of-533-million-facebook-users-leaked-online-2021-4`. [Accessed May 10, 2023].

REFERENCES

[11]   B. Krebs, "Facebook Stored Hundreds of Millions of User Passwords in Plain Text for Years," KrebsOnSecurity, March 21, 2019. [Online]. Available: `https://krebsonsecurity.com/2019/03/facebook-stored-hundreds-of-millions-of-user-passwords-in-plain-text-for-years/`. [Accessed May 10, 2023].

[12]   UNICEF, "Despite significant increase in birth registration, a quarter of the world's children remain 'invisible'," UNICEF, December 10, 2019. [Online]. Available: `https://www.unicef.org/press-releases/despite-significant-increase-birth-registration-quarter-worlds-children-remain`. [Accessed May 10, 2023].

[13]   Chainalysis, "The 2022 Global Crypto Adoption Index: Emerging Markets Lead in Grassroots Adoption, China Remains Active Despite Ban, and Crypto Fundamentals Appear Healthy," 2022.

[14]   Solana, "Solana's Energy Use Report: March 2022," Solana, March 25, 2022. [Online]. Available: `https://solana.com/news/solanas-energy-use-report-march-2022`. [Accessed May 10, 2023].

[15]   Galaxy Digital, "On Bitcoin's Energy Consumption: A Quantitative Approach to a Subjective Question," 2021.

[16]   Bitcoin Mining Council, "Global Bitcoin Mining Data Review Q4 2022," Bitcoin Mining Council, 2023.

[17]   J. Vazquez and D. L. Crumbley, "Flared Gas Can Reduce Some Risks in Crypto Mining as Well as Oil and Gas Operations," *Risks,* vol. 10, no. 127, pp. 1–12, June 16, 2022.

[18]   H. Ferreira de Mendonça, D. J. Cordeiro Galvão, and R. Falci Villela Loures, "What is the importance of regulation and transparency in the subprime crisis," *Banks and Bank Systems,* vol. 5, no. 1, pp. 32–46, March 18, 2010.

[19] "BT blames human error as it reveals £500m pension deficit gaffe," *The Guardian*, July 27, 2018. [Online]. Available: `https://www.theguardian.com/business/2018/jul/27/bt-blames-human-error-for-500m-pensions-accounting-gaffe`. [Accessed May 10, 2023].

[20] P. Champagne, *The Book of Satoshi*, e53 Publishing LLC, 2014.

[21] S. Nakamoto, "Bitcoin: A Peer-to-Peer Electronic Cash System," Bitcoin.org, November 1, 2008. [Online]. Available: `http://www.bitcoin.org/bitcoin.pdf`. [Accessed May 10, 2023].

[22] M. Friedman, "The Island of Stone Money," *Working Papers in Economics,* Vols. E-91-3, pp. 1–3, 1991.

[23] Chainalysis, "Chainalysis 2022 Crypto Crime Report," February 2022. [Online]. Available: `https://go.chainalysis.com/2022-Crypto-Crime-Report.html`. [Accessed May 10, 2023].

[24] J. L. Verhelst, Bitcoin, the Blockchain and Beyond, Jean-Luc Verhelst, 2017.

[25] N. Mehta, A. Agashe, and P. Detroja, *Bubble or Revolution*, 2nd ed., Paravane Ventures, 2021.

[26] B. Lashkari and P. Musilek, "A Comprehensive Review of Blockchain Consensus Mechanisms," *IEEE Access,* vol. 9, pp. 43620–43652, 2021.

[27] D. P. Oyinloye, J. S. Teh, N. Jamil and M. Alawida, "Blockchain Consensus: An Overview of Alternative Protocols," *Symmetry,* vol. 13, no. 1363, p. 35, July 27, 2021.

[28] B. Tapscott, "Reinventing International Clearing and Settlement," *Blockchain Research Institute,* pp. 1–51, January 2018.

[29] C. Burniske and J. Tatar, *Cryptoassets: The Innovative Investor's Guide to Bitcoin and Beyond*, New York, NY: McGraw-Hill, 2017.

[30] D. Tapscott and A. Tapscott, *Blockchain Revolution*, New York, NY: Portfolio Penguin, 2018.

REFERENCES

[31] Brave New Coin, "General Taxonomy for Cryptographic Assets,"
      Brave New Coin, February 8, 2018. [Online]. Available: `https://`
      `bravenewcoin.com/enterprise-solutions/taxonomy`. [Accessed
      May 10, 2023].

[32] CoinDesk, "Digital Asset Classification Standard Methodology,"
      CoinDesk, December 2022. [Online]. Available: `https://`
      `downloads.coindesk.com/cd3/CDI/Digital+Asset+Classificat`
      `ion+Standard+Methodology.pdf`. [Accessed May 10, 2023].

[33] C. Indices, "Digital Asset Classification Standard (DACS)
      Glossary," December 2022. [Online]. Available: `https://`
      `downloads.coindesk.com/cd3/DACS+-+Glossary+-+Final.pdf`.
      [Accessed May 10, 2023].

[34] CoinGecko, "The Global Crypto Classification Standard by
      21Shares & CoinGecko," February 7, 2023. [Online]. Available:
      `https://www.coingecko.com/research/publications/global-`
      `crypto-classification-standard`. [Accessed May 10, 2023].

[35] US Commodity Futures Trading Commission, "Bitcoin Basics," US
      Commodity Futures Trading Commission, 2019.

[36] Financial Stability Oversight Council, "Report on Digital Asset
      Financial Stability Risks and Regulation 2022," Financial Stability
      Oversight Council, Washington DC, 2022.

[37] Ernst & Young, "Accounting by holders of crypto-assets," Ernst
      & Young, October 12, 2021. [Online]. Available: `https://www.`
      `ey.com/en_gl/ifrs-technical-resources/accounting-by-`
      `holders-of-crypto-assets-updated-october-2021`. [Accessed
      May 10, 2023].

[38] M. D. Holdings, "Marathon Digital Holdings: Building America's
      Leading Enterprise Bitcoin Miner," Marathon Digital Holdings,
      January 1, 2022. [Online]. Available: `https://marathondh.com/`.
      [Accessed January 1, 2022].

[39] Coinbase, "Coinbase," Coinbase, January 1, 2022. [Online].
      Available: `www.coinbase.com`. [Accessed January 1, 2022].

[40] M. Kevin, "2021 Institutional Blockchain Investment Guide,"
      D-Core, 2021.

[41] K. Hyunjun, K. Kyungho, K. Hyeokdong, and S. Hwajeong, "ASIC-
      Resistant Proof of Work Based on Power Analysis of Low-End
      Microcontrollers," *Mathematics,* vol. 8, no. 1343, pp. 1–13, August
      12, 2020.

[42] B. Graham, *The Intelligent Investor*, First Collins Business
      Essentials edition 2006 ed., New York, NY: HarperCollins
      Publisher, 2006.

[43] B. Greenwald, J. Kahn, E. Bellissimo, M. Cooper, and T. Santos,
      Value Investing: from Graham to Buffett and Beyond, 2nd ed.,
      Hoboken, NJ: John Wiley & Sons, 2021.

[44] Bitcoin Mining Council, "Global Bitcoin Mining Data Review Q3
      2022," Bitcoin Mining Council, 2022.

[45] F. Arute, K. Arya, R. Babbush, D. Bacon, J. Bardin, and e. al.,
      "Quantum supremacy using a programmable superconducting
      processor," *Nature,* no. 574, pp. 505–510, October 23, 2019.

[46] J. Bier, *The Blocksize War*, independently published, 2021.

[47] V. Buterin, "The Meaning of Decentralization," Medium, February
      6, 2017.

[48] A. R. Sai, J. Buckley, and A. Le Gear, "Characterizing Wealth
      Inequality in Cryptocurrencies," *Frontiers in Blockchain,* vol. 4,
      p. 20, December 20, 2021.

[49] American Bankruptcy Institute, "Bankrupt Bitcoin Exchange Mt.
      Gox begins to Pay Back Account Holders in Bitcoin," American
      Bankruptcy Institute, [Online]. Available: https://www.abi.
      org/feed-item/bankrupt-bitcoin-exchange-mt-gox-begins-
      to-pay-back-account-holders-in-bitcoin. [Accessed May
      10, 2023].

[50] E. Rogers, *Diffusion of Innovations*, 5th ed., Simon and
      Schuster, 2003.

REFERENCES

[51] D. Chaum, *Blind Signatures for Untraceable Payments*, Springer, pp. 199–203, 1982.

[52] J. Pitta, "Requiem for a Bright Idea," *Forbes*, November 1, 1999. [Online]. Available: `https://www.forbes.com/forbes/1999/1101/6411390a.html`. [Accessed May 10, 2023].

[53] S. Haber and W. S. Stornetta, "How to time-stamp a digital document," *Journal of Cryptology*, vol. 3, no. 2, pp. 99–111, 1991.

[54] R. J. Anderson, "The Eternity Service," Cambridge University Computer Laboratory, Cambridge, 1996.

[55] A. Back, "Hashcash: A Denial of Service Counter-Measure," August 1, 2002. [Online]. Available: `http://www.hashcash.org/papers/hashcash.pdf`. [Accessed May 10, 2023].

[56] W. Dai, "B-money, an anonymous, distributed electronic cash system," 2004. [Online]. Available: `http://www.weidai.com/bmoney.txt`. [Accessed May 10, 2023].

[57] binance.com, "Binance," December 1, 2021. [Online]. Available: `https://www.binance.com/en`.

[58] S. Ammous, *The Bitcoin Standard*, Hoboken, NJ: John Wiley & Sons, Inc., 2018.

[59] M. N. Rothbard, *The Case Against the Fed*, Auburn, AL: Ludwig von Mises Institute, 1994.

[60] A. Fekete, *Whither Gold?*, 2nd ed., Pintax cvba, 1996.

[61] J. P. Morgan Asset Management, "FactSet," 2022.

[62] R. Dalio, *Principles for Dealing with the Changing World Order: Why Nations Succeed and Fail*, New York, NY: Avid Reader Press, 2021.

[63] S. Ammous, *The Fiat Standard*, The Saif House, 2021.

[64] L. Lamport, R. Shostak, and M. Pease, "The Byzantine Generals Problem," *ACM Transactions on Programming Languages and Systems*, vol. 4, no. 3, pp. 382–401, July 1982.

[65] M. Castro and B. Liskov, "Practical Byzantine Fault Tolerance," *Proceedings of the Third Symposium on Operating Systems Designs and Implementation,* pp. 1–14, February 1999.

[66] U.S. Court, "Securities and Exchange Commission v. Howey Co., 328 U.S. 293 (1946)," Justia, May 27, 1946. [Online]. Available: `https://supreme.justia.com/cases/federal/us/328/293/`. [Accessed May 10, 2023].

[67] Statista, "Number of cryptocurrencies worldwide from 2013 to February 2023," Statista, February 11, 2023. [Online]. Available: `https://www.statista.com/statistics/863917/number-crypto-coins-tokens/`. [Accessed May 10, 2023].

[68] J. R. Peden, "Inflation and the Fall of the Roman Empire," *Mises Daily Articles,* October 19, 2017.

[69] H. A. Amankwah, D. J. Goulding, E. Krausbeck, K. Mwenda and R. Schweigert, German Hyperinflation 1922/23, 1st ed., W. C. Fischer, Ed., Cologne, North Rhine-Westphalia: Josef Eul, 2010.

[70] F. Norrestad, "Value of assets on the balance sheet of the Federal Reserve from August 2007 to December 2022," Statista, February 11, 2023. [Online]. Available: `https://www.statista.com/statistics/1121448/fed-balance-sheet-timeline/`. [Accessed February 11 2023].

[71] J. Stodder, "Complementary Credit Networks and Macro-Economic Stability: Switzerland's Wirtschaftsring," *Journal of Economic Behavior & Organization,* no. 72, pp. 79–95, October 2009.

[72] M. N. Rothbard, *America's Great Depression,* 5th ed., Auburn, AL: The Ludwig von Mises Institute, 1963.

[73] D. Colander, Post Walrasian Macroeconomics: Beyond the Dynamic Stochastic General Equilibrium Model, D. Colander, Ed., Cambridge: Cambridge University Press, 2006, p. 440.

REFERENCES

[74] I. Schnabel and H. S. Shin, "Money and trust: lessons from the 1620s for money in the digital age," *BIS Working Papers,* no. 698, pp. 1–39, February 5, 2018.

[75] World Economic Forum, "Why the debate about crypto's energy consumption is flawed," World Economic Forum, 2022.

[76] PlanB, "Bitcoin Stock-to-Flow Cross Asset Model," Medium, April 27, 2020. [Online]. Available: `https://medium.com/@100trillionUSD/bitcoin-stock-to-flow-cross-asset-model-50d260feed12`. [Accessed May 10, 2023].

[77] PlanB, "Modeling Bitcoin Value with Scarcity," Medium, March 22, 2019. [Online]. Available: `https://medium.com/@100trillionUSD/modeling-bitcoins-value-with-scarcity-91fa0fc03e25`. [Accessed May 10, 2023].

[78] W. G. Council, "Above-ground stocks," World Gold Council, February 8, 2023. [Online]. Available: `https://www.gold.org/goldhub/data/how-much-gold`. [Accessed May 10, 2023].

[79] W. Woo, "Is Bitcoin In A Bubble? Check The NVT Ratio," *Forbes*, September 29, 2017. [Online]. Available: `https://www.forbes.com/sites/wwoo/2017/09/29/is-bitcoin-in-a-bubble-check-the-nvt-ratio/?sh=7ec603cb6a23`. [Accessed May 10, 2023].

[80] Datareportal, "Digital 2022 Global Overview Report," Datareportal, 2022.

[81] B. f. I. Settlement, "Triennial Central Bank Survey of Foreign Exchange and Over-the-counter (OTC) Derivatives Markets in 2022," Bank for International Settlement (BIS), October 27, 2022. [Online]. Available: `https://www.bis.org/statistics/rpfx22.htm`. [Accessed May 10, 2023].

[82] M. P. Richardson, J. Boudoukh, and R. F. Whitelaw, "The Best of Both Worlds: A Hybrid Approach to Calculating Value at Risk," *SSRN*, p. 12, November 1997.

[83] B. Gnedenko, "Sur La Distribution Limite Du Terme Maximum D'Une Série Aléatoire," *Annals of Mathematics,* vol. 44, no. 3, pp. 423–453, February 8, 1943.

[84] H. Hauge, "Introducing Binary Adjusted BDD, VOCD and Reserve Risk," *WORDS Bitcoin Journal,* 2019.

[85] World Population Review, "Bitcoin Mining by Country 2023," World Population Review, 2023. [Online]. Available: `https://worldpopulationreview.com/country-rankings/bitcoin-mining-by-country`. [Accessed May 10, 2023].

[86] Look Into Bitcoin, "Bitcoin Rainbow Price Chart Indicator," Look Into Bitcoin, [Online]. Available: `https://www.lookintobitcoin.com/charts/bitcoin-rainbow-chart/`. [Accessed May 10, 2023].

[87] R. de Best, "Number of identity-verified cryptoasset users from 2016 to November 2022," Statista, 2023.

[88] P. Moers, "Community Currency Systems: A Co-operative Option for the Developing World?", The Social Solidary Economy resources website, 1998.

[89] Federal Reserve Bank of Boston, Putting it Simply, Boston, MA: Federal Reserve Bank of Boston, 1984.

[90] Government of Iceland, "Energy," Government of Iceland, [Online]. Available: `https://www.government.is/topics/business-and-industry/energy/`. [Accessed May 10, 2023].

[91] S. Nakamoto, "Re: Current Bitcoin economic model is unsustainable," BitcoinTalk, 2010.

Index

A

Agency problem, 51
Airdrops, 156
Altcoin, 86
Anchoring effect, 214
Anonymous eCash, 291
Anti-Money Laundering, 197
Application-specific integrated circuit
    (ASIC), 145
ASIC-resistant, 147
Asymmetric encryption, 93
51% attack, 220
Automated market maker (AMM),
    154, 196

B

Basic Attention
    Token (BAT), 87
Bitcoin Core, 202
Bitcoin Golden Bull Ratio, 167
Bitcoin's dominance, 171
Bitcoin's lengthening cycles, 170
Bitcointalk.org, 82
Bit gold, 294
Blockchain, 90
Blockchain-based
    insurance, 235
B-money, 294
Bretton Woods, 17
Brokerage service, 196
Byzantine Generals problem, 77

C

Call option, 299
Chiliz (CHZ), 87
Cold storage wallets, 192
Cold wallets, 192
Confirmation bias, 212
Consensus mechanism, 97
Conservatism bias, 214
Consumer Price
    Index (CPI), 19
Correlation, 67
Credit risk, 238
Cryptoassets, 121
Cryptocommodities, 122
Cryptocurrencies, 122
Cryptography Mailing List, 82
Cryptotokens, 122
Currency, 9
Custody, 195

D

Decentralization, 229
The Decentralized Autonomous
    Organization, 105
Decentralized exchange
    (DEX), 182, 196
Decentralized Finance, 86, 128
Decentralized insurance, 235
DeFi, 86, 128
Developer risk, 226
DigiCash, 292

T. Jeegers, *Understanding Crypto Fundamentals*, https://doi.org/10.1007/978-1-4842-9309-6

Printed in the United States
by Baker & Taylor Publisher Services